NIETZSCHE'S *BEYOND GOOD AND EVIL*

Continuum *Reader's Guides*

Continuum's *Reader's Guides* are clear, concise, and accessible introductions to classic works of philosophy. Each book explores the major themes, historical and philosophical context, and key passages of a major philosophical text, guiding the reader toward a thorough understanding of often demanding material. Ideal for undergraduate students, the guides provide an essential resource for anyone who needs to come to grips with a philosophical text.

Reader's Guides available from Continuum

Aristotle's Nicomachean Ethics – Christopher Warne
Aristotle's Politics – Judith A. Swanson and C. David Corbin
Berkeley's Principles of Human Knowledge – Alasdair Richmond
Berkeley's Three Dialogues – Aaron Garrett
Deleuze and Guattari's Capitalism and Schizophrenia – Ian Buchanan
Deleuze's Difference and Repetition – Joe Hughes
Derrida's Writing and Difference – Sarah Wood
Descartes' Meditations – Richard Francks
Hegel's Philosophy of Right – David Rose
Heidegger's Being and Time – William Blattner
Heidegger's Later Writings – Lee Braver
Hobbes's Leviathan – Laurie M. Johnson Bagby
Hume's Enquiry Concerning Human Understanding – Alan Bailey and Dan O'Brien
Hume's Dialogues Concerning Natural Religion – Andrew Pyle
Kant's Critique of Aesthetic Judgement – Fiona Hughes
Kant's Critique of Pure Reason – James Luchte
Kant's Groundwork for the Metaphysics of Morals – Paul Guyer
Kierkegaard's Fear and Trembling – Clare Carlisle
Kuhn's The Structure of Scientific Revolutions – John Preston
Locke's Essay Concerning Human Understanding – William Uzgalis
Locke's Second Treatise of Government – Paul Kelly
Mill's On Liberty – Geoffrey Scarre
Mill's Utilitarianism – Henry West
Nietzsche's On the Genealogy of Morals – Daniel Conway
Nietzsche's The Birth of Tragedy – Douglas Burnham and Martin Jesinghausen
Plato's Republic – Luke Purshouse
Plato's Symposium – Thomas L. Cooksey
Rawls's Theory of Justice – Frank Lovett
Rousseau's The Social Contract – Christopher Wraight
Sartre's Being and Nothingness, Sebastian Gardner
Schopenhauer's The World as Will and Representation – Robert Wicks
Spinoza's Ethics – Thomas J Cook
Wittgenstein's Tractatus Logico Philosophicus – Roger M White

NIETZSCHE'S *BEYOND GOOD AND EVIL*

A Reader's Guide

CHRISTA DAVIS ACAMPORA
AND
KEITH ANSELL PEARSON

continuum

Continuum International Publishing Group
The Tower Building   80 Maiden Lane
   11 York Road   Suite 704
London SE1 7NX   New York, NY 10038

www.continuumbooks.com

British Library Cataloguing-in-Publication Data
A catalogue record for this book is available from the British Library.

ISBN: HB: 978-0-8264-7363-9
       PB: 978-0-8264-7364-6

Library of Congress Cataloging-in-Publication Data
Acampora, Christa Davis, 1967-
Nietzsche's Beyond good and evil : a reader's guide / Christa
Davis Acampora and Keith Ansell Pearson.
       p. cm.
Includes bibliographical references (p.).
ISBN 978-0-8264-7363-9 – ISBN 978-0-8264-7364-6
1. Nietzsche, Friedrich Wilhelm, 1844–1900. Jenseits von Gut und
Böse. 2. Ethics. I. Ansell-Pearson, Keith, 1960- II. Title.
       B3313.J43A23 2011
       193–dc22   2010046123

Typeset by Newgen Imaging Systems Pvt Ltd, Chennai, India
Printed and bound in India

CONTENTS

ACKNOWLEDGMENTS

The authors wish to thank their respective institutions for support and study leave, including Hunter College of The City University of New York and Warwick University. Acampora also wishes to thank the Institute for Advanced Study at Durham University and Warwick University, which provided support while she was writing portions of the manuscript, and colleagues and students who provided insightful and critical feedback, especially Gary Shapiro, David Cerequas, Adam Israel, Greg Zucker, Ben Abelson, Adele Sarli, Elvira Basevich, Jennifer Hyman and Frank Boardman. Greg Zucker also assisted with the index. The Hunter College philosophy department provided generous support for research assistance and manuscript preparation. For support and inspiration Ansell Pearson wishes to thank his many friends in the world of Nietzsche studies.

TRANSLATIONS AND ABBREVIATIONS FOR CITATIONS OF NIETZSCHE'S WORKS

Translations used in citations of Nietzsche's works are as follows. Titles are abbreviated using the following conventions:

A = *Der Antichrist* (1888); translated as *The Antichrist*. Trans. Judith Norman (Cambridge: Cambridge University Press, 2005).

AOM = *Vermischte Meinungen und Sprüche* (1879); translated as *Aphorisms, Opinions and Maxims*. In *Human All Too Human*, trans. R. J. Hollingdale (Cambridge: Cambridge University Press, 1986).

BGE = *Jenseits von Gut und Böse* (1886); translated as *Beyond Good and Evil*. Trans. Walter Kaufmann (New York: Vintage Books, 1966).

BT = *Die Geburt der Tragödie* (1872; 1886); translated as *The Birth of Tragedy*. Trans. Walter Kaufmann in *The Birth of Tragedy* and *The Case of Wagner* (New York: Vintage Books, 1967).

CW = *Der Fall Wagner* (1888); translated as *The Case of Wagner*. Trans. Walter Kaufmann in *The Birth of Tragedy* and *The Case of Wagner* (New York: Vintage Books, 1967).

D = *Morgenröthe* (1881; 1886); translated as *Dawn* or *Daybreak*. Trans. R. J. Hollingdale, *Daybreak: Thoughts on the Prejudices of Morality* (Cambridge University Press, 1982).

DD = *Dionysos-Dithyramben* (1888); translated as *Dionysian Dithyrambs*. Trans. R. J. Hollingdale (London: Anvil Press Poetry, 1984).

EH = *Ecce Homo* (1888); translated as *Ecce Homo*. Trans. Walter Kaufmann in *On the Genealogy of Morals* and *Ecce Homo* (New York: Random House, 1967). References to *EH* include the abbreviated chapter title followed by the relevant section number when applicable.

GM = *Zur Genealogie der Moral* (1887); translated as *On the Genealogy of Morality* and *On the Genealogy of Morals*. Trans. Walter Kaufmann and R. J. Hollingdale in *On the Genealogy of Morals* and *Ecce Homo* (New York: Random House, 1967).

GS = *Die fröhliche Wissenschaft* (1882; 1887); translated as *The Gay Science*. Trans. Walter Kaufmann (New York: Vintage Books, 1974).

HC = "Homer's Wettkampf" (1871); translated as "Homer's Contest." Translations are our own.

HH = *Menschliches, Allzumenschliches* (1878); translated as *Human All Too Human*. Trans. R. J. Hollingdale (Cambridge University Press, 1986).

HL = *Vom Nutzen und Nachtheil der Historie für das Leben*; *Unzeitgemäße Betrachtungen* II (1874); translated as "The Use and Disadvantage of History for Life" and "On the Utility and Liability of History for Life." Trans. Richard T. Gray in *Complete Works: Unfashionable Observations*, Vol. 2 (Stanford: Stanford University Press, 1995).

SE = *Schopenhauer als Erzieher*; *Unzeitgemäße Betrachtungen* III (1874) translated as "Schopenhauer as Educator." Trans. Richard T. Gray in *The Complete Works of Friedrich Nietzsche: Unfashionable Observations*, Vol. 2 (Stanford: Stanford University Press, 1995).

TI = *Götzen-Dämmerung* (1888); translated as *Twilight of the Idols*. Trans. Duncan Large (Oxford: Oxford University Press, 1998). References to *TI* include the abbreviated chapter title followed by the relevant section number when applicable.

UM = *Unzeitgemäße Betrachtungen* (when referred to as a group) translated as *Untimely Meditations* and *Unfashionable Observations*.

WP = "The Will to Power." This is not a book written by Nietzsche. Instead, it is a translation of a compilation of notes culled from Nietzsche's numerous unpublished notebooks across a long period of time. Students should cite it with caution, and when possible, the original German text should be closely compared. Our citations include reference to the German text from which translated material was selected. Trans. Walter Kaufmann and R. J. Hollingdale (New York: Vintage, 1968).

WS = *Der Wanderer und sein Schatten* (1880); translated as *The Wanderer and His Shadow*. Trans. R. J. Hollingdale in *Human All Too Human*.

Z = *Also sprach Zarathustra* (1883–1886); translated as *Thus Spoke Zarathustra*. Trans. Walter Kaufmann (New York: Viking Penguin, Inc., 1966). References to *Z* list the part number and chapter title followed by the relevant section number when applicable.

References to Nietzsche's unpublished writings are standardized to refer to the most accessible edition of Nietzsche's notebooks and publications, the *Kritische Studienausgabe* (*KSA*), compiled under the general editorship of Giorgio Colli and Mazzino Montinari. We also reference works not included in the *KSA*, which are part of the complete edition, published as *Kritische Gesamtausgabe* (*KGW*) (Berlin and New York: Walter de Gruyter, 1967–continuing). Unless otherwise indicated, translations from *KSA* and *KGW* are our own. Readers may access a digitized and further edited version of *KGW* (abbreviated *eKGWB*) at www.nietzschesource.org. A stable web address is used when citing that source.

In citations, Roman numerals denote the volume number of a set of collected works or standard subdivision within a single work, and Arabic numerals denote the relevant section number. In cases in which Nietzsche's prefaces are cited, the letter "P" is used and followed by the relevant section number where applicable. When a section is too long for the section number alone to be useful, the page number of the relevant translation is also provided. In the cases in which the *KGW* and *KSA* are cited, references provide the volume number (and part for *KGW*), followed by the relevant fragment number and any relevant aphorism (e.g., *KSA* 10:12[1].37 refers to volume 10, fragment 12[1], aphorism 37).

CHAPTER 1

NIETZSCHE'S LIFE AND WORKS IN CONTEXT

Much has been written about Nietzsche's life. It was a topic of choice for Nietzsche himself (see his *EH* and the prefaces he wrote to new editions of his works in 1886). A fascinating intersection of forces marks German history during Nietzsche's lifetime. The modern state of Germany did not even exist when Nietzsche was born in Röcken in 1844. It was not until 1871, when he published his first book, *BT*, that the diverse group of states and fiefdoms were finally and uneasily bound together militarily under Bismarck, although numerous failed confederations and alliances preceded the union. Great political unrest prevailed throughout Europe, and there was increasingly violent resistance to European colonization throughout Asia, Africa, Australia, and the Americas.

As industrialization rapidly spread, economic volatility ensued, and many countries saw the development of a new "middle class," which pushed for economic reforms and challenged long-established aristocracies. Socialism became increasingly popular and, consequently, feared. (Marx and Engels met in Paris in the same year Nietzsche was born.) German states were divided politically and religiously: a politically active Catholic minority struggled with the Lutheran Protestant majority. As Nietzsche was beginning his professorship at Basel in 1869, the First Vatican Council issued the doctrine of Papal infallibility, a move considered to be—at least partially—a response to pressures brought about by Bismarck's insistence that states formerly a part of the Holy Roman Empire of the German Nation should declare complete allegiance to Prussia. At the same time, the First Socialism Congress met in Basel.

Despite significant tensions and divisions, Germans were united linguistically and culturally, thanks to Martin Luther's translation of the Bible (which played a major role in the standardization of modern German),[1] and their deep appreciation for the accomplishments of German musicians (especially Bach, Haydn, Mozart, Beethoven, and Schubert), literary figures (such as Goethe, Schiller, and Hölderlin), and philosophers (such as Kant and Hegel). A dominant theme in Nietzsche's writings, particularly in *BGE*, is consideration of what it means to be part of a *nation* and whether and how that supports or interferes with the ability to see oneself as connected with a *culture*. The book includes numerous discussions of what it means to be German, in the sense of being part of the new "German nation" as compared with what it means to be German in the sense of being the heirs to (and standing on the shoulders of) Goethe and Beethoven. Nietzsche contrasts German nationalism with the sense of belonging to a tradition that exceeds any state's borders, largely what we might refer to today as the "Western tradition." This is only *partially* what he means by "good Europeans," because he thinks what constitutes the "Western tradition" is more than just traditional values and includes recognizing the entwinement of what is alien—or *unheimlich* (literally, *un-homely*)—with what might be considered most familiar, most our own (cf. the opening of *GM*).

In the same year as Nietzsche's birth, Ralph Waldo Emerson published the second series of his essays, which Nietzsche would later read with great enthusiasm. Also in that year, an assassination attempt was made on the life of the Prussian king, Friedrich Wilhelm IV, for whom Nietzsche was named and whose birthday, October 15, he shared. (The king was declared insane in 1858.) Nietzsche's father, Carl Ludwig, was a Lutheran minister who followed in the footsteps of *his* father. This vocational path stretched back at least four generations.

Elisabeth, Nietzsche's sister, was born less than 2 years after him. By all accounts she adored her brother but was deeply envious of the attention he received. She admired his intelligence, and even as a young child she chronicled it in the form of making lists of books in his library and noting his compositions. Later in life, Elisabeth was protective of her brother and took interest in the company he kept. She was especially jealous of Nietzsche's youthful relationship with Richard Wagner. She married a radical anti-Semite with whom she left Germany to found an Aryan colony in Paraguay. After her husband's suicide following a financial scandal, Elisabeth returned home where she lived with her mother and later cared for her ailing brother. Elisabeth is a notorious figure in Nietzsche scholarship. She carefully guarded her brother's literary estate, unscrupulously edited his notes for publication under the title *The Will to Power*, a book Nietzsche never wrote, and sought to have him recognized as the intellectual forbearer of what would become National Socialism. Famous pictures feature Hitler looking admiringly upon a bust of (a then deceased) Nietzsche, and one of the aged Elisabeth beaming with Hitler at her side.

A few months prior to Nietzsche's fifth birthday, his father died at the age of 35. Although the average lifespan at the time meant that someone who made it to their late-forties had lived a full life, Nietzsche's father's death was premature and might have resulted from an earlier stroke or injuries sustained in a fall off a ladder. Regardless, Nietzsche's family had little financial support thereafter, and his own health problems and difficulties with publishers meant, though he was far from destitute, financial hardship followed him for all of his life.

Nietzsche was educated at the famous Schulpforta, where he helped to found a musical society and pursued his own compositions. He deeply admired Schumann and Hölderlin. At Bonn, Nietzsche began his university studies as a student of theology, changing his course of study after one semester to philology. His extensive training in foreign languages and antiquity informs his understanding of the origins of modern ideas as well as alternative possibilities. Nietzsche finished his studies in Leipzig, where by chance he came upon the works of Arthur Schopenhauer (1788–1860) in a bookshop. He was deeply struck by Schopenhauer's thesis about the nature of willing, which regards will as the basis of reality and music as the highest art—ideas Nietzsche would wrestle with throughout his career. *Beyond Good and Evil* includes some of Nietzsche's most sustained discussions on will and on pessimism, and one can see this book as Nietzsche's testing ground for his ideas about will to power and asceticism that he develops in his later *GM*. In the year following his discovery of Schopenhauer, Nietzsche read F. A. Lange's *History of Materialism*, which attempts to wed materialism with

Kantian philosophy. Nietzsche greatly admired the book and cites it numerous times in his notebooks. From it, he also became acquainted with various developments in astronomy and chemistry, including the work of mathematician and physicist Boscovich (1711–1787) whose work Nietzsche mentions at a prominent point in part I of *BGE*.

In 1868, Nietzsche became personally acquainted with Richard Wagner (1813–1883) at a dinner party at the home of Wagner's sister. Eventually, Nietzsche became a regular guest at the Wagner's home in Tribschen, spending numerous birthdays and holidays there, and he worked to raise funds for Wagner's Bayreuth concert hall. Years later, Nietzsche broke off the relationship and wrote sharp criticisms of his former mentor but retained admiration for him. These ambivalent feelings are reflected in *BGE*, and in Nietzsche's discussions of artists generally. Further discussion of this occurs in our chapters on parts I and VIII.

Tremendously important developments in science occurred during Nietzsche's lifetime, particularly among German physicists, biologists, and astronomers. In 1850, Clausius formulated the second law of thermodynamics and a theory of gases. In the same year, Helmholtz made important contributions to understanding nerve impulses and subsequently published important works on optics and auditory sensations. A Neanderthal skull was found in a cave near Düsseldorf in 1856 and evolutionary biology and embryology emerged as distinctive areas of research. Spencer's "The Development Hypothesis" (1852) deployed the word "evolution" for the first time in the context of developmental biology; Darwin's "On the Origin of Species by Natural Selection" was published in 1859 (both are mentioned in *BGE*). Other prominent German scientists during this time included Ernst Haeckel, a zoologist and natural philosopher who developed a fundamental law of biogenetics, and Wilhelm Wundt, author of *Physiological Psychology* (1873) and widely recognized as a founder of experimental psychology. The same Wundt published a survey of contemporary philosophy in an 1877 issue of *Mind*, a journal still highly regarded today.[2]

Nietzsche met the editor of *Mind*, George Croom Robertson, in a guesthouse in 1877. At the time, Robertson was preparing the English translation of Wundt's review for publication, and he apparently told Nietzsche his *Untimely Meditations* were mentioned.[3] A curious feature of the article is that one of the ways it measures current trends in the discipline is by charting the number of lectures given for each of the main subject areas in philosophy. This data was supposed to indicate how the history of philosophy, which the author generally finds *unphilosophical*, has overtaken other areas of the discipline. The entire issue of the journal is noteworthy, since it treats many themes prominent in Nietzsche's writings, particularly the later works.[4]

Nietzsche maintained a lifelong interest in contemporary scientific theory, considering for a time giving up his philological studies in order to pursue chemistry.[5] His discussions of "science"—*Wissenschaft*, which includes but extends beyond the physical sciences—should be read in this context and mindful of Nietzsche's interests in the development of culture. This plays an important role in Nietzsche's critique of "the prejudices of the philosophers" at the beginning of *BGE*, and we shall see, is at the heart of the book.

The full text of *BGE* was completed in 1885 and published in 1886, just after Nietzsche's prose poem *Z* was published. At the time, Nietzsche wrote a letter to Burckhardt in which he claims that *BGE* "says the same things as my *Zarathustra*, only differently, very differently."[6] This is rather difficult to fathom; the works are *so* different, and not simply in their form. Rather than seeking to create some sort of elaborate concordance, we can draw on Nietzsche's statement to acknowledge that *BGE*, for all its specificity of detail in some places, is essentially like *Z* in its character as a philosophical quest, *the same philosophical quest*, which has vital implications. *What* Zarathustra *thinks* matters essentially for *how* and even *that* he lives. *Beyond Good and Evil* has the same sense of purpose, though not for a fictional character but rather for Nietzsche, perhaps also for his readers. The two books share this core project, but they differ significantly in *tone*, as Nietzsche notes in his *EH*: while *Zarathustra* was a "yes-saying" book, the books following it were "no-saying," or as he elaborates, "*no-doing*" (*EH, BGE* 1). Readers should keep this in mind when trying to flesh out Nietzsche's philosophical project—he thinks of it as an activity, *a doing*, not a meditation to be conducted before the fire in his nightclothes, not a thorough-going analysis that exposes the nature or being of thought, not a set of illustrations upon illustrations that all bring us increasingly closer to a non-hypothetical plateau of all thinking or complete understanding. "No-doing" for Nietzsche is "the great war—conjuring up a day of decision." (*EH, BGE* 1).

There is a considerable bit of melodrama in Nietzsche's characterization of *BGE* as he extends martial metaphors to include discussion of recruitment, courage, and toughness required for the task it sets: "One has to have guts merely to endure it; one must never have learned how to be afraid" (*EH, BGE* 2). It is unhelpful to dwell for too long on just how momentous Nietzsche thinks his project is, for it encourages us to simply anticipate and herald these "great events" without actually experiencing them. But it is worthwhile to keep in mind that it is precisely the latter that Nietzsche anticipates for those who appreciate his task—it is literally gut-wrenching to learn that one's points of pride are base, empty, and miserably misguided; it can be exceptionally disorienting to have this experience. Notice how Nietzsche has recourse at various times to describing his project in terms of a seafaring voyage and all the unpleasantness and uncertainties that go with it—nausea, the loss of horizon, thirst for clean water and land.

Early in 1885, Nietzsche arranged to have the fourth part of *Z* published privately. Meanwhile, he worked on the draft for a fifth book to be added to a new edition of *GS*. Between 1885 and 1886, Nietzsche experienced significant financial difficulties exacerbated by struggles with his publisher to whom he had made a loan. The publisher eventually repaid the loan, and rights to Nietzsche's books were sold to another publisher. Nietzsche decided to take advantage of the change by publishing new editions of his works. He wrote a series of new prefaces, including ones for *HH, BT, D*, and *GS*, and he negotiated to have the first three books of *Z* published together in a single volume for the first time. For the second edition of *GS*, he added a fifth book and an appendix of poems and songs. All of these new editions were finally published in 1887, just prior to Nietzsche's completion of his *GM*, which he claims in *EH* is a "clarification of *Beyond Good and Evil*." Thus, *BGE* stands at the leading edge of a particularly productive and important period in Nietzsche's philosophical life. It takes up virtually every theme he treats in later writings and presents them in a unified narrative. It is one of Nietzsche's richest and most insightful texts and is best appreciated when considered whole, which is precisely our approach in the following chapters.

CHAPTER 2

OVERVIEW OF THEMES

Nietzsche's aphoristic style sometimes leads readers to think of his texts as assemblages, perhaps lacking much organization other than their collection under large themes. Scholars contribute to this impression when they pluck lines from across his corpus. Nevertheless, *BGE* has a definite organization and complex structure which can be grasped when looking at it whole. The book is composed of a preface and nine parts, or chapters, which cover everything from the classic problems of philosophy—What is the self? What is knowledge and how do we know?—to freshly coined psychological analyses and investigations—What is the religious nature? And what is noble? What follows are synopses of these parts with highlights of significant sections. Chapters for each part discuss its relation in the context of Nietzsche's overarching concern to imagine and practice future philosophy.

Preface: Like much of the book, Nietzsche's preface is humorous, pithy, singular, and tantalizing. Teasing his reader he asks, "Supposing truth is a woman—what then?" If philosophers have been dogmatists, as Nietzsche suspects, then they have not been experts when it comes to women (note the switch to the plural here) since truth as a woman has not allowed herself to be won and every dogmatism finds itself discouraged and deflated. Philosophical dogmatism is the theme of the preface's opening gambit, and dogmatism is evident in folk superstitions such as the "soul" and the "ego," in the seductions of grammar, and in generalizations from human, all too human, facts. The fundamental error of philosophy—one to which Nietzsche insists we should not be ungrateful—is that of Plato and his invention of the pure spirit and the good in itself. These are transcendent notions bereft of human blood and bone and have given rise to a Platonism for the people in the form of Christianity. This error stands truth on its head and denies what is most basic to life, namely, perspective. Why should we be grateful for this? Because, Nietzsche thinks, it has created in European civilization "a magnificent tension of the spirit" and "with so tense a bow we can now shoot for the most distant goals." He places himself in opposition to the attempts made so far to unbend this bow (e.g., by means of Jesuitism and the democratic Enlightenment) and allies himself with the cause of "good Europeans" and "free (very free) spirits."

Part I, "On the Prejudices of the Philosophers": With a "rendezvous of question marks" Nietzsche suggests the activity of truth-seeking might be similarly scrutinized—what is truth-seeking really? Why do we do it? How does it stand in relation to other desires (wills, drives)? And he considers tendencies of philosophers and their kinds of problems and questions. Because his scope includes the history of philosophy since Plato, Nietzsche's remarks are necessarily general, but they are often astonishingly penetrating in isolating particular tendencies, false dilemmas, and dead ends. Several key concepts are introduced and utilized, including the hypothesis of "will to power" and the claim that "psychology shall once again be the queen of the sciences." This part focuses on Nietzsche's assessment of philosophy and his philosophical task: calling into question the value of truth and knowledge and its relation to the evaluation of "life." Three key concerns inform the organization and content: Arthur Schopenhauer's philosophy as exemplary of Nietzsche's reflection on the relation between philosophies and the philosophers who write them; the history of certain philosophical problems, including the distinction between the real and the apparent (and how these are known); the nature of human psychology and freedom; and developments in biology and evolutionary theory and applications of these researches in moral, social, and political philosophy. These concerns guide his explorations in the rest of the book and immediately bear on problems in contemporary philosophy including direction for a proper philosophical naturalism, the relation between philosophy and science, and the normative force of claims to truth.

§1 Introduction of the "problem of the value of truth."
§2 The "faith in opposite values" offered as paradigmatic "pre-judgement" or "prejudice" that directs philosophical

thinking and inhibits pursuit of what is identified in section 1; an introduction to the question of the normative value of truth by raising the possibility of a higher value in "life."

§3 Consciousness conceived as "channelled instinct," an extension of rather than distinct from instinct. The means of such "channeling" is valuation, including beliefs and "physiological demands for preservation of a certain type of life."

§4 Focus on the issue of what is life-promoting, first in consideration of necessary fictions.

§§5–6 Philosophy viewed as personal expression of a dominant drive, which is presented in abstract form along with the pretense of universality, a "prejudice," and the perspective of the ruling drive in the individual philosopher. Conception of individuals as collection of drives; in the case of philosophers, "*who he is*" is the "order of rank [of] the innermost drives of his nature."

§§7–9 Examples of preceding discussions with specific points of comparison in Hellenistic philosophy: Epicurus, Stoics. Introduction of the notion of the development of the history of philosophy as both tragic and comedic. Philosophy characterized as ultimately an intense expression of "will to power" in its desire to "creat[e] the world," and identify "the causa prima."

§10 Consideration of the "problem of the 'real and the apparent world'" and how its approach indicates either weariness or vitality. Significance of the role of the senses (cf. §§7–9, 10, 14, and 15).

§11 Consideration of the method and influence of transcendental philosophy and importance of belief in truth in "the perspective optics of life." Distinction between finding and inventing.

§12 Consideration of the influence of the concept of the atom, particularly the atomistic conception of the soul (contrast with §6). Anticipation of "new versions . . . of the soul-hypothesis" as "invention" that might lead to "discovery."

§13 Primary interest of organic being might be maximal expenditure of strength rather than conservation; introduction of concept of "will to power." (cf. §3, 6, 9).

§§14–15 Distinction between interpretation and explanation underscored; return to discussion of role of senses in knowledge (cf. §10), sensualism, and a "noble way of thinking."

§16 Consideration of "immediate certainties" and the complexities of and host of assumptions made about such candidates, as for example, René Descartes' "I think." Reorientation of primary metaphysical questions to psychological ones.

§17 The "I" or "ego" as a result of interpretative process, neither cause nor origin of thought, the latter as remnant of "soul atomism" (cf. §12).

§18 Attraction of some philosophical problems is the lure of refutability (linked with sensation as described in §19).

§19 Complexity of the activity simply named "willing": "pluralities of sensations," a "ruling thought," "affect." All willing as a dynamic of commanding and obeying, considering the complexity of subjectivity (cf. §§6, 12, 17), which is *felt* as a tense unity; freedom of will tied to "sensation of power" in this relation. Individual as "social structure composed of many 'souls'"; morality pertains to its commonwealth and "the doctrine of the relations of supremacy under which the phenomenon of 'life' comes to be" (cf. §§2, 4, 6, 13).

§20 Organic and atavistic character of concepts; grammar as reflective of a structure of world-interpretation, which distinguishes and constricts range of possible concepts; also linked with physiological conditions.

§21 Consideration of causation and free will debate, further underscoring distinctions between description, interpretation, and explanation. Instead of "free" or "unfree" wills, strong and weak ones (cf. §19).

§22 Key assumptions in all higher learning as "bad modes of interpretation," particularly concern for "lawfulness" (contrast with "will to power" [cf. §13]).

§23 Moral prejudices as impediments to analysis of human "soul," the nature of thought and will, and the relation between will and action (properly "psychology" in the ancient sense); form of study also perverted, which might better mirror morphology (drawn partially from "psychology" in modern sense) in light of will to power hypothesis just introduced; difficulty of the task considering what philosophy *has been*, our habitual inclinations, and our constitutional capacities. Overcoming these could be strange and sickening, yet profound.

Part II, "The Free Spirit": This part provides us with one of the most comprehensive portraits of not only the "free spirit," which occupied Nietzsche's concern in many of his earlier works, but also his philosophy as a whole at this point. Included are discussions that refine Nietzsche's views on truth and perspectivism, interpretation, the development and problem of morality, his proposition of will to power, and his conception of the possibilities for philosophy and how the free spirits engage it. Taken as a whole, it becomes clear that Nietzsche significantly breaks with his earlier conceptions of free spirituality or freemindedness.

§24 Though knowledge often seems so important to us, we are also willfully ignorant, since much of life depends upon simplification and falsification. This differs from the adage that "ignorance is bliss," since Nietzsche considers ignorance as a *refinement* of our will to know, which suggests it can be deliberate superficiality, which for Nietzsche is informed by insight and affirmation of life.

§25 Against martyrdom for truth, which poses as pure and selfless, but which can take the most cruel forms and embody intense personal hatred. Contrasts "good, free solitude" with being a "compulsory recluse." Once again compares philosophy to tragedy [cf. §§7–9] with the martyr providing a spectacle akin to the satyr play.

§26 Development of the notion of solitude in which the "choice" seeks refuge from the rule, but those who seek knowledge *cannot* live this way, because they need to study what is "average." Compare hybrid images here with discussions of hybridity and barbarism in parts VII and VIII.

§27 Introduces importance of *tempo* of thinking and the need for subtlety in interpretation.

§28 Continues discussion of tempo in language; considers rhythms of living, both cultural and physiological, and the connection between *what* can be conveyed and *how* as linked with expressive possibilities, drawing on musical examples and analogies. Free-spiritedness playfully associated with *presto*.

§28 Further develops ideas raised in 25 and 26, exploring the dangers of independence in the forms of loneliness and isolation. Zarathustra might provide an object lesson.

§29 Development of concerns about interpretation, translation, and being understood. The attempt to control this is expressed in the distinction between the esoteric ("looks down from above") and exoteric ("sees things from below"). An important section for appreciating Nietzsche's interest in how distance creates different perspectives and how different constitutions have different forms of nourishment, pollution, and poison.

§30 "Taste for the unconditional" as the worst, since it neither venerates nor despises with subtlety, and one who has it "forge[s] men and things in such a way" as to "vent" their "wrathful" and "reverent" attitudes. Even an unconditional taste against such unconditionality can develop; both are folly and signs of youth.

§31 A brief history of the development of morality from its "pre-history" to its "supramoral" possibilities. Key distinctions turn on the value or disvalue of consequences (prehistoric) and intentions (morality in the "narrower sense"), and the fundamental shift that could occur with recognition that "the decisive value of an action lies precisely in what is *unintentional* in it." Recalls the vision of "sail[ing] right over morality" in *BGE* 23. Emphasis on intention as monumental prejudice. Compare the "living touchstones of the soul" with *BGE* 263.

§33 Morality of selflessness and emphasis on disinterestedness in aesthetics and contemplation more generally challenged as duplicitous; they are pursued because "they please."

§34 One of the most direct challenges to the reigning value of truth, the concern that inaugurates the book: "It is no more than a moral prejudice that truth is worth more than mere appearance." Offers a direct, concise statement of what is called "perspectivism": "there would be no life at all if not on the basis of perspective estimates and appearances" (cf. §§2, 10, 11, 21, 24); and rejects the distinction between the true and apparent worlds, the ultimate conclusion of idealism, replacing it with an assumption of "degrees of apparentness [. . . and] different 'values,' to use the language of painters."

§35 A lament over the well-intentioned but ultimately fruitless (not to mention dangerous) linkage of truth with goodness.

§36 Most elaborate account and justification for Nietzsche's "proposition" that "our entire instinctive life [can be explained] as the development and ramification of *one* basic form of the will—namely 'will to power.'" Considers conscience and morality of method.

§37 Aphorism involving an interlocutor who expresses concern that Nietzsche's proposition eliminates god in favor of the devil, which Nietzsche dismisses.

§38 The variety of interpretations of the French Revolution, the divergent causes it is supposed to have advanced, leads to the "disappearance of the text" such that it can mean anything (and thus nothing). This offers evidence that its rally for freedom has been ultimately successful, which Nietzsche regards as an assassination of the very possibility of nobility generally (cf. §§46 and 239).

§39 Insights and traits of free thinkers identified, including acknowledging the fact that neither happiness nor unhappiness are arguments for or against a view. Invokes Stendhal's "banker" as "dry, clear, and without illusions."

§40 Frequently cited section on masks, as necessary to protect the "delicacy" of the profound (Nietzsche's examples: "love and extravagant generosity"), and as necessarily projected by those around a "profound" spirit.

§41 Return to the theme of independence in terms of not "remaining stuck" to people, fatherlands, pity, science, virtues, or even our own "detachment."

§42 Baptism of the "new philosophers" as *Versucher*: seekers, attempters, and tempters (cf. §§210 and 227).

§43 New philosophers as still "friends of truth" who "love their truths" but who do not wish their taste to be shared by everyone (cf. §221).

§44 Most elaborate and detailed account of the free spirit in all of Nietzsche's writings; distinguishes his conception from that of the "levelers" and "free thinkers." Key characteristics:

they do not want to be misunderstood, do not give "freedom" the highest value, are anti-democratic and anti-modern, exercise unparalleled conscience, and have a concern for humanity as such. Also notable: distinguishes free spirits from the *very* free spirit, for which he is a herald and addresses directly in the end.

Part III, "What Is Religious": Nietzsche the brilliant psychologist is at work in this book as he focuses attention on questions of religion and the religious nature, and dissects with acumen and startling turns of phrases religious cruelty, the religious neurosis, and the differences between different religious mentalities. Readers expecting Nietzsche to be simply and unequivocally anti-religious are in for a shock however, since Nietzsche dissociates himself from "free thinking" about religion. For the philosopher, as the free spirit understands him, religion has tremendous uses and is an important means in the cultivation (or "breeding") and education of the human being.

§45 Introduction to what is religious and what is required for those who go in search of knowledge of the history of the human soul.

§46 Focus on "original Christianity" and the cruelty of the Christian faith; Pascal as example of the suicide of reason. Important reference to the "slave rebellion in morals." (cf. *GM* I).

§47 On the conditions of the possibility of "religious neurosis"; Schopenhauer's thinking as an example from recent philosophy of the religious crisis and its question mark; Wagner cited as Schopenhauer's most convinced adherent.

§48 The difference of religious attitudes between northern and southern Europe.

§49 The gratitude that characterizes Greek religion.

§50 How different temperaments worship God differently: Luther, St. Augustine, and female saints.

§51 The riddle of the saint: Why is it that even the most powerful have bowed worshipfully before him?

§52 Contrast between the Old and New Testaments.

§53 Why atheism prevails today; contrast between the growth of the religious instinct and the lack of satisfaction with theism.

§54 Modern philosophy since Descartes described as "episte-mological skepticism"; anti-Christian but *not* anti-religious. Problem of the "I" and the subject addressed again.

§55 The great ladder of religious cruelty; Nietzsche attends to three rungs on it as most important.

§56 Pessimism and eternal recurrence; the latter presented as the "ideal" of the most world affirming human being.

§57 How the great religious concepts of the past, such as God and sin, are part of humanity's childhood and yet new "toys" for humanity to play with and learn from may be needed in the future.

§58 How modern existence, with its industriousness and pride, prepares people for a life of "unbelief." Thinly disguised attack on "free thinking" approaches to religion such as bourgeois Protestantism.

§59 The value of being "superficial"; important discussion of artists and their falsifying of the image of life. Important link to piety or "the life in God" where piety serves as a means of beautifying man; the will to *un*truth at any price where truth is too hard to accept.

§60 Nietzsche claims a human being who loves man for the sake of God has flown the highest and yet gone astray most beautifully. Does this mean man should be loved for what he simply is? What kind of love would love of the overman be?

§61 Account of the philosopher as free spirits understand him and his link to religion. Religions play a vitally important part in the project of man's cultivation and education. Religion has many valuable "means" Nietzsche spells out.

§62 When religions don't see themselves as means of cultivation and education but rather as ends in themselves they become dangerously dominant, and humanity is thwarted since much that ought to be allowed to perish is preserved. Christianity as calamitous example: the doctrine of the equality of all souls before God has led to the flourishing today of a sickly and mediocre creature, "the herd animal."

Part IV, "Epigrams and Interludes": This curious part might be regarded as the "heart" of the book in at least two respects. Nietzsche's original plan for *BGE* was a large collection of aphorisms, a "sentence book." Reasons for interest in this form of writing are conveyed throughout the book as he highlights how aphorisms can crystallize moralities and the "heart's desires" they embody. Our chapter applies and develops these themes.

Part V, "Natural History of Morality": Nietzsche performs a twofold task of advancing the cause of a science of morality in the form of a naturalistic psychological history of morality and laying out in clear and emphatic terms the nature of his opposition to the morality that prevails in Europe today. For his first task, he criticizes attempts to establish ethics or morality on a rational foundation, which he regards as misguided and naïve. He pursues his second task in exposing the errors and dangers of "herd animal morality," which he thinks today takes itself to be morality incarnate, as if history has all along been moving in the direction of values of equality and compassion as part of some telos of our evolutionary becoming.

§186 The developing "science of morals" cast as a crude level of evolution. Sets out the terms of opposition to any and all attempts to supply morality with a rational foundation insofar as all are insufficiently critical.

§187 Moralities to be understood as a "sign language of the affects."

§188 Crucial section for appreciating the extent to which Nietzsche thinks freedom is based on the acceptance and affirmation of *constraints*, hence the concluding statement on the need for self-respect and what it requires.

§189 Another treatment of the "industrious" spirit.

§190 On Plato, especially on what does not really seem to belong to him and comes from Socrates: Plato's morality. Contrast between the "noble" Plato and the "common" Socrates.

§191 The ancient theological problem of faith and knowledge presented as an opposition between instinct and reason; the role of Socrates in this. Another contrast drawn between Plato and Socrates: Socrates as great ironist (cf. *TI* "The Problem of Socrates").

§192 Elliptical section on learning: for example, how an individual science develops. Lesson: we are much more artists in our learning than we commonly suppose (i.e., we are falsifiers).

§193 On the two-way relationship between waking life and dreams: dreams influence waking experiences, dreams also exert influence on how we live.

§194 How differences between human beings manifest themselves. Focus is on how human beings regard the possession of something good rather than the order of rank of the goods they recognize.

§195 On the Jews and their "inversion of values" as marking the commencement of the slave rebellion in morality (cf. §§250–1).

§196 Parable centered on how innumerable dark bodies can be inferred beside the sun and that will never be seen by anyone.

§197 On misunderstanding the beast of prey and the human of prey (e.g., Cesare Borgia).

§198 Examination of the nature of moralities addressing themselves to the individual and his or her happiness and a criticism of their unconditional character.

§199 Existence of "herds" and herd instinct of obedience, regarded as a feature of human existence since time immemorial. Important for understanding the strange limits of human evolution, the moral hypocrisy of those who command in Europe today, the European herd human being, and why the appearance of Napoleon and his effect is such an exception to the norm.

§200 The weak character of human beings of mixed or diversified descent and whose instincts are at war with each other (cf. part VIII). Examples provided of rarer cases in which the inherited desire for carrying out a war against oneself leads to a stronger type of human via self-overcoming.

§201 Fear and timidity as "the mother of morality" and how we have been weakened by the dominance of one type of morality, which today takes itself to be "morality."

§202 Theme of the entire part emphasized: contemporary European morality is herd-animal morality and mistakes itself for "morality" in itself. Concentration on a single and fixed "morality" is dangerous for the future health and flourishing of the human animal (cf. *GM* P: makes the present live at the expense of the future).

§203 Dramatic conclusion offering Nietzsche as having a different faith, directed toward *new philosophers* who will revalue and invert eternal values. Task is to teach the human being that its future depends on human will and a new cultivation that will end the accident and nonsense that has ruled in history to date. Crucial section for understanding Nietzsche's project of a revaluation of values.

Part VI, "We Scholars": This part continues discussion of what constitutes "free thinking" (from part II), and develops the notion of dominating philosophy and the kind of person it would take to do it. "Dominating" refers to strength of will required to perform the task of creating values, and it characterizes the relation between philosophy and other kinds of inquiry. While Nietzsche's comments might seem a bit rambling and pedantic at times, he is trying to make razor thin distinctions (e.g., between different forms of pessimism in §§207 and 208) as well as project a task he thinks is only barely possible given our modern condition of a hybridity of tastes, democratic ideals, and fixation on objective truth-seeking (elaborated in subsequent parts).

§204 Introduces the subject of the relation between philosophy and science; focus on "philosophers of reality" and "positivists" as resigning themselves from "the masterly task and masterfulness of philosophy."

§205 Concern for the philosophers' development: "proper level, the height for a comprehensive look, for looking around, for looking down" (cf. §§30, 36, 56–7, and 62); emphasis on "over-all value judgment" and what is required *to be in the position* to make a judgment about the value of life, the risks and dangers such entails.

§206 Virtues, diseases, and bad manners of the "scientific man," who neither begets nor gives birth, contrasted with the noble type, dominating, authoritative, and self-sufficient. Greatest danger in their quest for the common: annihilation of what is "uncommon," "unbending the bow" (cf. §§P, 193, and 262), and introducing a "religion of pity" (cf. §§62, 82, 171, 202, 222, 225, 260, 269–71, and 293).

§207 Question: Is the objective spirit not a person *because* he is a mirror, or does he mirror because he lacks what is "personal?" In being objective, he must strip away everything personal, but in doing so ends up losing humanity; danger of hospitality (cf. 41).

§208 Rejection of skepticism and its perceived relation to pessimism. The skeptic as unable to say "yes" or "no," lacking *judgment*. Diagnosis of modern condition as sick and exhausted on account of *mixture* of different types, and unable to will or to feel the pleasure of willing. "Dynamite" image conjured (cf. *EH*); call for "grossen Politik."

§209 Consideration of a "stronger type of skepticism," which "despises and nevertheless seizes"; prepared in "the German spirit" via inheritance (e.g., Frederick William I to Frederick the Great), sublimated, spiritualized, and crystallized (cf. §186). Suggestions for considering what it is to be a man (both human and, apparently, "virile").

§210 Further distinction between skepticism (the stronger type) and criticism as evident in the future philosophers, who will have these as *dimensions* while not being of that *type* (future philosophers as multi-faceted and multi-capacitated). Key difference: their "certainty of value standards, the deliberate employment of a unity of method, a shrewd courage, the ability to stand alone and give an account of themselves." Future philosophers will have a commitment to and practice *experimentation*, and can be thought of as exceedingly "scientific" in that respect, although they will not make use of the same kind of experimentation that characterizes "objective" inquiry.

§211 Adoption of the specific characteristic perspectives of the earlier types discussed (and including many others), conceived as preconditioning and expanding the perspective of future philosophers, necessary for their task of "*creating values.*"

§212 Focus on philosophy in specialized sense as concerned with "a *new* greatness of man" and thus *necessarily* at odds with its contemporaries. The case of modernity is especially difficult because of the complexity and hybridity of modern human beings, modern tastes and types, especially for democracy, as well as the weakening of will as previously described. Conception of greatness in terms of excess, over-fullness, over-richness.

§213 Future philosophers as embodying both *presto* (cf. §§27 and 28) and severity (in judgment), and how this is especially linked with their disposition toward *necessity* (§213; cf. §188). Orders of rank of soul corresponding to orders of rank of problems, and the philosophical type as rare and requiring cultivation.

Part VII, "Our Virtues": This part explores the relation between capacities and tastes in a case study of the European legacy. Nietzsche practices the experimentation he flagged in part VI, utilizing the method of collection announced at the beginning of part V. "Our virtues" refers to both the status of what is considered moral virtue (as bad taste) and the virtues we've acquired in the process of getting to this rotten condition. Whereas the previous part was a further development and expansion of the earlier part on "The Free Spirit," this part draws resources from and expands the ideas introduced in part III on the essence of the religious by focusing on our psychic conditions and potentialities. Ignobility is part of our descent (our ancestry) and is tied to the condition of our sensibilities. This is partially a matter of bad breeding (a mixture of psychic types, miscegenation), such that now we have a taste for everything; yet, this is where our future lies because it gives us "secret access" to the circuits of instinct, which are crucial for us to understand if we want to project an alternative to the concept of greatness we currently hold.

§214 Virtue conceived as a relation between inclination and need, a radical transformation of what counts as "good conscience."

§215 Astronomical analogy drawn to suggest that modernity is oriented and illuminated by two suns "in which we perform actions of many colors."

§216 Return to the concept of Christian and neighborly love and the imperative to "love one's enemies" (cf. §§201, 67, 174, 162, 60, and 197): "we learn to *despise* when we love, and precisely when we love best."

§217 Reference back to the type that takes morality as pose.

§218 Call to study how the "norm" fights against the higher type (rather than study of deviant types).

§219 Higher spirituality as a "synthesis of all" "merely moral" "acquired through long discipline and exercise" with a "mission to maintain the *order of rank* in the world."

§220 The "interest" in all things allegedly disinterested; "choosier" spirits don't dwell long. Truth as a woman, not to be violated.

§221 Against the unconditional and bringing moralities to bow to the order of rank.

§222 Pity (cf. §§202, 206, 224, and 225) linked with self-contempt.

§223 Hybrid European; trying to achieve a perspective that affords *laughter*.

§224 Semi-barbarism provides "secret access" yet a "historical sense," including "having a taste for everything"—inherently *"ignoble"* (cf. positive conception of "free spirit" in §44 and danger of hospitality in §§41 and 233.) Shakespeare as a synthesis of tastes unappreciable by ancient Athenians. But with the "historical sense," we experience measurelessness, cannot feel, taste, love. Sexual imagery conveys the new philosophy has something to do with seduction and the control of/direction of desire (cf. §§131 and 220), part of the attempt to lure and achieve some measure of bliss. Insofar as nothing can be foreign and strange to us anymore, nothing can be truly "ours." Cf. travels in §44 and dangers of hospitality (§41, etc.); "drop the reins" at infinity (and this in contrast with Kant's conception of sublime).

§225 Pleasure and pain no argument (cf. §§46, 124, and 293), no measure, not opposites as we see in tragedy §229; "our pity" in contrast with "their pity," religion of pity; the discipline of suffering "Die Zucht des Leidens"; pity the pity of those who want to abolish suffering (while they want to increase it).

§226 Important section on "immoralism." Contrary to appearances, immoralists remain "men of duty" and dance in their chains.

§227 On free spirits and the perfection of their principal virtue of "honesty." On how every virtue ultimately leads to stupidity and how free spirits need to beware of this. Reference to "we last Stoics." Fear of being misunderstood and being mistaken for others. Is this not the fate of all innovators?

§228 On the boring character of all moral philosophy to date and on why there is a need to think of moral questions and problems as calamitous and fateful (the future of humankind is at stake). The idea of promoting the "general welfare" represents no real ideal or goal, not even an intelligible concept, but only an emetic. The need to recognize an order of rank between human beings and moralities.

§229 Important section on the extensive character of cruelty which extends to intellectual activity and the search for knowledge. It is a piece of clumsy psychology to suppose that cruelty only comes into being at the sight of the suffering of others—there is also an abundant enjoyment of one's own suffering.

§230 On the fundamental will of the spirit or mind, which has cultivated Protean arts and artifices of assimilation, incorporation, and self-deception and as a way of aiding the feeling of growth and increased power. Mind/spirit compared to a stomach. This will to simplification, appearance, and surface can be countered with a different inclination, the sublime one of the seeker of knowledge who demands profundity and multiplicity. This is represented by the "extravagant honesty" of free (very free) spirits. On the need to translate the human being back into nature so as to become master of the numerous vain and enthusiastic interpretations that have been painted over the "eternal basic text of *homo natura*" (Nietzsche makes a reference to the 'sealed' ears of Odysseus, but in fact only the ears of his sailors were sealed so that they would not hear the sirens' song or the pleas of Odysseus for the ship to change course).[1]

§231 On learning and how it changes us. But is there not at the bottom of us something that cannot be taught, some granite of "spiritual *fatum,*" such as predetermined decisions and answers to predetermined questions? Nietzsche gives the cardinal problem of "man and woman," as an example.

§§232–9 Notorious and playful presentation of Nietzsche's "truths" about "woman as such"; contains an unfashionable attack on "modern ideas" for their shallowness, including (in §239) "scholarly asses" of the male sex who wants woman to defeminize herself and imitate all the stupidities of European man.

Part VIII: "On Peoples and Fatherlands"—this part further develops the ideas of our ancestry, decadent heritage, and future possibilities. Wagner is offered as an exemplar of a mixture of types, and Nietzsche analyzes him as both a modern *type* and an *individual* with distinct possibilities. Nietzsche engages a variety of distinctively modern and contemporary concerns, including nationalism, programs for racial purity, and cultural decadence.

§240 On Wagner's music, especially the *Meistersinger*, which is interpreted as providing insight into the German character as one that as yet has no "today."

§241 What it means to be "good Europeans"; imaginary conversation between two patriots.

§242 Locates a "physiological process" taking place in Europe's democratic movement; Europeans become increasingly similar, a supra-national and nomadic type is emerging. Democratization of Europe produces two different main types of human being.

§243 Short parable on the constellation of Hercules expressing the hope that a new type of human is emerging.

§244 Lessons on German "profundity."

§245 Continuation of the exploration of German character through music.

§§246–7 Examination of German language, writing, and style.

§248 Two types of genius.

§249 Maxim on how every people has its own hypocrisy that it calls its virtues.

§250 What Europe owes to the Jews, including the "grand style in morality."

§251 The "European problem" defined as the cultivation of a new caste to rule Europe; important reflections on anti-Semitism and Jewish assimilation.

§252 Why the English are not a philosophical race.

§253 Why the plebeianism of modern ideas is due to England.

§254 The superiority of the French national character.

§255 Contrast between northern and southern European temperaments in relation to music.

§256 The "insanity" of nationalism conceals the fact that Europe wishes to become one. Great Europeans from Napoleon and Goethe to Schopenhauer and Wagner have worked towards a new synthesis preparing the way for the European of the future. Wagner as not simply a German patriot but part of the European movement towards unity.

Part IX, "What Is Noble?": Explores the possibilities for nobility, given the inheritance and descent of modernity. Nietzsche's finale ultimately attempts to create a perspective that comes close to the view that might be enjoyed by the *very* free spirits of §44. Mindful of the limitations of such a perspective, Nietzsche endeavors to draw on the capacities he identifies as characteristic of free spiritedness in previous parts. Especially important is the perspective readers are able to achieve on how Nietzsche thinks about the formation and maintenance of orders of rank, and once this becomes possible, Nietzsche begins to destroy his own text much like a Mandala sand painting, which is destroyed as soon as it is finished. This suggests that the title question *what is noble?* is not as much answered as it is given to the *reader* to ask and explore.

§257 How the "enhancement" of the type "man" has allegedly been secured and the origins of aristocratic societies.

§258 Further insight to "aristocratic radicalism." A healthy aristocracy experiences itself not as a function of society but as its meaning and highest possible justification.

§259 Definition of "life" as resting on appropriation, injury, overpowering, and exploitation. Appeal to honesty about the basic facts of "life" and how European consciousness resists instruction on this issue.

§260 Outline of the two basic types of morality: master and slave moralities. Note that in all higher and mixed cultures the two interpenetrate and can even be found together in the same human being. Reference to love as passion and the "gay science."

§261 Why the noble human being lacks vanity. Further differences between master and slave moralities enumerated.

§262 The evolutionary history of aristocratic societies and their decline; appearance of the "individual" that is obliged to be its own lawgiver; dangers of the morality of mediocrity.

§284 What is required for living with proud composure in which one can employ at will one's affects and one's pro and con, including the four virtues: courage, insight, sympathy, and solitude.

§285 The greatest thoughts are the greatest events and what is great as thought and an event is always the last to be comprehended.

§286 Quotation from the final scene of Goethe's *Faust* in which the soul of Faust rises to heaven. Nietzsche supposes an opposite type that also has height and free vision but looks down.

§287 What the word "noble" can still mean for us today; the noble soul is one that has reverence for itself.

§288 On virtue as "enthusiasm" or the possession of "spirit."

§289 Lesson on the hermit and the philosopher (the philosopher has been a hermit) in which the hermit holds that one writes books precisely in order to conceal what one really harbors. Every philosophy is a "foreground philosophy," and there can be no final stopping place in philosophy. This is why every philosophy conceals another one and every word is a mask.

§290 The profound thinker is more afraid of being understood than misunderstood.

§291 Another section on man as falsifier or forger (e.g., in the domain of morality), thus there may be more to the concept of art than is typically supposed.

§292 Definition of the philosopher as a "fatal" human being.

§293 Pity has value when it comes from a master type of human being but little or no value when it is expressed by those who suffer and preach it. Contemporary Europe is marked by a pathological sensitivity to pain (cf. §225). Another reference to the "gay science."

§294 The order of rank among philosophers is to be determined by the rank of their laughter.

§295 In praise of the "genius of the heart"; Nietzsche speaks of himself as the last disciple and initiate of the god Dionysus.

§296 Nietzsche laments the fact that his thoughts—colorful, young, and malicious—are already becoming immortalized and fixed as "truths."

"From High Mountains": Nietzsche's *Aftersong*—Nietzsche brings the book to a final close with this song to friends: the friends he has surpassed and the new friends he now awaits; bending of the bow and striking of the arrow; noon as the curious time of the shortest shadow and when one becomes two; arrival of Zarathustra and marriage of dark and light (beyond the metaphysical opposition of good and evil).

CHAPTER 3

PART I: "ON THE PREJUDICES OF THE PHILOSOPHERS"

one really has to wait for the advent of a new species of philosophers, such as have somehow another and converse taste and propensity from those we have known so far (BGE 2).

Nietzsche cleverly and eloquently opens part I claiming his project entails a "rendezvous of question marks" (*BGE* 1). *Questioning* is his chief objective; and he intends to do it as deeply and thoroughly as possible, trying not to shrink away just when it becomes most difficult. Nietzsche repeatedly raises the question *what is the value of truth*—how has truth come to be valued as it is, and where has that led us? In contemporary philosophical language, *what is the normativity of truth*? And further—concerning philosophy, science, and other forms of inquiry—how does the *will to truth* stand in relation to other values and desires? Is it really most primary in terms of what ultimately motivates such work? This new focus of inquiry is what Nietzsche links with the practice of "intellectual conscience," discussed at length in the chapters on parts VI and VIII.

In assessing others' philosophic projects, Nietzsche looks for how their views are indicative of a judgment concerning the value of life, and he explores relations among certain kinds of judgments (and conditions prior to judgment) from a metaphilosophical perspective to demonstrate how and why, in the history of philosophy, we have made very little progress in resolving some of our most ardent concerns, including: *what is the ultimate nature of reality? what is the status of human freedom?* and *what is the nature of change, growth, and development?* Further, he considers various conditions that would have to occur in order for things to be otherwise, in order for there to be a future philosophy that does not simply reiterate and repeat these errors of judgment. One such condition is recognition and development of *a new kind of taste.* Precisely what Nietzsche means by "taste" and why it matters are complicated and multi-dimensional issues. Only rarely does Nietzsche mention discussions of "taste" in the history of philosophy, as for example, when he refers several times (in ways that are somewhat ill-informed) to Kant's conception of "disinterestedness" in his *Critique of Judgment.* Sometimes, Nietzsche appears to be discussing taste in a rather pedestrian sense—the ordinary enjoyment that people seek out in their everyday experiences, such as the taste for newspapers and beer. These observations might seem irrelevant, although it becomes clear Nietzsche intends something more, even *these* "loves" are relevant for *his* analysis. This stands in sharp contrast with Kant's concern with a kind of taste for something beyond what is merely "pleasing," and with the views of others who claimed to be identifying and distinguishing *refined taste.*[1] Nietzsche is interested in these other senses too; he just doubts they are unrelated to his broader concern about values and how they shape objects of inquiry and motivate action. The topic recurs throughout *BGE*, ultimately leading to exploration of the concluding question "What is noble?"

From the start, we notice there are at least three dimensions to judgment Nietzsche explores: (1) the relations between *judgment of the value of life* and *judgment of the value of truth and knowledge*; (2) conditions for judgment and "prior," unconscious motivations influencing conscious, stated motives—*prejudices*; and (3) operations of judgments of taste as illustrative of the conditions identified in "2" and ultimately reflective and indicative of judgments of the value of life, as in "1." Much of *BGE* explores how these three dimensions of judgment function and are related in the case of philosophy, and Nietzsche anticipates various changes that might have to occur in order to effect new possible ways of thinking. Part I introduces a host of terms and key ideas that Nietzsche develops, combines, and advances in the rest of the book, so it is necessary here to deviate from the format of the rest of the book, which largely traces developments as they appear in the text.

WILL TO TRUTH, WILL OF LIFE

The question Nietzsche lays at the feet of his readers, put simply and starkly, is: *What in us wants truth?* (*BGE* 1; cf. *BGE* 11, *BGE* 16). He asks repeatedly, and shows how the pursuit of truth takes curious turns. He does not *deny* truth; rather he challenges dominant assumptions we have about the good of truth and its normative force: *Why not prefer untruth?* An initial response is obvious: we want truth because it is useful; it helps us get on in the world. Nietzsche doesn't deny this. But why not stop there? There is very much involved in "getting on" in the world that depends on *untruth*, or at least on overlooking "the truth" of some things. Practically speaking, truth matters, but so does untruth.

Untruth can take a variety of forms and connote different senses,[2] including: (1) *simplification*—we might think of this as a kind of *partiality*: "untrue" because incomplete; (2) *artificialization*, which helps us better capture or sort out experience: untrue because the ordering we use to make sense of something is not really to be found *in the world itself*; (3) *invention* or *fabrication*, or an exercise of creatively producing images of all sorts: untrue because such images are not direct representations of anything particular in nature. Thus, we can see it is possible for something to be untrue while not absolutely and completely false.[3] Untruth, in these senses, has its practical advantages; it is unavoidable and admits of a variety of senses and degrees.

Conversely, the same could be said for truth—it has various referents and admits of a scale. Nietzsche challenges the simplistic but enduring mistake of assuming that truth and untruth are opposite values rather than there being various gradations, "shades" of truth and apparentness (see ahead in *BGE* 32 and discussion of the "will to appearance" in our Chapter 9 [part VII]). Nietzsche sums up this worry in section 2 in which he discusses the "faith in opposite values." Throughout part I, and periodically the rest of the book, Nietzsche examines other instances of how the "faith in opposite values" generates other false dilemmas that push philosophers into dead-ends, such as the question of human freedom, for example, whether we are absolutely free or absolutely unfree, discussed below. Overcoming the "faith in opposite values" is important not only for gaining greater subtlety in our judgments concerning truth but also for surmounting a potentially harmful aversion to untruth.

At least since Plato, as he notes in the preface, truth has come to have intensive moral values attached to it—truth is good; untruth is bad, at times evil, and should be avoided if not eradicated. These attachments of moral and epistemic values also have certain affective associations. We presume that what is "good" is *good to want* (and have) and what is bad is not; and when we cannot have the good, we feel bad, deprived, and wish it were otherwise. This is a rather unfortunate circumstance if it should turn out to be the case that untruth is not only inevitable but also advantageous, since we would potentially avoid (and feel bad about) what could in fact be good for us.

We have mentioned there are certain specific practical advantages of untruth in the fuller senses outlined above—consider the enormous gain we enjoy through applications of the artificial structures of physics in engineering. But Nietzsche has in mind more general, broader advantages of untruth and the difference our affective attachments to it might make. These concerns are linked with what Nietzsche has to say about the "will of life," which he contrasts with the "will to preserve life" and various other motivations that might be thought prominent in human experience such as the pursuit of happiness or pleasure, safety, or security. Moreover, Nietzsche thinks *this* will (to life, which can have various degrees of strength or intensity) is also a powerful source of motivation in forming "pre-judgments," *prejudices* about which we are generally unconscious, but nevertheless direct what we judge as true, real, and good.

WILL AND AFFIRMATION OF LIFE

Even though we might highly value truth—enough that we are willing to sacrifice very much for it—Nietzsche speculates that, "For all the value that the true, the truthful, the selfless may deserve, it would still be possible that a higher and more *fundamental value for life* might have to be ascribed to deception, selfishness, and lust" (*BGE* 2). Nietzsche thinks although philosophers often claim to value truth above all else, it might nevertheless be the case that a will of life is higher or has greater force and influence, and *that* will also wants untruth when it is a condition of life (cf. *BGE* 24). We can see this expressed not only in our conscious motives but also physiologically (*BGE* 3; cf. *BGE* 23). At least two questions arise: *what is the nature of what we are calling "will" here?* and *how does Nietzsche's idea of human motivation as driven by "will of life" compare with some sort of "instinct" for self-preservation?* Nietzsche addresses both of these concerns in part I, and he pursues them further throughout the book and his writings that follow.

We cannot understand what Nietzsche means by "will" and why he discusses it without recalling Nietzsche's admiration of and disagreements with Schopenhauer (1788–1860), whose works he read with relish many times. Schopenhauer basically accepted Kantian idealism: what we know as "the world" is the product of the organizational structure and shaping forces of mind such that we "know" things insofar as they *appear* to us, insofar as they are *phenomena*; there is no knowledge of the world as such (in itself), independent or "outside" of human thought.[4] But unlike Kant, Schopenhauer thought it possible to bridge the phenomenal world of appearances and the noumenal world of things in themselves: for Schopenhauer, appearances are objectifications, representations of the world as will, the ultimate reality. We can *know* this by virtue of our felt experience of ourselves as embodied and willfully causing bodily action: in action we both sense our will as the cause of those actions and see the objectifications of will that result (i.e., the movements of the body). Thus, we have access to *immediate* knowledge, according to Schopenhauer, of the noumenal world—will. All that appears to exist is a representation of will, the fundamental basis of everything. Unlike other philosophers who consider will an important part of the soul that facilitates its development toward full completion and perfection, Schopenhauer thinks will is all there is, and it is essentially purposeless striving. This lies at the heart of his pessimism: will does not have any particular aim, and it is not leading toward some ultimate perfection. There is desire, yearning, want, and nothing more. The world of appearances presents us with many different individual entities, but behind it all there is nothing but striving will.

While immensely influenced by Schopenhauer, Nietzsche had his own ideas about the concept of will and the activity of willing, which are indicated in part I, such as in his critiques of "immediate certainties" (*BGE* 16) and the distinction between the real and the apparent worlds (*BGE* 10); his complex conception of soul (*BGE* 6, 12, 17, and 19), and his challenge to the ideas of causality upon which Schopenhauer's views depend (*BGE* 21). But what are most indicative of Nietzsche's pull away from Schopenhauer are his views about the complexity of what we synthesize and bring together under the simple term "will" (*BGE* 19), and his rejection of Schopenhauer's particular form of pessimism (discussed more fully in part III, Chapter 5). However, there's an important twist to note right away: Nietzsche's main problem with Schopenhauer's pessimism is *that he does not take it far enough*, he isn't *honest enough* to pursue it to its final conclusions (such honesty, in the form of what Nietzsche calls "intellectual conscience," is discussed in Chapters 7 and 8). Thus, in many respects, Nietzsche retains a deep commitment to a central dimension of Schopenhauer's philosophy (particularly, his view that the world itself is valueless and lacks ultimate, positive purpose), but he tries to take those ideas even further. Nietzsche thinks his own conception of the world as will to power accomplishes this and allows him to explore a host of questions Schopenhauer did not, *could* not, including "the problem of morality" (see Chapter 7 on part V) and how it is possible nevertheless to affirm life, to love it.[5]

Before turning directly to the issue of Nietzsche's pessimism, we should clarify the claim that Nietzsche does not preserve the distinction between appearances and reality that plays a major role in the views advanced by Kant and Schopenhauer. Thus, Nietzsche's "will to power" is not his candidate or substitute for the "in-itself," the real world of *noumena* behind everything else. "Will to power" is *descriptive* of the overall tendency of what he calls "life"—everything seeks expansion of life, its conditions to live (*BGE* 6, 13, and 23). It is also important to notice here that "expansion" and "preservation" are not necessarily identical; indeed, sometimes (perhaps often) expansion is pursued even at the risk of preservation, as Nietzsche writes in the section in which he formally introduces the idea of "will to power" (it also appears briefly in *BGE* 3, 6, and 9): "physiologists should think before putting down the instinct of self-preservation as the cardinal instinct of an organic being. A living thing seeks above all to *discharge* its strength—life itself is *will to power*; self-preservation is only one of the indirect and most frequent *results*." We return to these ideas in greater detail below in consideration of what Nietzsche thinks it would be possible to recognize if we were not blinded by some of the specific prejudices and views toward life he thinks have characterized much of philosophy and were *free to* conceive our own selves, motives, and future possibilities in new and different ways.

Challenges we face in rising to this task include pessimism—the view that life is not worth living—and nihilism—the view that there are no values, that nothing has any value (including life). For Nietzsche, these are gravely serious matters because they bear quite directly on the nature of our constitutions. He is interested in the psycho-physiological effects these have: these dispositions and beliefs express the relation of drives we are (*BGE* 6). A pessimistic constitution can be indicative of a life form in decline, in which the entity is not so strongly motivated by continuation or preservation much less *cultivation* and enhancement of *life*.[6] Such an organism might be dysfunctional, with disintegrating instincts, what Nietzsche calls a "weaker" will (*BGE* 2; cf. *BGE* 21). Someone who expresses nihilism might lack reasons to pursue anything in particular, have any particular sort of order, and prefer anything above anything else. Nietzsche thinks modern human beings are especially susceptible to these conditions.

All human beings have faced pessimism. There is plenty in life that is difficult. We all suffer, and in the end, we all die. Moreover, this cycle—including the various turns that make up the momentous occasions in our lives—just repeats itself in countless iterations: it is the same drama just with different actors, as Nietzsche writes in *WS* 58. Viewed from the perspective of life (and all eternity), our problems, challenges, and accomplishments are utterly mundane and insignificant. And it is not just our own suffering that induces stress and distress: the suffering of others also bothers most of us, compounding our suffering as we suffer because of the fact that others do. Our disposition toward suffering is especially telling, Nietzsche thinks, of our judgment of the value of life. Given suffering, which seems inescapable, is life worth it? Whether we answer "yes" or "no" is indicative of the relative strength of our constitutions, he suggests, indicative of the relative strength of will to power we express.

Most of us find ways to console ourselves, compensate for, or redeem suffering. Familiar strategies include distracting ourselves (e.g., celebrity gossip and politics), escaping it (e.g., alcohol and other narcotics, or religious fixation on an "afterlife"), and ignoring it by putting on a cheery face (though this might be the least successful strategy given how pervasive and persistent suffering can be). Another approach is to seek *redemption* or compensation for suffering, which might utilize one of the other strategies above, as for example, in the redemption of the life of suffering in this world through a perfectly cheerful afterlife. We shall discuss this at greater length in the next chapter when considering Nietzsche's thoughts about how art might offer a kind of redemption in this life rather than an afterlife, and thus potentially be a way of overcoming pessimism without escaping or ignoring it, which was a theme explored in his first book.

As previously mentioned, we should not think pessimism is all bad; on the contrary, Nietzsche describes his own aspirations as achieving a "pessimism of strength" (*GS* 370; cf. *BT* "Attempt at a Self-Criticism"), and he reports he arrives at the perspective of eternal recurrence through his effort "to think pessimism through to its depths and to liberate it" (*BGE* 56). Whereas in *BT* Nietzsche casts Homer as giving the ancient Greeks a hard-won cheerful veneer, which is instructive provided we do not mistake it for ignorance or naiveté, he considers Schopenhauer as providing a dose of brutally honest sobering reality at a time when there is far too much mindless optimism and distraction in the forms of blind convictions about human moral progress, dreams of transcendence of human limitations by virtue of technological advancements, and optimism that science will ultimately lead to human perfection and solutions to all our problems. The challenge Nietzsche tries to meet involves exploring how it is possible to draw on the benefits of each: a sobering look at what we are entitled to believe about the nature of our existence and the exercise of our human creative capacities in the course of maximally esteeming precisely *this* life. This entails a great deal of reflection on *who* and *what* we are and how and why we value what we do.

CONDITIONS OF JUDGMENT: OUR CONSTITUTIONS

Nietzsche thinks what we refer to as "consciousness" and endeavor to distinguish from unconscious, non-reflective "instinct" is in fact a variant or extension of the latter (*BGE* 3) insofar as what we call "instinct" channels and guides what we think and how. Thus, Nietzsche had great interest in studies of heredity, morphology, and evolutionary biology.[7] Throughout part I, Nietzsche considers the "prejudices of the philosophers" in terms of what he calls "a desire of the heart" (*BGE* 5), which is abstracted and refined, justified after the fact, and presented as though it were pure, objective, and independent of any personal need, wish, or interest. Rather than *discoverers* of truth, philosophers are actually *advocates* for their prejudices even though they do not wish to be called such. What Nietzsche calls *conscience* would have them admit as much and wear their prejudices on their sleeves. This last point is especially important, because Nietzsche is not suggesting that if philosophers really want to get at the truth they should avoid all prejudice.

As for the form of these prejudices, Nietzsche thinks some are motivated by settling personal grudges or feuds (suggested in the case of Epicurus: *BGE* 7), while others refer back to a desire for life—that is, for more of it, namely to *expand*; or for less of it, that is, to *flee* (cf. *BGE* 28 and *GS* 340). Four key sections in this part provide the basis for a much richer appreciation for how Nietzsche thinks about the human constitution and its capacities for judgment of the sorts identified at the head of this chapter. In section 6, Nietzsche writes that what "characterizes" (*bezeichen*) the philosopher is his "morality," which "bears decided and decisive witness to *who he is*—that is, in what order of rank the innermost drives of his nature stand in relation to each other" (*BGE* 6). Earlier in the same section, Nietzsche offers the idea that *what* we are is a composite of drives, each of which has sought to rule the others and articulate the world from its perspective: "every single one of them would like only too well to represent just *itself* as the ultimate purpose of existence and the legitimate *master* of all the other drives."[8] In short, one way to look at what we are is as a site of struggle among these drives, each of which seeks to order the constitution of the whole and set the terms for action. Since "every drive wants to be master," we can analyze philosophies as indicative of characters of orders person are, particularly what drives rule and how they establish relations among other drives.

How Nietzsche describes drives and their relations as constitutive of the "soul"[9] bears some significant similarities to that of Plato's Socrates: he conceives it as an arrangement of many parts, whose order is indicative of what rules the whole. Moreover, Nietzsche considers better and worse ways this occurs, in terms of *how* ordering is achieved, the means used to achieve it (his next book, *GM*, offers an in-depth analysis of how the ascetic ideal functions in that way); *what* particular order is achieved; and *how* the particular order is maintained (how whatever rules continues to do so). But whereas Plato's Socrates appears to think there is a good and just order, Nietzsche is concerned with analyzing how such arrangements come to be, how estimations of the value of life play a role in ordering, the fragility and stability of such arrangements, and how conceptions of soul bear on the other concepts we have. This latter concern is particularly evident in section 12, which also provides insight into how Nietzsche ends up talking about "soul" in the first place, even though he is hostile to many things metaphysical and prefers the modern scientific conception of the human to its religious counterpoint.

A specific prejudice Nietzsche examines at the core of philosophy is what he calls "the atomic need"—a longing to determine the fundamental "stuff" of the universe great and small—and he thinks this need is a major culprit in mangling thinking such that it has led to the pursuit of a set of dead-ends. In section 12, Nietzsche considers Boscovich's arguments against the concepts of "substance" and "matter" in which he develops a theory of non-material, dynamic force-points or particles in contrast with the Newtonian conception of corpuscular atoms.[10] Even though Boscovich might have managed to vanquish the notion that one needs the atom to offer an account of substance, he did not eradicate the "atomic need," which Nietzsche thinks is metaphorically transferred and lives on in all sorts of forms, including our conception of ourselves. What Nietzsche calls "soul atomism" is a manifestation of this need (cf. *WS* 9–11), which seeks to identify an indestructible eternal core of things. But getting beyond this need does not necessarily mean giving up on the idea of a soul. Nietzsche suggests that there might be ways of revising the "soul hypothesis," including conceiving a "mortal soul," or "soul as subjective multiplicity," or "soul as social structure of the drives and affects" (§12), and in fact, he tests out several of these in the book. Doing this conceptual replacement work is one dimension of a wide-ranging set of activities, inclinations, and cultivated capacities Nietzsche envisions as future philosophy, and it will take us virtually the rest of the book to identify and collate them. For now, we note Nietzsche associates this work of creating new (more adequate and fruitful) conceptions with a form of artistic power, the precise nature of which is uncertain even for Nietzsche, though he will try to draw increasingly more precise distinctions between such activity and its contrasts. Two helpful indications of what this might entail are available to us at this point as this allows us to make some quick observations about Nietzsche's empiricism and naturalism.

In section 10, Nietzsche discusses the age-old philosophic argument of how to distinguish and reconcile the world of appearances and the world as it really is. Nietzsche thinks this exhausting problem can lead to nihilism: consider the debate that leads Parmenides to conclude that "all is one" and the apparent world of change (the world of our experience) is an illusion; the developments of modern empiricism and idealism reflect the very same concerns that motivated the earliest Greek thinkers, Plato, the Epicureans, and the Stoics [cf. *BGE* 7–9]); yet others evince what is described above in terms of an affirmative will ("stronger and livelier thinkers who are still eager for life"), arguing for "perspective" and denying the (ultimate) reality of the sensual world. Nietzsche calls these "skeptical anti-realists and knowledge microscopists,"[11] who are anti-modernists wishing to retain an ancient sense of human nobility they find lacking in the modern "village fair motleyness and patchiness." While admiring their skepticism, Nietzsche thinks they do not follow their ideas far enough, namely to the point of questioning the value of truth and the basis of nobility, such as he anticipates possible: "A little *more* strength, flight, courage, and artistic power, and they would want to *rise*—not return!" (*BGE* 10).

In other words, instead of resorting to retrograde ideas, the anti-realist rebels against modern philosophy might have created new conceptions of human existence and its possibilities.

Nietzsche's apparent admiration for the "sceptical anti-realists" of section 10 stands in contrast with his apparent praise of "sensualism" in section 15, which has been the subject of significant discussion in the Nietzsche literature, particularly as it bears on Nietzsche's naturalism and his assessment of the aims, methods, and results of science. There is a sizeable body of secondary literature that *relies upon* certain assumptions about the meaning of Nietzsche's claim, "Sensualism, therefore, at least as a regulative hypothesis, if not as a heuristic principle," and engaging it would take us too far afield from the main focus of this chapter, but we can make a few points about Nietzsche's apparent ambivalence about "sensualism" here.[12] In *BGE* 14, Nietzsche contrasts the noble thought of Plato who "mastered the senses" by dulling and containing sense evidence with those who are captivated by sense evidence, thinking it supplies the basis of explanation rather than interpretation— Nietzsche associates *this* with "popular sensualism." But he further contrasts this with a different sort of imperative stance associated with the idea of "sensualism . . . as a regulative hypothesis." In setting these views side by side, we can see there is a significant difference between them: "*was sich sehen und tasten läßt—bis so weit muss man jedes problem treiben*" (only what can be seen and felt—every problem has to be pursued to that point; *BGE* 14) and "*wo der Mensch nichts mehr zu sehen und zu greifen hat, da hat er auch nichts mehr zu suchen*" (where one cannot find anything to see and to grasp he has no further business; *BGE* 15).

The first concerns *the extent to which* a problem is pursued by those holding the view of popular sensualism; the second is about the *limits of problems* when guided by sensualism as a regulative ideal. Nietzsche is certainly not rejecting the value of sense experience, but neither is he limiting knowledge to whatever can be the subject of empirical investigation nor is he simply *endorsing* scientific explanation.[13] Instead, he calls readers to reconsider the relation between invention and discovery, and this might be the best way to understand what is at stake for Nietzsche in the possibilities for revised conceptions of the soul hypothesis.

In sections 11 and 12, Nietzsche suggests a new relation between inventing and discovering—in which *erfinden* might eventually lead to *finden*—could provide cues for possible applications of the philosophical creative power previously mentioned. In this case, it is important to not think of invention as *sheer* (trivial or capricious) invention; the creation of new soul hypotheses would not necessarily be pure fiction. That Nietzsche anticipates such revised concepts will be inventions rather than discoveries is consistent with what he says about truth and what he has suggested about the limits of human knowledge, particularly as it is sought in philosophy. But at this point in the text, Nietzsche has yet to give much indication of how inventions might lead to discoveries, so we must continue to try to make sense of what this might mean as we move through the book.

The contrast between *invention* and *discovery* is complemented by Nietzsche's distinction between *interpretation* and *explanation*. Nietzsche thinks even the formalized sciences provide us with what are interpretations, not explanations of the phenomena investigated—as much as philology, which was trying to formalize its methods so as it make itself a science, provides interpretations of its objects of investigation, so too does physics. (It will take some work for Nietzsche to distinguish better from worse interpretations, but it is clear he does think there are differences; the fact that there are many interpretations does not mean all interpretations are equally valuable.) Moreover, such descriptions are always organized to suit our purposes or interests. We continue to place more faith, namely faith in the possibility of "world explanation" in physics because of an abiding faith in the senses. This is curious if we recall Nietzsche's discussion from section 13, since faith in the senses should have been irremediably shaken *by science* (Nietzsche offers the works of Copernicus and Boscovich as examples of what can undermine our senses of both the cosmic and the microscopic). So, these scientific discoveries should have at least challenged the sense-perceptive basis of science and empiricism, and yet they did not. That we continue to have such faith that science is, in fact, supplying *explanations* rather than *interpretations*, shows the stubborn nature of our prejudices.

Nietzsche suggests his own conception of soul in section 19 in which he claims that "our body is but a social structure composed of many souls [. . .] in all willing it is absolutely a question of commanding and obeying, on the basis, as already said, of a social structure composed of many 'souls.'" This section not only helps us better understand Nietzsche's conception of human subjectivity (with possible implications for a different conception of agency) but also sheds light on his hypothesis, discussed below and in the next chapter, that "the world defined and determined according to its 'intelligible character'—it would be 'will to power' and nothing else" (§36).

In section 19, Nietzsche discusses the complexity of willing, which we are inclined to think of as simple in its composition because we utilize a single word to describe what is a multifaceted process, another of our prejudices Nietzsche singles out in part I. This complexity is comprised of at least three aspects: sensations, thoughts, and affects. Cautiously, Nietzsche writes, "let us say that in all willing there is, first, a plurality of sensations." Moreover, every episode of willing is organized in terms of "a ruling thought": "let us not imagine it possible to sever this thought from the 'willing,' as if any will would then remain over!" And "above all," Nietzsche claims, there is *affect* in willing. It includes "straining of attention" focusing on the object or aim willed, and an "unconditional evaluation that 'this and nothing else is necessary now.'" Such affects are appropriate to a commander, but in this case what is commanding and what is being commanded are not two separate and distinct entities: all commanding is a commanding over something else within oneself that "renders obedience" or is believed so. Thus, it seems, all willing involves both commanding and obeying: "we are at the same time the commanding *and* the obeying parties." (As an aside we can note this is partially offered as counter-evidence to the faith in opposites and the prejudice that something cannot be both simultaneously [§2].) These characteristics— commanding and obeying—have accompanying sensations, which are in tension. Along with acts of will comes the duality of sensations of "constraint, impulsion, pressure, resistance, and motion." But we grow accustomed to disregarding these oppositions "by means of the synthetic concept 'I.'"

What we call "will" has its appearance (as *Anschein*) in the feelings that accompany obedience to commanding, and we mistake this for the *cause* of the feelings. We might rightly see Nietzsche as offering a *phenomenology of willing* here, which also focuses on the psychological dimensions of motivation rather than an explanation of willing.[14] The terms of this sort of experience and where it leads us philosophically and psychologically also direct us to Nietzsche's hypothesis of will to power. He seems to think the appearance of will emerges secondarily in enjoyment derived in the "success" of willing, in "an increase of the sensation of power, which accompanies all success." Notice that what is significant is the *sensation* of power and not necessarily actual achievement of power. This can be compared with the description of the "sovereign individual," mentioned in *GM* II:2, who is distinguished by his immense "sensation of the feeling of power" among other things. Overcoming obstacles produces a sensation we call willing; the pleasure of that sensation is intensified in taking ourselves to be the *cause* of such triumphs.

As Nietzsche further elaborates the relation between the "synthetic concept of the 'I'" and willing, he claims these multiple activities of commanding and obeying, presenting obstacles and overcoming them, involve us in thinking not only of a soul but of various "under-wills" or "under-souls" struggling and competing to rule. In this way, we are like social structures of many souls, an idea that harkens back to Nietzsche's discussion of soul atomism in section 12. And if we are social structures then willing itself (as expression of the activity and interrelation of the various parts of the "commonwealth" we are) is subject to moral consideration. There is, in other words and as philosophers much earlier and later would consider it, an *ethos of the self*, the soul, which coordinates with the order of rank it is and the character of the ordering thus maintained.[15] In this respect, Nietzsche claims, "it is only a matter of *strong* and *weak* wills" (§21) rather than "free or "unfree" ones. Souls are conceived by Nietzsche as social structures subject to order of rank in accordance with the relative strength of their constitutive drives. This order of rank reflects the values of the drives that dominate, and this is what amounts to what can also be called taste—it consists of a set of priorities among drives that characterize and orient the activity of any particular organism or organization in question. What we want and what we value matter very much for Nietzsche, because those things determine or give shape to how we live (i.e., that for which we have a taste orients what we pursue, what we define as meriting risk, and what we avoid).

JUDGMENT AND TASTE

For this reason Nietzsche thinks his contemporary evolutionary theorists who attribute to the whole species the ultimate value of self-preservation, particularly conservation, simply fail to account for the complexity of human valuation and the ways in which it conditions life (§13). In this respect, Nietzsche focuses his attention on a nexus of judgment, value, and taste. Judgment concerns not only the true and the false but also the *value* of the true and the false: why pursue truth, what in us wants the truth, why might we also pursue untruth? What we judge and how we exercise judgment are related to conditions of life, what makes it possible for us to live *and how*. Other philosophers had considered this in the past, of course, most famously (for our purposes) Kant, who distinguished forms of judgment, including the kind of judgment that leads to knowledge (pure reason), judgments about what we ought to do (practical judgment), and judgments of the beautiful and sublime (aesthetic judgment). But Nietzsche opposes this separation, denying there are separate "faculties" or realms of judgment. He considers instead hierarchies of interests (often in terms of *aims of drives*) that coordinate with orders of rule of the various parts making up individuals, as we shall see further below and throughout the book.[16]

Nietzsche thinks the kinds of lives we prefer and seek are fundamentally related to tastes, as reflected in his early claim that philosophy is not merely the love of wisdom, as the tradition often identifies it, but also involves having "sharp taste."[17] Thus, his discussion of the multifaceted nature of "Judgment" is essentially related to questions of taste, particularly and ultimately whether one has a taste for life (cf. §9). Much like Plato,

Nietzsche distinguishes noble tastes from those that are base, although (as evident in §14), he greatly differs with Plato about *what is noble and how it is determined.* In conceiving human willing as the expression or unfolding of a complex interaction of obeying and commanding parties, we can see Nietzsche's perspectivism as linked with the constitution of what philosophers call "the subject": that which says "I" refers to whatever happens to be the ruling party in the mix. A perspective is a viewpoint from a position of commanding or obeying, shaped by the interests and values of that party. Subjects view the world from the perspectives of their ruling drives, and these drives can be distinguished in terms of what they want; that is, they are defined in terms of what they seek or pursue, or, finally, what they value. A will to truth is the expression of merely one of many such drives, which include making money, politics, and so on (§6). Drives may be piqued, agitated, or strengthened by popular opinion—they come to be strengthened by virtue of being widely shared among a number of subjects, and they rule in this way. What Nietzsche thinks is distinctive about philosophy is that moral valuations predominate and establish ranking orders among the other drives. Again, since willing, as discussed in section 19, is encompassed in the "sphere of morals" and "morals [are] understood as the doctrine of the relations of supremacy under which the phenomenon of 'life' comes to be," philosophical perspectives can shape or condition *ways of life, possibilities for living*, and not merely different ways of thinking. This idea is contained within our conception of what constitutes an *ethos*: it is the set of values that gives rise to whole ways of being. This idea cues us to what Nietzsche has in mind at the end of part I when he writes, "psychology shall be recognized again as the queen of the sciences" (§23). He refers, at least in part, to an ancient sense of the study of the soul, although he is obviously departing from the conception of the soul as attributed to Plato or later to the "soul atomists."[18]

The philosophers of the future, it seems, if they are identical to those who will endeavor to articulate "a proper physio-psychology" (§23) will practice psychology in the sense of exploring the nature of the human soul, with particular attention to the command structure that emerges in the context of willing (§20) and mindful of the conceptual quagmires Nietzsche identifies in this part. There can be no value-less willing, no thinking without willing, and therefore no philosophy free of values. Thus, it would seem, whatever the future philosophers do, it cannot be free of prejudice. The "free spirits" related, if not identical to, the future philosophers, therefore cannot be *free* or rid themselves of values. Their task must be somehow otherwise defined.

When we look at Nietzsche's critiques of values and judgments we see he measures them in relation to the conditions of life they support. What kind of taste is cultivated so as to direct life in a certain way, bring out certain qualities or characteristics rather than others?[19] *What* is thereby strengthened or weakened, and how? As we shall see, particularly in later chapters, Nietzsche seems to envision philosophers potentially playing roles in actually cultivating new tastes. Thus, future philosophers do not simply try to understand the world; they seek in some major respects to *change it*, and not just by helping others know better, though this seems to be a dimension of what part I describes, but also potentially in order to *act differently* because *they want different things*. Motivating different action does not simply turn on argument; it requires cultivation and coordination, or direction of desire. Nietzsche's assessment of the condition of modern human beings turns on the difficulty of this task.[20]

Taste is relevant insofar as *what we want* determines the direction of our attention and energy, and *what we love* (what wins out as wanted most) does this even more so. Thus, as he puts it in section 5, "wishes of the heart" motivate our interpretations of the world, our metaphysical systems and conceptual structures. Nietzsche is concerned to further investigate the nature of such desires, how we come to have them, and their various possibilities, because he does not advocate simply following one's heart's desire. As previously discussed in relation to his investigations of our prejudices, Nietzsche thinks we need to exercise a good deal more "conscience" in understanding the origin and nature of our prejudices. Moreover, the content of those judgments—*what is valued and why*—also deserves scrutiny, particularly in relation to the degree to which such loves are compatible and conjoined with a love of life. Very much like the Platonic Socrates of the *Republic*, Nietzsche is concerned about "right tastes" (e.g., *Republic* 410–12), although what makes a taste *right* or otherwise "good" is a matter for considerable reflection, and much of *BGE* explores just that concern right up until the very end with the questioning of what is noble.

NIETZSCHE'S HYPOTHESIS AND HIS NEW PSYCHOLOGY

There may be no more popular association with Nietzsche's philosophy than the notion that he is a philosopher of power. While familiar, Nietzsche's views on power are generally not well understood. By way of concluding this chapter, we introduce Nietzsche's self-proclaimed "proposition" concerning "will to power."

Insight on Nietzsche's curious idea can be gained negatively: "will to power" is neither a substance nor a description of people's motivations. Nietzsche does not postulate some ultimate *will* that is behind and responsible for all (Schopenhauer's view). As discussed above, in section 19 Nietzsche highlights the fact that what we call "will" is a complex of thinking, feeling, and affect. Thus, "will to power" is chiefly defined as a psychological and physiological perspective or orientation and not first and foremost a political aim or objective. Finally, it is not an imperative or normative view about the value or desirability of getting power *over* others, although subduing, dominating, and exploiting are each manifestations of will to power (*BGE* 230, see Chapter 9).

The idea of "will to power" is formally introduced in section 13, where Nietzsche challenges "physiologists" and their idea of an "instinct of self-preservation" as the most influential instinct directing the behavior of organic life. In commenting on the theory of conservation, Nietzsche refers to what he understands of debates in the nascent evolutionary theories. Nietzsche agrees with those such as Rolph and Roux who think organisms seek *expansion*, or growth, rather than their own preservation at virtually all costs.[21] This serves as a clear indication that Nietzsche is not simply discussing a psychological tendency of human beings. He experiments with a variety of ways of elaborating these ideas in his notebooks and later writings. From the very first to the last, he attempts to makes sense of the world in terms of struggling forces, which result in various *interpretations* rather than political projects: "The will to power *interprets*" (*KSA* 12:2[148]).[22] Such interpreting:

> defines limits, determines degrees, variations of power. Mere variations of power could not feel themselves to be such: there must be present something that wants to grow and interprets the value of whatever else wants to grow. Equal in *that*—In fact, interpretation is itself a means of becoming master of something. (The organic process constantly presupposes interpretations.) (ibid.)

In the end, what we designate with the word "life" is, according to Nietzsche, "the tremendous shaping, form-creating force working from within which *utilizes* and *exploits* 'external circumstances'" (*KSA* 12:7[25]). There is no *substance* or *core* that wills. There is simply this activity; what exist are centers of force ("dynamic quanta") situated in relation to others, and *what they are* is constituted in and by their relations. What we call "the individual" is "itself [as] a struggle between parts (for food, space, etc): its evolution is tied to the victory or predominance of individual parts." Its passing occurs in the context of "an atrophy, a 'becoming an organ' of other parts" (*KSA* 12:7[25]).[23]

Since Nietzsche's physics of interpretation and incorporation conceives human beings (and all entities) as pluralities of relational affects, by living, by taking any action at all, we play a role in creating reality. And the same holds true of our interactions with others. We not only participate in shaping social reality, but through engaging others, eliciting affects, and being involved in relations with them, we are constituted by and participate in constituting others as well.

In *Thus Spoke Zarathustra* Nietzsche's character Zarathustra articulates alternative ways of conceiving what a human being is, how it develops, and how such conceptions might be relevant for reflections on the aims of humanity as such. It is helpful to keep these possibilities and their prospect in mind when reading *BGE*. The activity of the future philosophers and free spirits, the nature of future philosophy, and the orienting force of new possible conceptions of nobility are certainly related to such ideas. Thus, as we approach the end of Nietzsche's first chapter, which considers a variety of impediments to our development, we might be reminded of some of these alternatives Nietzsche considered previously.

In the second book of *Z*, the part titled "On Self-Overcoming," Nietzsche offers his first elaboration of the idea that all existence is characterized by will to power in a speech addressed to "you who are wisest," the "lover of truth." The desire to render intelligible what is true, good, and real is described as a manifestation of will that ultimately seeks power. Zarathustra observes will to power in life as establishing a dynamic of obeying and commanding. Every being aims at commanding, and what cannot command obeys. He describes this activity as experimental and risky: even what might be considered greatest will yield, will risk itself for the sake of power: "And as the smaller yields to the greater that it may have pleasure and power over the smallest, thus even the greatest still yields, and for the sake of power risks life." The dynamic that characterizes life is described as one of creation and recreation. The process does not simply characterize discrete relations. "Life" itself whispers in Zarathustra's ear that it is: "*that which must always overcome itself.*" Everything is connected in the paradigm of self-overcoming.

Within this paradigm Nietzsche's Zarathustra offers an alternative account of redemption.[24] The overcoming being Zarathustra anticipates does not become the measure of all things but engages an activity of esteeming, of willing, that aims at determining value. This enterprise is *redemptive* because it seeks to replace or re-stamp values that hitherto have been received. A particularly curious feature of Zarathustra's conception of redemption is that it is organized, at least partially, in terms of the past: "All 'it was' is a fragment, a riddle, a dreadful accident—until the creative will says to it, 'But thus I willed it.' Until the creative will says to it, 'But thus I will it; thus shall I will it'" (Z:II "On Redemption"). Zarathustra's redemption takes the form of a creative *backward* willing. In such a case, one wills the past as if it were one's own responsibility, as if it were the result of one's own willing it to be so. This is not merely reconciliation with the past or passive acceptance of what has transpired; rather it is at least partially reconstituting the past along the lines of that which one affirms. Thus, the past becomes one's own insofar as its significances and relations that serve as the bases for value become essentially related to one's own perspective. A perspective thus transformed by the reconstituted past potentially revises or reorients future interpretations. These ideas lie at the heart of Nietzsche's interest in history and the kind of historical development that he associates with genealogy. Throughout *BGE*, we shall see Nietzsche appropriating the past as well as scrutinizing past *appropriations* by others.[25] To be able to engage in this sort of activity is a kind of liberation as Nietzsche sees it. The idea of will to power is meant to provide a new way of looking at the world that potentially facilitates new inventions that might lead to new discoveries. It does not involve *being free from* the past, starting from scratch, retaining no trace or influence of what one has been—such is impossible: there is no such "blank slate"—but it is being *free to* utilize the past in certain ways even though the success or failure of one's endeavors in such projects is undetermined and uncertain. We explore this further in the next chapter.

Emphasis on this possibility of the concept of will to power allows us to see that Nietzsche conceives his project, his "prelude to philosophy of the future," specifically as a kind of action, a doing; and the stakes of this enterprise are not only possible different ways of living but *the very possibility of living* (this partially explains Nietzsche's penchant for melodrama). He regards his project as so dangerous because he thinks it can undermine the conditions of life. As we make our transition from part I to part II, we can take further stock of just what Nietzsche's project seems to be and how he is pursuing it. One thing we can clearly recognize at this point is that a facet of his "doing" is an "undoing," a loosening of some sense of security we might have in the thought that even though we might not yet have answers to our philosophical and scientific questions, we are nevertheless making progress, or that progress is at least possible. Nietzsche challenges both the desirability of this goal and its likelihood.

In part I Nietzsche endeavors to lend credence to his claim that "The power of moral prejudices has penetrated deeply into the most spiritual world, which would seem to be the coldest and most devoid of presuppositions and has obviously operated in an injurious, inhibiting, blinding, and distorting manner"

(*BGE* 23). Part I describes this power as immense and irresistible and how human thought, especially Indo-European thinking, is almost entirely directed by prejudgments that close us off from and inhibit certain kinds of inquiries, and others that send us down dead-ends, sometimes with disastrous consequences. But our situation must not be absolutely hopeless, for even though it might well be that "the falsest judgments are the most indispensable for us" (*BGE* 4), it is still the case that we can recognize, along with Nietzsche, the lack of justification we have for some major assumptions that direct both metaphysics and physics, and we can at least attempt to avoid some of these errors or draw on more adequate assumptions. As discussed above, these enduring concepts and features of thought include: our assumptions that "the things of highest value must have another origin" (i.e., an "other-worldly" character); our understanding of the basic order of thought on the basis of the principle of non-contradiction (sorting what is from what isn't, existence vs. non-existence, what is and is not the case, etc.) because of our "faith in opposite values" (*BGE* 2); false dilemmas, such as whether the will is free or (its opposite) unfree (*BGE* 21) and the division of the world into "the real" and "the apparent" (*BGE* 10); the unjustified assumption that there must be an "ego," an "I" that is the responsible cause for, and the agent of, the activity thinking (*BGE* 17), a "superstition," which has saturated even our grammar such that we can't get along without subjects that stand behind and are thought to be the causes of activity (*BGE* 17, 6, and 20); our reification of what we perceive as cause and effect (projecting a kind of agency onto "nature" or "the world" [e.g., *BGE* 21]); and our tendency toward atomism, which extends not only to nature but also to our conception of individuals, which are (at the least!) complex and synthetic (*BGE* 6, 12, 16, and 17–21). The examples Nietzsche discusses are not merely isolated cases of erroneous thinking that ought to be avoided; rather they are indicative of much larger problems for traditional philosophical projects.

Finally, Nietzsche makes at least three claims about the nature of thinking that shed further light on how such "prejudices" matter: (1) concepts grow organically, not in isolation (*BGE* 20); (2) consciousness is not something wholly separated and isolated from what we regard as instinctual: our ideas are influenced by and "channeled by [our] instincts" (*BGE* 3), and these have physiological and evolutionary conditions (*BGE* 20 and 23); and (3) valuations orient our ideas, even logic (*BGE* 3). In the case of philosophers, this is even more exaggerated, since there are whole moralities at work (*BGE* 6, cf. 8–9, and 19; consider also, for example, the normativity of truth: *BGE* 1–4, 10, 13, and 23). Nietzsche announces from the start that he is involved in questioning "the value of truth," the *will to truth* (*BGE* 1). These are not just the musings or momentous deep thinking of Nietzsche himself, but rather a place we have arrived in late modernity (as suggested in the preface and repeatedly through the use of the first person plural "we"). Nevertheless, Nietzsche thinks he is pursuing something extraordinarily profound (*BGE* 1 and 23), and in a manner that is like none other. We get the sense Nietzsche thinks he (or someone in the future) can somehow get out of the "orbit" of thinking that has constituted philosophy thus far and accounts for why "the most diverse philosophers keep filling in a definite fundamental scheme of possible philosophies" (*BGE* 20). Does Nietzsche somehow think he will help us get out of this scheme or expand it beyond recognition? This will be a question we will pursue throughout the book.

We are thus primed to encounter Nietzsche's discussion of "The Free Spirit" or "The Free Mind" in part II. We now can see that we are not talking about a special form of metaphysical freedom; neither are we talking about simply ridding ourselves of all prejudices, and we are certainly not pursuing a social or political campaign for freedom in the democratic sense. In fact, we can already recognize why it might be that Nietzsche thinks democratic ideals are problematic and dangerous given his politics of the soul we have just glimpsed. In particular, the notion of the importance of rank ordering of desires is in tension with the inclination to treat everything as equal, the same, to not give priority to rule of what is distinguished as what is best. How this stands in relation to the ideas of another philosopher who similarly seemed to have an interest in the "politics of the soul," Plato, will be explored in the next two chapters (on parts II and III) as we begin to see Nietzsche's fuller development of what he earlier introduced as the possibility for "refinement of the 'soul hypothesis'" (§12) and how such might sharpen the "question of morality" (part V), which is one of the main problems of the book.

CHAPTER 4

PART II: "THE FREE SPIRIT"

Part II of *BGE* is usually translated as "The Free Spirit," and most of the English-language scholarship on Nietzsche uses the phrase, but it could also be translated "the free mind" or "free-mindedness," and it is in this chapter we find one of the most comprehensive, concentrated accounts in all of Nietzsche's writing of his own positive views. Virtually every topic of consequence in the book is raised in this part; many ideas vital to popular interpretations of Nietzsche, such as his perspectivism and his hypothesis concerning will to power, receive direct articulation here. Readers also witness Nietzsche trying to push himself to practice the intellectual conscience mentioned in the preceding chapter. In so doing, he forsakes certain facets of his earlier conception of the free spirit (a kindred of Voltaire), and strives to achieve a perspective somewhat freer of *moralized* prejudices, those assessments and orientations treated in the prior chapter. Three major sets of concerns form the basis of our discussion: (1) Nietzsche's views about *knowledge* (especially §§24–5); (2) related considerations about *understanding*, including interpretation, masks, and intelligibility (especially evident §§26–8, 30, 34, and 40); and (3) how his considerations of knowledge and understanding bear on the *future possibilities for philosophy*, particularly philosophical engagement *beyond good and evil* (e.g., development beyond the morality of intention [31–3]; Nietzsche's "proposition" of will to power [36], the "new philosophers" [42–3] and how they might arise [29, 41, 44], and how we are to understand this vision as it relates to the free spirit [35]). We discuss the "free spirit" in detail toward the end of the chapter. We can note for now that although Nietzsche envisioned a series of his writings as thematically exploring the "free spirit,"[1] part II of *BGE* is the only substantial part of any single work that bears that title, and it was written at a time when it seemed Nietzsche had concluded his "free spirit" series (prior to writing *Z*). As a portrait or at least a sketch of future philosophers becomes clearer in this part; we will explore the notion in relief as compared with his earlier writings.

KNOWLEDGE: WILL TO TRUTH AND THE WILL TO IGNORANCE

Part II opens with a bit of irony when in section 24, Nietzsche invokes Jan Hus (1369–1415), "*Oh holy simplicity!*". The Latin phrase he cites is a common one underscoring human naiveté. Despite our commitments to truth (indeed, perhaps even because of such), we live in states of simplification (*Vereinfachung*) and falsification (*Fälschung*), as the foregoing part illustrated. Nietzsche opens his discussion on the "free spirit" with the suggestion that there are many ways in which our minds are *not free* insofar as we are constricted by significant prejudices that amount to perversions and falsifications of thought. But these impediments to freethinking also serve the purpose of providing another sense of freedom achieved through creativity and invention. As we shall see in a section below, this partly involves not compulsively or stubbornly clinging to contradictions and problematic concepts identified in the first part. In this respect, Nietzsche repeats his concerns about contradictions he uprooted in the first part of the book (e.g., the contradiction in terms of the notions of "immediate certainty," "absolute knowledge," and "thing in itself," references to major concepts in the history of modern philosophy, particularly in the views of Descartes, Hegel, and Kant). This is the hallmark, but not the limit, of independence for Nietzsche, and it is an important step on the route to intellectual conscience. As we will see, Nietzsche thinks that instead of securing a foundation for knowledge, we have created for ourselves a foundation of ignorance (*Unwissenheit*) that allows knowledge to rise further (cf. §10) for the enjoyment of life. This will to ignorance, or *unknowing*, this will to lacking certainty and truth should not necessarily be conceived as precisely the *opposite* of the will to knowledge (again, following Nietzsche's critique of opposing values [§2]); instead, it is rather "its refinement" or purification.

We can see "refinement" as having at least two dimensions: as purification it involves an attempt at cleansing the moral stain of untruth, falsification, and artificiality; and as refinement it seeks a certain kind of knowledge resembling skepticism, which is critical of certain ways of thinking and their products. Nietzsche's practice of this activity, however, does not terminate with the conclusion that no knowledge is possible; neither does it claim to have discovered the real or true path to knowledge. It offers a refined understanding of knowledge and a different route to achieve it, which involves the practice of intellectual conscience. This is possible, Nietzsche thinks, with the acquisition of a certain kind of taste, a kind of love, namely that for *life*. The dynamic between the will to knowledge and the will to ignorance is given a somewhat different twist later on in section 230 in part VII, "Our Virtues," so we return to this notion later. For now, it is worth noting the ironic way part II begins, since in the section following the opening with Hus, a martyr burned at the stake that influenced Martin Luther, Nietzsche specifically cautions against becoming a martyr for truth.

Nietzsche's chapter on the free spirit also assesses the past relationship between science and philosophy and envisions its future. What has been said about science in the preceding chapter and the issue of whether Nietzsche is an advocate of scientific reasoning or its staunchest critic and destroyer must be read in this light. When Nietzsche writes that "until now" science has had to build itself on a foundation of ignorance, he seems to be suggesting a new relation is possible in the future, a new course that perhaps begins with his own book. "Until now," Nietzsche tells us, science emerged out of and rested upon a "solidified granite foundation of ignorance, the will to know rising up on the foundation of a much more powerful will, the will to not know, to uncertainty, to untruth!" This relation, contrary to what we might believe and contrary to what Nietzsche's contemporary "Free Thinkers" (*Freidenker*) might have thought,[2] is not one of direct opposition—replacing untruth with truth, ignorance with real knowledge—but rather "its refinement." The will to untruth is an expression of our tendency to simplify and falsify, which Nietzsche thinks serves life. Pursuit of untruth provides a measure of perceptible freedom, a sense of bravery, a touch of lightness that makes it possible to be joyful, to take delight in life. Even "the best science" will "best know how to keep us in this *simplified*, utterly artificial, well-invented, well-falsified world"; it remains "unwillingly willing" to embrace error in this sense precisely because "being alive—it loves life!" Envisioning what such a project might entail and how it encourages us to think about the value of truth itself are difficult challenges Nietzsche begins to address in this part.

Thus, in section 25, Nietzsche expresses deep concern about those who would sacrifice their lives in the name of truth itself (rather than, perhaps, for particular *truths*). He emphasizes the importance and priority of questioning one's views rather than clinging to one's convictions strictly on the basis of a commitment to truth, particularly when such convictions are harmful to life such that one must sacrifice life in order to cling to them. So here Nietzsche underscores the importance of questioning for life as essential to life, an idea that the very first section raised as a dangerous possibility.

Those who secure the "good solitude" for themselves and those who seek it willingly are contrasted with those forced into solitude because of their inability to engage their enemies or because of persecution. Spinoza and Bruno are cited as examples of the latter that, because they became "compulsory recluses," ended up as "vengeance-seekers and poison brewers," who exhibit the "stupidity" of "moral indignation." The latter in a philosopher, Nietzsche claims, is a sure sign that "his philosophical sense of humor has left him." We might imagine that part of what constitutes such comedy is the gaiety and lightness summoned in the prior section (§24). As Nietzsche considers how martyrs for truth become degenerate (suspicious, resentful, "poisonous"), he suggests the kind of freedom he envisions is a condition for being good (gives one a *right* to be good), more precisely, for *remaining* or *staying* good. This is surely relevant to the title: in this passage, we have a different sense of 'good' than the sense we are supposed to get beyond, which is invoked in the opposition of "good and evil."

The appropriate response to the degenerate philosopher appears to be laughter, for he puts on a show like a satyr play, "an epilogue farce" (§25). This recalls an earlier set of passages in part I in which Nietzsche also evokes the satyr play and the ass (§§7–9). Satyr plays in ancient Greece followed series of tragedies and provided what might be regarded as comic relief from the drama that preceded them. A philosopher's desire to sacrifice himself for the truth is not so much something to be lamented as it is a comic event that also reveals, in the end, the "order of rank the innermost drives of his nature stand in relation to each other" (§6). His will is weak, as evident in his inability to affirm life (§21). And with that, we know that "the long, real tragedy *is at an end*" (§25). This, Nietzsche claims, entails "assuming that every philosophy was in its genesis a long tragedy."

The reference to actors and the satyr play recalls Nietzsche's earlier discussion of Epicurus and his view of the Platonists as *Dionysiokolakes* (§7), which he follows with a citation from the ass festival (§8).[3] As Kaufmann points out in his translation of *BGE*, the Greek term here is ambiguous, since dramatists could be regarded as followers of Dionysus, the god of the theatre and the deity thought to be behind each mask, and Plato is known to have failed in the practical application of his moral and political views in his counsel of the tyrant Dionysos of Sicily. Nietzsche's expression here also calls to mind the conclusion of his first edition of *GS*, whose fourth part (and original conclusion) ends with a section entitled "Incipit tragodia"— *let the tragedy begin*—a section in which readers are introduced to Zarathustra, the protagonist of the book Nietzsche wrote between publication of the first edition of *GS* and *BGE*. In these works we can see how Nietzsche thinks philosophy involves a kind of tragic undergoing (we meet the title character Zarathustra as he descends among humankind, an episode to which we find allusion in §26) and overcoming.[4] By the time Nietzsche writes *BGE* Zarathustra has died,[5] but *his* is not a tragic ending: the philosophy that emerges from his tragic beginning is still unfolding in Nietzsche's works.

Nietzsche's examples of decadents who become poisonous are interesting, and these are revealing of his ideas about knowledge and his own project. Bruno (1548–1600) is the sort of figure we might imagine would have appealed to Nietzsche, and one attractive to those sensualists mentioned in the first part (§§14 and 15). Bruno was martyred for his support of the ideas of Copernicus (cf. §12). He was shunned from nearly every academic community because of his opposition to Aristotle, he advanced the view that the world was eternal and ever-changing, and he anticipated a theory of relativity in his arguments against Aristotle's notions of opposites: "there is no absolute up or down, as Aristotle taught; no absolute position in space; but the position of a body is relative to that of other bodies. Everywhere there is incessant relative change in position throughout the universe, and the observer is always at the center of things."[6] In a play he wrote, which evokes themes of satyr plays, Bruno features the "ass of Cyllene," which skewers superstition. The "ass" is everywhere, not only in the church at the time of the ass festival (and at other times) but also in all other public institutions, including courts and schools. Bruno was a skeptic, particularly about theological matters in which scientific reasoning offered evidence contradicting matters of faith, and he was an advocate of free thought. We might, then, think he would be a perfect model for a free spirit. And he was—but *not* the sort Nietzsche appears to be advocating. Bruno was an icon for the "free thinkers" (*Freidenken*) movement,[7] with which Nietzsche explicitly contrasts his free spirits in section 44, as discussed below, but before moving on to this we press further on how Nietzsche thinks about understanding and the routes to achieving and expressing it.

UNDERSTANDING: MASKS, INTERPRETATION, AND INTELLIGIBILITY

It can be difficult to pin Nietzsche down, to know just what he is talking about, and sometimes, this seems to be exactly what he wants. There is plenty of evidence in this part of the book that Nietzsche is interested in indirect communication. This opens further opportunities for exploration, particularly if we consider Nietzsche's comments about "masks" (§40) in relation to his conception of tragedy (and philosophy *as* tragedy) as well as the musical and temporal dimensions of the text, all with an eye toward deepening our understanding of Nietzsche's ideas about perspective and the revaluation of *appearances*.

While part I of *BGE* was about unmasking the prejudices of the philosophers and challenging the integrity of those specific masks, Nietzsche's goal was not simply to eliminate masks or even necessarily bring about their willful replacement. Sometimes Nietzsche intends to deceive, as he himself tells us. Thus, it is plausible and reasonable to expect that he dons masks in his texts (e.g., §30). And it becomes clearer, once we appreciate his conception of the "soul as subjective multiplicity" and its development, that he thinks masks are inevitable, unavoidable, and that individuals in some respects bear resemblance to characters in the ancient Greek plays (§40). We would do well to pay attention to this, not so as to disclose evidence of Nietzsche's free-wheeling inventiveness, leading us wherever he or we want to go, but rather to appreciate the dramatic context of masks and Nietzsche's view about the relation between philosophy, drama, and music.

In *BT*, Nietzsche dramatizes the tragic effect resulting from the dynamic tension of creation and destruction in the opposition of the artistic forces of the Apollinian and Dionysian. "Apollo" and "Dionysus" are names Nietzsche gives to formative tendencies that characterize both human culture and the creative forces of the world more generally. Ancient Greek tragic art, on Nietzsche's account, created an arena in which the best was drawn out of each opponent, in a dynamic through which neither was allowed to dominate. In contrast with Aristotle, who thought the pleasure of tragedy was the result of a kind of purging (*catharsis*), and Schopenhauer, who thought that tragedy stills the strivings of the Will, Nietzsche thought the pleasure of tragedy stemmed from a productive potency, the expression of creative power, which could invest a human being with significance that was unattainable solely through the idealized imagery of the Apollinian or the rapturous ecstasy of the Dionysian (*BT* 22; cf. *BT* 7). We might contemplate how this is possible by considering further the relation between the masked and the mask. Dionysus, god of the theatre, was thought to be behind each masked character. The god Dionysus himself is not visible, and appears only through and by virtue of masking; he is the god of formlessness, destruction, sometimes chaos. Apollo is the god of appearance, form and light, illumination, and sometimes intellection. United in the context of a tragic work of art, the Apollinian mask does not simply cover or hide the real Dionysus who lies underneath. Together, Apollo and Dionysus create a real character, one true in the sense of true to human existence, sometimes in an idealized or exaggerated form that heightens awareness of certain, very human, characteristics and their possibilities for both glory and ruin. So when Nietzsche champions donning masks, he is not advocating hiding or necessarily engaging in deception. He is, at least at times, invoking this form of creative activity that taps a distinctive kind of productive power.

Tragic art, according to Nietzsche, dramatizes the struggle between competing perspectives of the individualized and undifferentiated, the intelligible and the mysterious. It symbolizes the entire process of human creative appropriation of opposition and resistance. It offers a spectacular display of superficial images, playfully built up and destroyed in a single work.

One of the most common interpretations of Nietzsche's *BT* is that it advances the claim that tragic art collapsed with the diminution of the Dionysian.[8] But we can see this tells only half the story. If we focus on the effect the alleged abandonment of Dionysus has upon the most crucial element of the tragic— namely, the productive power of the *union* of the opposing contestants—then we see that Nietzsche's concern is for both the Dionysian *and* the Apollinian. Certainly, Nietzsche thinks the Dionysian is valuable, and Dionysus makes an appearance at the end of this book and in Nietzsche's later works, but readers should avoid hastily concluding that Nietzsche admires tragedy *simply* or *exclusively* because it gives the Dionysian its expression. Tragic art is so powerful, Nietzsche claims in his early work, because it creates a contest of equally fundamental forces in which, to cite "Homer's Contest," the opposing parties "incite each other to reciprocal action as they keep each other within the limits of measure" (*HC* p. 789).[9] Readers encounter this idea of the importance of opposites, their relations, and their dynamic interrelations throughout *BGE*, as for example, in the interplay of the will to truth and the will to ignorance in section 24, and his return to it in section 230.[10] With these ideas in mind, we might look back to a set of passages that were bypassed in the previous chapter, sections 7–9, since they shed further light on the idea of the philosopher as a certain kind of actor (all people are actors of some sort), and philosophy perhaps plays some role in bringing about a new relation between appearance and reality, truth and falsity, through appreciation for the relation between the mask and the masked.

Recall that Nietzsche thinks it possible to discern the "order of rank the innermost drives of [a philosopher's] nature stand in relation to each other" (§6) according to the morality he holds. As a case in point, he offers a brief analysis of the Hellenistic philosopher Epicurus (341–270 BCE). Epicurus was known for his materialism (diametrically opposed to the idealism with which the Platonic philosophers would be associated) and along with that his naturalism. Epicureans not only provided an account of what we are (i.e., nothing but material atoms in a certain arrangement) but also an ethics oriented around practices to facilitate shedding irrational fears and desires, especially those associated with the fear of death.[11] In his *De Finibus* ("On Moral Ends"), Cicero criticizes Epicureanism, particularly its ethics. This section of *BGE* is clearly related to the nearby section 9, where Nietzsche mentions other Hellenistic philosophers, namely the Stoics for whom virtue was the good life achieved through self-commanding. In this case self-control was viewed as having the ultimate worth and constituting the greatest power, and pity was discouraged.[12]

Sandwiched between these sections is a curious reference in Latin to the ass festival, mentioned above. It is strange that Nietzsche would interrupt the flow of his text here, but it is not as much of a diversion as it might initially seem. In referring to the ass festival, Nietzsche at the same time makes reference to the even more ancient satyr play. So, following the reference to philosophers as actors and their works as theatrical play (§7), Nietzsche alludes to a facet of ancient drama that seems especially apropos for his critique—the buffoon in the satyr play. Much as the foolishness of the satyr play followed the deadly serious ancient Greek tragedies, Nietzsche thinks that the even the most serious, somber, and dramatic metaphysical views are eventually followed by the levity of the satyr play of the philosophers' convictions (cf. *GS* 1 and other passages on actors and superficiality). That convictions are figured as actors in a satyr play means Nietzsche views them as buffoonish and comical. Moreover, this is also a clear allusion to his *Z*, where Nietzsche uses the figure of the ass as one that solely says "yea-yuh" to everything and thus to nothing of any genuine significance.

Even philosophers who endeavor to avoid superficial trappings by getting "back to nature" face problems on Nietzsche's view. As it becomes clearer still, Nietzsche is not claiming that the philosopher should have no values or that he should strive for the kind of *supposed* objectivity of the scientist. In the first place, Nietzsche does not think this is possible (recall, even the quest for what is definite or for what is true, as opposed to merely apparent, reflects some kind of estimate, which could very well be mere folly [§3]). And in the second place, values are what give direction and organization to whole philosophical metaphysical views. The problem is that philosophers fail to recognize their truck with and responsibilities *for* values. A great example of this is the Stoic dictum to live according to nature. This is at once laughable and pitiful to Nietzsche. The Stoics placed great emphasis on cultivation of self-control based on fairly strident moral views—they sought a kind of *natural justice* within themselves and the world. But *nature*, Nietzsche claims, is neither just nor unjust—rather, from a human perspective it is tremendously *wasteful* (e.g., fish lay thousands of eggs resulting in just a few animals that survive to adulthood), *indifferent* (there is no temperance in earthquakes such that 'innocent' lives are spared), *purposeless* (although the temptation to see it otherwise is great, as discussed below), "without mercy and justice," and at once "fertile" in some respects while also "desolate." Given these conflicting, opposing, inconsistent, and unpredictable characteristics, how could we possibly divine a rule for life from this? Living itself, Nietzsche suggests, takes the form of— it simply *is*—"estimating, preferring, being unjust, being limited, wanting to be different" (§9). Thus, in a certain sense living an individual life seems to involve distinguishing oneself from the whole. And even if the Stoic maxim could be revised to take this into account so as to claim that we should "live according to life," what could that possibly mean—how could we *not* do *that*?

What Nietzsche thinks is really going on with the Stoics is that they wish to impose *their* morality on nature itself (not just on other human beings, although obviously on them too). Because they have already decided that nature itself embodies Stoic values, they are incapable of seeing it any other way. The Stoic case is extreme, only because of the rigid control it expects of its adherents. But, in fact, every philosophy works this way— "it creates the world in its own image." This drive toward world-making is both tremendously creative and tyrannical, exhibiting the form of all drives seeking power (which Nietzsche gives the name "will to power"). At the end of section 9, Nietzsche claims philosophy is the most tyrannical drive toward this ultimate form of creative activity. We might further suppose that if this is so, then it is potentially the most powerful and certainly among the most interesting.

In *BT* 6 Nietzsche provides a powerful description of how in early tragic art (until the time of Euripides), Dionysian music finds its reflection in the Apollinian in which the appearance of Will is the form of its longing, and desire is brought forth. The Apollinian depends upon the music, and the music endures the conceptualization manifest in the Apollinian. Euripides is supposed to have initiated a new contest in which an emaciated Dionysus is pitted against a Cycloptic Socrates (transmogrified by his atrophied rationality) in a struggle in which neither can emerge as truly better for having engaged in the fight. Nietzsche seeks a route to revivifying the tragic *agon* which, in his first book, he imagines as potentially realized in innovations Wagner brings to the opera when he makes music (which lacks a visible form) itself a character capable of interacting with others who appear, take shape. Though he abandons the specific course to this end, we might well recognize Nietzsche's goal as constant. Revivifying the tragic *agon*, reactivating a grand contest that makes it possible to say "yes" to life, continues to be part of Nietzsche's project for most of his philosophical career, and his invocation of the artist and his task as artistic at the end of part III should attune us to this fact. But in the writings after *Z* it also appears that Nietzsche becomes increasingly ambivalent about, and perhaps eager to look beyond, the tragic. For example, in *BGE*, although the philosopher may appear a tragic or comedic figure, Nietzsche scouts a perspective from which this, and all human trials and tribulations, would appear as laughable (worthy of "divine laughter" [§30]). As we shall see, however, it is not clear whether Nietzsche thinks such a perspective, something like a god's eye view that he seems to reject in other places in the book, is really possible. Moreover, Nietzsche also seems ambivalent about the kind of reaction such a perspective might elicit: it might just as well provoke rage or pity. This is a concern discussed at the end of part III and in our own chapter on part IV. Questions remains though concerning *how* such artistry occurs and whether and how this is relevant to the sense and extent to which Nietzsche thinks the task of the future philosophers is "to form *man*" (§62) Before we leap to that question, we should further consider how Nietzsche begins to anticipate future philosophers and their possible emergence from a perspective *beyond good and evil.*

INTERPRETATION, PERSPECTIVE, AND VALUE

In sections 26–31, Nietzsche explores several related ideas he previously introduced, including the idea that orders of rank of drives are definitive of character (§6) and how the notion of the soul as "subjective multiplicity" might be more adequate than the conception of soul as atomic (§12). He does this in consideration of how "lovers of knowledge" emerge, express their *taste* for knowledge, and face challenges that threaten their development. Section 26 begins with a simplistic image of a "choice human being" who "saves" himself from the "many" or the "crowd." The image of the lonely (noble) philosopher who finds the common "rabble" beneath him is familiar enough in the history of philosophy, and Nietzsche is perhaps appealing to those inclined to think that way. But rather than endorsing this view of the philosopher, Nietzsche unravels it, makes it more complex, and undermines the ideas of what such a person really seeks as well as his or her own integrity or stability. Moving from the simplistic notion of the noble and base at the beginning of section 26, Nietzsche conjures images of people who are rather like hybrid figures, mixtures of base and common elements: Cynics are cast as those who are able to gain some distance on themselves and recognize what is base within, combinations of types (e.g., Galinani as a mixture of "billy goat and ape," figures with a scientific head placed on an ape's body, those who are like satyrs, half-man, half-goat).[13] The purpose of this section seems to be to highlight the difficulties of perceiving the exception and rule, high and low. But also problematic is the determination of such values and distinctions. It seems clear Nietzsche is staking out the view that "whenever anyone seeks, seeks, and *wants* to see only hunger, sexual lust, and vanity as the real and only motives of human actions" (cf. §23), and without disgust or dismay, that person is onto something, has an insight that is valuable for the "lover of knowledge."[14] One can detect yet another revision to and deviation from a classical view of philosophy, namely the Socratic conception of philosophical pursuit as a form of self-knowledge. Given the propensity to hybridization of organic being Nietzsche advances, self-knowledge is rather elusive if not impossible. Further, it is not only difficult to understand oneself, it is also difficult to be understood, as Nietzsche discusses in section 27. Thus, if one thinks of philosophers as those who have some mission to impart knowledge to others, this is a problem. Part of the trouble is that differing orders of rank have different orders of ruling, different ways of maintaining the orders they are. One way of considering the relations among the multiple parts is in political terms, like Plato's Socrates in book VIII of the *Republic*, and as when Nietzsche describes individual constitutions in terms of commonwealths, as discussed in the previous chapter. Another way to appreciate differences among constitutions is by virtue of their temporal registers (§§27 and 28), what one might call the music of their souls, harkening to an even earlier philosophical notion allegedly held by the Pythagoreans.[15] We return to the importance of tempo in later sections of the book (especially the chapters on parts IV and VIII.) For now, we note that Nietzsche calls attention to the fact that some move and think swiftly, some slowly; some leap, and thus have difficulty understanding others unlike them. But Nietzsche also challenges the views that one *wants* to be understood *with ease*—rather, Nietzsche admits he tries to make his work difficult to understand (§27), and at least part of the reason for this is that he is encouraging the disuse of a good number of familiar terms and concepts. The challenges of interpretation Nietzsche elaborates here stem, in part, from his view that there are different orders of rank of the parts of the soul (§30), that these orders are difficult to discern with any confidence, and this makes communication among the parts and among other orders difficult.

Another challenge posed to inquiry and explication of the world is that the opposition of the real and the apparent (discussed in the previous part) does not seem to hold. Nietzsche suggests our desire to say "yes" or "no" to any appearance of reality (as discussed in §34) is linked with the youthful "taste for the unconditional" to which he draws attention in section 31. We approach the world and cope with it on the basis of "perspective estimates and appearances" (§34; cf. §§2 and 3, where

Nietzsche mentions "foreground estimates" and "provisional perspectives"). In terms of their *value*, Nietzsche claims, "it is no more than a moral prejudice that truth is worth more than mere appearance"; moreover, this is a particularly harmful prejudice if it should turn out that untruth is a condition of life, as Nietzsche thinks it is. Thus, he questions the diametrical opposition of the true and the false, particularly when indexed to good and evil. But rather than simply obliterating the distinction between true and false or undermining any basis for valuing one over the other, Nietzsche contemplates the replacement of the dualism with a continuum: "Is it not sufficient to assume degrees of apparentness and, as it were, lighter and darker shadows and shades of appearance—different 'values,' to use the language of painters?" Again, the idea here is not to rid the world of claims to truth or falsity or replace epistemic values with aesthetic ones but rather to develop a more subtle appreciation for the different kinds of claims we might make, their utility, and their value, and in this respect to recognize as potentially quite valuable what is fictional, merely apparent, and literally false but useful. Questioning the motivations and necessity of judgments such as these and developing openness to reconsidering some of our most cherished beliefs about the world and ourselves is one facet of the new kind of conscience Nietzsche anticipates for his free spirits and future philosophers.

Nietzsche's contemporary "free thinkers" took their independence of mind as one of their hallmarks. The difficulty of genuinely achieving such a state should by now be clearer, and Nietzsche repeatedly undermines both the conception of independence and its possibility. In section 29, Nietzsche describes the process of achieving independence metaphorically as entering "a labyrinth" in which lurk "dangers" that can lead to one being "torn piecemeal by some minotaur of conscience." There are two things to flag about this passage, to which we will return in this part and in later chapters. The reference to the humanoid Minotaur and the labyrinth certainly evokes the story of Theseus and Ariadne and the eventual relationship of Ariadne and Dionysus, which is mentioned at the end of *BGE*. The other point of note is the word Nietzsche uses for independence: "unabhängig" (literally, not stuck, not dependent), and

Nietzsche returns to this idea and elaborates it at the end of part II, as we discuss below.

BEYOND THE MORALITY OF INTENTION

Following Nietzsche's elaboration of the challenges facing the spirit that might develop and ripen as he anticipates, Nietzsche begins to look toward the future. It is an indication of our youthfulness that we have "a taste for the unconditional" in which we "venerate or despise without that art of nuance which constitutes the best gain of life" (§31). This recalls our earlier discussion of Nietzsche's concern for taste, the relation between tastes and forms of life, particularly a life informed by a positive estimation of the human condition. The morality of good and evil, based on its diametrical and radical opposition and its "faith in opposite values" (§2) evinces the kind of taste Nietzsche identifies in section 31. But readers detect a glimmer of hope in his account, since the following sections 32 and 33 link this with a kind of immaturity that he anticipates we just *might* be able to overcome.

Section 32 is particularly important for appreciating Nietzsche's title *Beyond Good and Evil* and what it might entail. In it, he provides a sweeping history of the development of morality as such, a version of which he provided in earlier writings, and which he elaborates in much greater detail later in the book (part V) and in subsequent volumes (especially *GM*).[16] It is useful to note that Nietzsche does not present himself as offering a *comprehensive* or even *necessary* account. He provides instead at least two models for responsibility, articulating them just enough to aid in imagining a third. This section should be read in light of others in which Nietzsche anticipates different conceptualizations for key notions such as the soul, the cosmos, and our place within it. But Nietzsche is not just interested to coming up with new ideas; he is keen to consider the relation between the way we think about these basic concepts and how our thinking informs other, perhaps seemingly unrelated ideas, and how these influence action and even whole ways of life.

The two types of ways of thinking about the relation between action and value are exemplified in works of ancient literature and modern moral philosophy; thus, Nietzsche associates the latter with a specifically "moral period," whose reasoning would appear alien to the characters in ancient literature.[17] He writes, "During the longest part of human history—so-called pre-historical times—the value or disvalue of an action was derived from its consequences [. . .] it was the retroactive force of success or failure that led men to think well or ill of an action" (§32). Nietzsche associates this with a "pre-moral" history, in part, because it presumed a somewhat less complex form of agency and attendant culpability. The development of what we might recognize today as morality obviously required multiple steps that Nietzsche regards as both inventive and conservative in some respects. The inventive dimension results in new depth in the conception of the human soul insofar as modern moral reasoning inserts a new entity (or facet) *behind* the action, as the *cause* of the action: *intention*; and it attaches value to *that* regardless of consequence. This is conservative in the sense that it is "an unconscious aftereffect of the rule of aristocratic values and the faith in 'descent'" in which what matters most is one's origins, or, to use a term that will be prominent in Nietzsche's subsequent work, the *genealogy* of an action. It is interesting to notice that this is no gradual progression of greater understanding based upon ever more expansive horizons: Nietzsche describes it instead as "a reversal of perspective!" that involves a "narrowness of interpretation." It is at once ingenious (as testimony to human creative power) and calamitous (resulting in a prejudice of value that produced some of the most destructive self-loathing and self-denial imaginable). Thus, Nietzsche inquires whether we are on the threshold of yet another "reversal" of perspective that would produce another "fundamental shift in values," what he "negatively" describes as *extra-moral* (*aussermoral*), outside of or beyond the moral.

This section provides us with much to consider about Nietzsche's overall goals and his routes to achieving them. One thing we might notice is that it is not simply that Nietzsche turns his back on morality and encourages others to do the same, but rather he anticipates a movement in human development that would render contemporary moral deliberations obsolete, one that would invalidate its norms and judgments. The other important facet to notice is how Nietzsche speculates this might occur, what it entails: another reversal of perspective. We might imagine this would occur on the basis of a widening rather than narrowing of view, though this is not quite clear. How it might be a broadening is suggested in Nietzsche's repeated appeal to a "life" perspective, but he also suggests even further intensification of the penetrating view that resulted in the postulation of intent, a "growth in profundity" insofar as one might regard intent and what is conscious as "surface and skin—which, like every skin, betrays something but *conceals* even more" (§34). In trying to cast an eye beyond the morality of intention, Nietzsche speculates, "the decisive value of an action lies precisely in what is *unintentional* in it." This requires seeing intention as "a sign and symptom that still requires interpretation," which, in large measure is what Nietzsche endeavors to do throughout much of the book, and as we soon see, one of the ways he attempts to do this is through shaping a new perspective that frees us, makes it possible for us to see, feel, and think differently. Nietzsche's free spirits claim such a perspective and herald those who might philosophize from it.

PHILOSOPHERS OF THE FUTURE

Section 42 announces the arrival of a new species of philosopher, "the philosophers of the future," whom Nietzsche also calls *Versucher*—attempters, experimenters. This name for the future philosophers draws together a cluster of ideas raised in earlier sections and also recalls Zarathustra's description of human society: "'Human society is a trial [*Versuch*]: thus I teach it—a long trial [*Suchen*]; and what it tries to find is the commander [*Befehlenden*]. A trial [*Versuch*], O my brothers, and *not* a 'contract.' Break, break this word of the soft-hearted and half-and-half!'" (Z:III "On Old and New Tablets," 25). In section 36, Nietzsche describes an experiment [*Versuch*] he thinks the "conscience of method demands" and which leads him to "posit[ing] the causality of the will hypothetically as the only one," speculating that "all organic functions could be traced back to this will to power." We gain insight here as to what the experimentalism of the future philosophers might be (more is suggested later in part VI): it involves experimenting with hypotheses following from the conscience of method that emerges in the wake of the critique of the "prejudices of the philosophers."

Yet more is connoted with the German word *Versuch* (as Kaufmann notes): *Versuch* also conveys a sense of "temptation." Kaufmann's *Z* translation, cited above, obscures this sense, which is easily recognized once we see the German text added to the passage. Human society, human association is a temptation, a lure. It is not that we should avoid it altogether, as we see in section 41, but we should resist getting stuck there. However, Nietzsche's text, considered as a whole is ambiguous about the extent to which *temptation* plays a role. In part VI he cautions against the *Verführer* (§205), the seducer (and he is critical of the seductive nature of pretenses to disinterest and altruism in §33), and yet something of the sort is suggested in the value-creating power of the future philosophers, whose great contribution to human welfare is that they make it possible to want something other than what we currently do, to *feel differently* about what is good, what is *desirable*. The philosophers of the future not only have different tastes; they become the new standard bearers of taste. This is explored further in part IX, where Nietzsche inquires into what might constitute a new sense of nobility. For now we can take notice of the fact, as many philosophers have previously, that taste does not become shared on the basis of an argument, demonstration, or proof. Taste is minimally about what one judges to be good, *experiences* as good in the sense of heightening and enhancing one's life. Directing desire in the way that the future philosophers are conceived as doing later in the book (e.g., §§61 and 211) involves some measure of seduction that draws upon the refined simplification and falsification highlighted in the opening section of part II and vivified in the portrait of Dionysus at the end of the book (§295).

We are now in a better position to understand what is said about "commanding" and "independence" in section 41, where Nietzsche writes: "One has to test oneself to see that one is destined for independence and command [*Befehlen*]." Here, Nietzsche uses the same term he did in the passage from *Z* cited above, and readers might recall that he discussed commanding earlier in section 19: "we are at the same time the commanding [*Befehlenden*] *and* the obeying [*Gehorchenden*] parties." The *Versucher*-philosopher is surely not strictly a commander over others. There is nonesuch pure and simple as

Nietzsche considers it. (This, however, does not necessarily mean Nietzsche is not thinking of commanding as having some sort of control over others, only that such need not necessarily be *only* what he is thinking.) To further explore both the free spirits' and future philosophers' relation to others we can recall the earlier discussion about independence (§29).

In section 41, Nietzsche returns to *Unabhängigkeit*.[18] We have already noted the choice of terms as interesting because he could have used the more positive term *Selbständigkeit*[19]—literally, able to stand by oneself, for oneself. Instead, he uses the negation of a term now commonly used in medicine and psychology for addiction, *Abhängigkeit*. Literally, clumsily, *Unabhängigkeit* means to be in a condition of not hanging on to (or being stuck to) something. When Nietzsche provides examples of what might constitute the "most dangerous games" one must play to see whether one is destined or determined to command, he lists a variety of things one must endeavor "not to remain stuck to." The difference this makes is that Nietzsche is not suggesting that we have *no* attachments, or that we truly stand alone. Instead, he is saying we shouldn't get *stuck*, or more precisely, shouldn't *remain* stuck. We might very well need other persons and draw near to people we love; we might need a sense of connection to a homeland; we might take pity on others, or even all of humankind (§225); we might yearn to practice science and have virtues. Nietzsche's point is that we should not remain stuck there—or anywhere. This idea is part and parcel of his critique of the taste for the unconditional (e.g., §31). Nietzsche's ideal, if one is indicated here, is not one who simply stands alone but rather one who doesn't get stuck anywhere for too long, not even (as the *selbständig* person might) to our own detachment. Attachments are good, necessary; we form them in relation to our tastes. The problem occurs when we do not let go even when we have outgrown them or have good reasons to form other associations we let these attachments define who we are and we make them an essential part of our being.[20] So, the free spirits Nietzsche envisions do not long to be free of human community, if they did, hospitality could not be their greatest danger, as it is described in section 41 and implied again in section 44.

In light of these remarks, we can better appreciate what Nietzsche means when he says that we should "take a stick and give any eyewitness a sound thrashing" when there appear "actions of love and extravagant generosity" (§40). The idea is to rid the witnesses' memories of such loving and generous actions not because they are bad or shameful but rather because they are so enticing that they might draw us in such a way that we get stuck where and when we should move on. Hospitality can be the downfall of a rich spirit, particularly if we recall from section 13 that "a living thing seeks to *discharge* it strength." In Zarathustra's language, the overman seeks to be rich enough so as to be constantly overflowing, to engage in gift-giving. But there is difficulty in discerning at what point one's giving away gives way to one's own destruction.

The organic metaphors of growth, maturation, and culti-vation are significant in the concluding section 44, though their use is somewhat curious for the purposes to which Nietzsche appears to be putting them. When we cultivate a garden, we do not expose it to the harshest conditions in order to strengthen or improve it, and yet that seems to be how he thinks about "the plant man." Exposure to danger and risk are—somehow—the way human beings improve and become stronger. Is this just the result of Nietzsche's idealization of the heroic individual? Surely so, to some extent; but we can also see how this idea is compatible with what Nietzsche thinks constitutes esteeming life as he anticipated in the first part of the book. It is worth thinking more about what is being valued here, how, and why, particularly in Nietzsche's claims that:

> we think that this has happened [cultivation of the plant man] every time under the opposite conditions, that to this end the dangerousness of his situation must first grow to the point of enormity, his power of invention and simulation (his 'spirit') had to develop under prolonged pressure and constraint into refinement and audacity, his life-will had to be enhanced into an unconditional power-will. We think that hardness, forcefulness, slavery, danger in the alley and the heart, life in hiding, stoicism, the art of experiment and devilry of every kind, that everything evil, terrible, tyrannical in man, everything in him that is kin to beasts of prey and serpents, serves the enhancement of the species 'man' as much as its opposite does. (§44)

This is consistent with what he writes at the end of part I, where he suggests that, "If [. . .] a person should regard even the affects of hatred, envy, covetousness, and the lust to rule as conditions of life, as factors which, fundamentally and essentially, must be present in the general economy of life" he might further conclude, no matter how sickening it might be, that these same conditions "must, therefore, be enhanced if life is to be further enhanced" (§23; cf. §§2, 26, and 188). In this light we can see Nietzsche's "free spirits" are clearly distinct from humanists, the likes of which Voltaire might be thought to be representative.

FREE SPIRIT REDUX

The original 1878 publication of *HH*, subtitled "A Book for Free Spirits" [Ein Buch für freie Geister], was dedicated to Voltaire, so when Nietzsche gently chides Voltaire in section 35, he is clearly indicating a shift from his earlier thinking about his "free spirits" and their relation to the *Free-thinkers* to whom they might bear resemblance. We are now in a position to mark these distinctions more clearly and consider what Nietzsche thought his own free-spiritedness or -mindedness led him to pursue. While Nietzsche clearly is not a humanist as many free-thinkers were, he is also not a misanthrope. Loving life, as Nietzsche imagines it, includes even the affirmation of things that from the humanist perspective look lamentable, pitiable, and even abominable. The *Freidenker* share a faith in the power and goodness of human reason as the route to truth. While Nietzsche embraces replacement of Luther's "worm of conscience" (the bad conscience) with the "conscience of reason," he rejects unconditional thinking. Like the *Freidenker*, Nietzsche affirms independence and a certain kind of autonomy, but he conceives of this as freedom from attachment (not self-standing). Nietzsche embraces freedom from the grip of morality, which stands in some tension with the humanism of most *Freidenker*, but he arrives at this position thinking that it might be possible to get *beyond* it. All of this is captured in his thought experiment of the will to power to which we now return.

We have already elaborated some of the important sources for Nietzsche's thought of will to power and its content in the discussions of sections 13 and 23 above. Here, we want to explore it as exemplary of Nietzsche's own free-spiritedness or -mindedness and how he might construe this as an outcome of his practice of intellectual conscience, which we highlighted above. Immediately, we are invited to join a *Versuch*, to suppose that we give up our intellectual props, what we take for granted as "given," to "suppose nothing else were 'given' as real except our world of desires and passions and we could not get down, or up, to any other 'reality' besides the reality of our drives—for thinking is merely a relation of these drives to each other" (§36; cf. §§16 and 19).

Nietzsche asks whether this could provide a sufficient basis for understanding the world in which the relations of our affects provide insight to a "*pre-form* of life" in which "all organic functions are still synthetically intertwined along with self-regulation, assimilation, nourishment, excretion, and metabolism" (ibid.). Nietzsche thinks his experiment is not only justifiable but also required on the basis of intellectual demands for simplicity and consistency—he claims his is an attempt to find a single form of causality rather than having to rely on several. While this might seem to violate his prohibition on unconditionality, Nietzsche makes it clear that he is not dogmatically insisting that *there be* only one form of causality but rather that before we postulate several sources, we should "push to the limit" even "to the point of nonsense" of what we have and not simply recoil when we do not like the way things are going. He calls this the conscience of method and the moral of method: it is a practice of seeking that maintains its commitment to truth even if it undermines other cherished beliefs, or the foundations of the inquiry itself.

Nietzsche then reconsiders the conception of will as efficient (in ways that are somewhat in tension with his earlier discussion of willing in §19). If we "push it to the limit" as described above, then we have to further experiment (again, *Versuchen*) with "the hypothesis" of will as the sole causality, the idea that only will can affect will, not "stuff," and all effects, insofar as they depend upon some active force, are the effects of will.[21] It is on this basis of reasoning that Nietzsche supposes what he calls his "proposition": "our entire instinctive life [is] the development and ramification of *one* basic form of the will—namely, of the will to power." It is significant that Nietzsche takes unusual care here in identifying a positive view he claims *and* a fairly detailed account of how he reached it.[22] On this basis he arrives at the perspective he claims at the end of the section, the one from which we might imagine the book is written (recalling the claims of §23): "The world viewed from inside, the world defined and determined according to its 'intelligible character'—it would be 'will to power' and nothing else."[23] Looking further ahead to the fifth book of *GS*, written and published just after *BGE*, we can see how knowledge of pushing to the limits in this way is empowering and liberating, for it strengthens one's ability to command and thereby lessens one's need to be commanded by others, as for example, in the *need* for the unconditional.

Section 347 of *GS* critically scrutinizes faith, dogma, and what Nietzsche calls fanaticism in terms of the organization of the commanding/obeying structure he articulates repeatedly in *BGE*. While we are all orders of command and obedience, *what* commands and *what* obeys, *how* commanding occurs and exercises its control in relation to the other parts, the *extent to which* we consciously identify with what commands, and the felt quality of power we experience all vary considerably and provide the bases for the distinctions of types Nietzsche describes throughout his works. In the case of the believer, Nietzsche thinks this command structure is so dilapidated and dysfunctional that the only way it can experience the pleasure of power is, perversely, by being subject to it, by being commanded: "the less one knows how to command [*befehlen*], the more urgently one covets someone who commands, who commands severely" (*GS* 347). What Nietzsche describes as the "free spirit par excellence" is someone with "such a pleasure and power of self-determination [*wäre eine Lust und Kraft der Selbstbestimmung*], such a *freedom* of the will [*eine Freiheit des Willens denkbar*] that the spirit would take leave of all faith and every wish for certainty, being practiced in maintaining itself on insubstantial ropes and possibilities of dancing even near abysses." Having explored the ways in which the free spirit is *free*, as described in *BGE* part II, we can appreciate that how the free spirit encountered in later portions of *GS* has developed an organization and relation of affects (which Nietzsche identifies both with strength [*BGE* 21] and health [*HH* P:4]) that allow him to be *free of the need* to be commanded, to identify with and experience the powers of command within himself. While this resembles other conceptions of autonomy in the history of philosophy, it is distinctive in its recognition of complexity, flexibility, and content (i.e., the pleasure in living, feeling oneself to be a power in the world such that one does not need to seek out or cling to unconditional supports).[24] How this stands in contrast to the perspective, tastes, and needs of the religious being is explored next.

CHAPTER 5

PART III: "WHAT IS RELIGIOUS"

The German title of the chapter is *Das religiöse Wesen* and could also be translated as religious "essence," "nature," "matter," or "disposition." In it, Nietzsche continues in part the analysis of religious matters he conducted in his free spirit trilogy (1878–1882).[1] The analysis of the religious "essence" in *BGE* focuses its attention not on the objects of religious dread and longing but on the religious being.[2] What is the history of the problem of "science and conscience" (*Wissenschaft* and *Gewissen*) in the soul of the religious human being? Given his reputation as a free spirit, atheist, and self-proclaimed anti-Christian, the reader might expect that Nietzsche is simply going to be hostile toward religion, but this is far from the case and the great surprise of the material contained in Nietzsche's nuanced and complex work. The chapter is also notable for its enigmatic presentation of the eternal recurrence (§56), the second such presentation in Nietzsche's published corpus outside of *Z*. It is not insignificant that the thought is presented as an "ideal" of a type in a chapter devoted to religion.

THE INTELLECTUAL CONSCIENCE

Nietzsche opens the chapter in section 45 by speaking of the human soul and its limits, of its history to date and "as yet unexhausted possibilities," and says this is the "predestined hunting ground" of a born psychologist and lover of the "great hunt" such as himself. He confesses to feeling isolated in this great task; scholars, he says, cannot be relied upon since the "great hunt" also contains "great danger" and here scholars lose "their keen eye and nose." Nietzsche soon makes it clear in the section that his concern is with the psychology of the religious human being, and to work on this problem one might need an "intellectual conscience" as "profound, wounded, and monstrous" as that possessed by Pascal. Here we are dealing with a "swarm of dangerous and painful experiences," and to survey the psychological field of problems such experiences throw up one needs a "malicious spirituality" capable of arranging the material and forcing into formulas.

Pascal held that even if the Christian faith was not capable of proof, it is the fearful possibility that it is in fact true that should compel us to prudently become a Christian. Pascal is a figure that fascinates Nietzsche. In *AOM* 408 he mentions him as one of several figures from whom he will accept judgment,[3] while in *EH* ("Why I am so Clever" 3) he describes him as "the most instructive victim of Christianity," and in a note from 1887 as "the admirable logician of Christianity" (*KSA* 12:10[128]; *WP* 388). Pascal embodies in his intellectual being what characterizes Christian faith from the start, as Nietzsche makes clear in the next section (§46): "a sacrifice of all freedom, all pride, all self-confidence of the spirit," and, at the same time, "self-mockery, self-mutilation." The Christian faith is marked by a cruelty and self-mutilation ("religious Phoenicianism"), which afflicts a conscience that is over-ripe, manifold, and pampered. Here we have a peculiarly religious psychology in which, Nietzsche says, "the subjection of the spirit" must hurt indescribably. Without the Christian faith, Pascal thought, we would become, no less than nature and history, "a monster and chaos," and this requires our negation of nature, history, and man (*KSA* 12:9[182]; *WP* 83). Pascal employs moral skepticism as a means of exciting the need for faith and for it to be justified. In short, Christianity breaks the strongest and noblest souls and Nietzsche says in a note of 1887–1888 that he cannot forgive Christianity for having destroyed a man like Pascal (*KSA* 13:11[55]; *WP* 252; see also *KSA* 12:5[25]; *WP* 276 on the gloominess of the strong, such as Pascal and Schopenhauer).[4]

Intellectual conscience is the key to understanding important aspects of Nietzsche's philosophy: how it works, what drives it, and the questions it poses and makes central. It is a curious conscience in a way: it tells us what is wrong or faulty in our ways of living, thinking, and feeling and rejects in principle anything that has been merely inherited and passed down and on (whether consciously or not). It aims to give us a set of methods and tasks by which we can become those that we are, supposing we *want* to become them. What is the case for Nietzsche is that we do *not* know; we don't know what we claim to know (this is especially true with respect to the whole field of "morality"). We in modern Europe, he says, claim to know what Socrates confessed he didn't know, namely, what morality is. Nietzsche construes the intellectual conscience as the superior form of conscience, the conscience behind our conscience (*GS* 335). As the practice of genuine science it challenges practical reason and the attempt to use knowledge to satisfy the heart's desire (*A* 12). The intellectual conscience demands that we do not accept anything on trust and that we question existence. Nietzsche writes on this most potently in *GS* 2:

> To stand in the midst of the "discordant concord of things," and of this whole marvellous uncertainty and rich ambiguity of existence *without questioning*, without trembling with the craving and rapture of such questioning . . . this is the feeling I look for in everybody. Some folly keeps me persuading that every human being has this feeling, simply because he is human. This is my kind of injustice.

In *GS* 319 Nietzsche speaks of making our experience a matter of conscience for our knowledge, which entails practicing a type of honesty (*Redlichkeit*) that is quite alien to founders of religion and moral systems. It requires listening to the sounds of one's being and being conscientious through knowledge: "What did I really experience? What was going on inside and around me? Was my reason bright enough?" Those who are thirsty for reasons and knowledge want to face their experiences as sternly as a scientific experiment, "hour by hour, day by day!" They want to be their own experiments and guinea pigs. In *GS* 324 Nietzsche speaks of the great liberation in terms of life being an experiment for the knowledge-seeker, which is to be practiced not as a duty, a disaster, or a deception, but rather a world of dangers and victories in which heroic feelings have their dance and playgrounds. With the principle "Life as means to knowledge" one can live not only bravely but also gaily or cheerfully. We do not live in fear of life or wish to shield ourselves against misfortunes and wrong turnings simply because we are confident in our possession of intellectual resources and physical strength and that will enable us to profit from all experiences, good and bad. In *GS* 335 Nietzsche addresses the issue of how difficult it is for us to follow the Delphic oracle, "know thyself," and observe ourselves adequately. The aphorism is entitled "Long live physics!" and its opening questions make it clear that by physics Nietzsche simply means the methods and techniques of observation and self-observation. At the end of the aphorism he argues that we can no longer posit valuations and ideals either in ignorance of what we discover to be lawful and necessary in the world or in contradiction to it. This attraction to "physics" places a constraint on creation, and what compels and binds us to it is our honesty or probity. Nietzsche is subjecting our claim to being sincere and upright to the scrutiny of the intellectual conscience. We need to put our claims to sincerity or rightness to the test, and in part this test is "physics" where it denotes learning the physiognomy of moral judgment and evaluation (e.g., its prehistory in the instincts, the likes and dislikes, etc.). "Physics" is shorthand for knowledge and its practices. The Latin *probus* means "good": in this aphorism Nietzsche's basic task is to push us to the limits of what it means to be good or just. In short: one can never be good or just enough, the scope for self-deception and dishonesty is immense. For Nietzsche, knowledge requires thinking against oneself and refashioning the heart's desire (see §23 on the "hearty conscience").

This problem of "knowledge and conscience" is given a prominent place in *BGE* III and returns as an important theme in later chapters, notably, when Nietzsche addresses himself to the task of the future philosopher. As one commentator has noted, the new philosopher is faced with the task of forging a new conscience on the basis of new knowledge (e.g., life as will to power): "Hardness of conscience is a Christian attainment not to be abandoned but transformed into a post-Christian conscience, intellectual conscience or the vice by which the mind rules the heart" (see *BGE* 230 on being "hardened in the discipline of science").[5]

REVALUATION OF ALL VALUES

Nietzsche makes two main points in section 46. The first key point is that the faith of original Christianity is not the faith of a Luther or a Cromwell, "or some other northern barbarian of the spirit," but rather the faith of Pascal since it amounts to a continual suicide of reason. Right from its inception, then, Nietzsche contends, Christian faith is a form of sacrifice (of freedom, pride, self-confidence, etc.). It rests on a pampered conscience. This conscience, however, has bred within us qualities such as doubt and suspicion, which can now be utilized by free spirits to carry out the "self-sublimation" of morality and to question the universalist claims and hegemony of "morality." Nietzsche, for example, will go on in the book to make use of the honesty of the intellectual conscience in his call for man to be translated back into nature (*BGE* 229–30). The second key point he makes concerns the revaluation of all values of antiquity promised by the paradoxical formula, "god on the cross." Here Nietzsche touches on a topic that will occupy him in the first essay of his next work, *GM*, and the idea that in ancient history there took place a slave revolt in morality. He notes at the end of section 46 that the last great slave rebellion took place with the French Revolution. The Oriental slave took revenge on Rome: on its noble and frivolous tolerance and its "catholicity" of faith. The psychology of the slave can be understood in terms of a need for the unconditional; what outrages the slave about the masters is the latter's freedom from the fanaticism of faith, "that half-stoical and smiling unconcern with the seriousness of faith." Nietzsche thus points out that "Enlightenment" about faith is what outrages since it has eschewed the need for the fanatical and unconditional.

Let's focus on the two terms Nietzsche uses to explain the slave revolt: inversion and revaluation. The formula "god on the cross," Nietzsche says, amounts to the boldest "inversion" (*Umkehren*) yet seen in history; it also promised a "revaluation" (*Umwerthung*) of the values of antiquity. What is being "inverted"? And what is an act of inversion? To invert is literally to turn upside down, so in this case Nietzsche is getting at the fact that the slave revolt inverts a previous moral order and set of perspectives of the world (perspectives on suffering and cruelty, on good and bad, on what is noble and base), but it does so in a manner that remains in thrall to that which it seeks to overcome or conquer: it is essentially reactive ("the meek shall inherit the earth" as a declaration of revenge, for example). A revaluation by contrast suggests a new positing of values and a break with previous values (good and evil over good and bad, humility over self-confidence). The two are closely linked of course in Nietzsche's mind. He sees his own revaluation project not so much in terms of the creation of new values—that is to come in the future and after the revaluation—but more in terms of humanity performing a supreme self-examination (*EH* "Why I am a Destiny" 1). The task is to reverse prevalent valuations that reversed ancient valuations and thus conduct an immanent or internal criticism: what claims to be "eternal" will be shown to be historically specific; what claims to be absolute will be shown to be perspectival; in short, our "morality" will be shown to be mendacious, hypocritical, and dishonest.[6]

Nietzsche stresses the fact that because Christian language is essentially dead for us moderns, we no longer can feel the gruesomeness of the formula "god on the cross" as it would have struck a classical taste. But he wants us to reimagine its "horrible" and "questionable" character. What in fact characterizes modern man is not so much the task of revaluation but rather the temptation of a new European Buddhism, and it is this movement Nietzsche seeks to uncover and take to task in his next book, *GM*. Today, Nietzsche observes in a note of 1885–1886, Christianity has declined in fearfulness and we see emerging an "opiate Christianity," one that is intended to soothe diseased nerves and has no need of the fearful solution of "god on the cross." This explains why Buddhism is gaining ground in Europe (*KSA* 12:2[144]; *WP* 240).

Section 47, along with sections 50 and 51, treat the enigma presented by the figure of the saint and we will take them together. In section 47 Nietzsche focuses on Schopenhauer and Wagner as two recent examples where this enigma reveals itself. In Schopenhauer's case there is the fixation on the question of how a denial of the will to life through a saintly existence is possible. Nietzsche contends that this question seems to have been the one that inspired Schopenhauer to become a philosopher. In Schopenhauer this is not the moral saintliness of the compassionate person, but rather the ascetic saint who secures the highest insight into the nature of reality. The world and the people in it are disowned. The highest good sought by philosophers from Plato to Kant does not consist in feeling universal love but in the denial of the will. This is Schopenhauer's doctrine of renunciation. The transition to it can be explicated as follows:

(a) The compassionate person "knows the whole" and "comprehends its inner nature"; all that exists is involved in a constant passing away, a vain striving, and a continual suffering. Wherever we look we see a suffering humanity, a suffering animal world, and a world that passes away (*WWR* I p. 379).

(b) We now reach the point at which this "knowledge" becomes a quieter of all and every willing, and where the will now turns away from life, "it shudders at the pleasures in which it recognizes the affirmation of life."

(c) At this stage we attain to a state of voluntary renunciation, resignation, true composure, and complete will-lessness. Seeing the vanity of all existence we now wish to deprive desires of their sting, to close the entry to all suffering, "to purify and sanctify ourselves by complete and final resignation" (ibid.).

Schopenhauer is basically tracing a path from virtue to asceticism. One has to develop an aversion to the will and know this as an eternal truth. This means renouncing nothing other than one's "inner nature," including one's sexual impulses: "voluntary and complete chastity is the first step in asceticism or denial of the will to life." The human being who remains in a state of delusion is like someone who lives life as a circle of red-hot coals with a few cool places that console him. The human being of true wisdom sees himself in all places, hot and cold simultaneously, and so freely withdraws from life. The saint effects the transition from virtue to asceticism through a rigorous and exacting practice of self-discipline, involving not only fasting but self-castigation and self-torture. Only through constant privation, and the suffering this entails, can the saint kill that which he abhors and knows to be the source of all human misery and suffering. Moreover, Schopenhauer goes so far as to say that the saint positively welcomes every suffering that comes to him be it through chance or the wickedness of others, including every injury, every ignominy, every outrage, and every humiliation. Why? Because they provide him with the opportunity of proving to him that he longer affirms the will.

There are several questions one can ask about Schopenhauer's "deduction" of the saintly existence, including how compatible it is with the rest of his system in *The World as Will and Representation* (e.g., if Schopenhauer is right about the fixity of intelligible character, how can someone with an inborn sinful character become saintly?). However, this need not detain us here. Instead, let us return to Nietzsche in *BGE*. Nietzsche's focus is explaining how the whole phenomenon of the saint has exerted such an extraordinary attraction on human beings of all types and ages, including philosophers. His answer, "beyond any doubt," is that it carries with it the air of the miraculous, such as "the immediate *succession of opposites,*" of states of soul that are judged morally in opposite ways (§47). It appears as something palpable to us that the sinner or bad person has suddenly and miraculously been transformed into a saint or good person. As a result, the psychology developed to this point in intellectual history suffers shipwreck, and Nietzsche wonders whether this was because hitherto this psychology has been developed under the dominion of morality, that is, the system of thought that believes in opposite moral values and reads and interprets them into the texts and facts (see *BGE* 2 on these opposites). Nietzsche invites us at the end of the section to consider that what might be at work here is a "mistake of interpretation" and "lack of philology" or close and slow reading. Throughout his works, Nietzsche emphasizes the need to read well and actively seeks to cultivate the right readers (see, for example, *D* Preface, *GM* Preface; and discussion of part IV).

THE RELIGIOUS INSTINCT

In section 51 Nietzsche's focus is on probing why the most powerful individuals have equally been drawn to the saintly figure and bowed before him. His answer is that they see in the saint, consciously or not, a will to power expressing or manifesting itself no matter how perverse and monstrous this will to power is. As such, the powerful were honoring something in themselves when they honored the saint. In addition, the powerful ones learn a new fear before the figure of the saint: such is his miraculous and elevated state above nature that the thought arises in them that there has to be some reason for this existence of ascetic self-denial and anti-nature, as if he possessed some "inside information." It is the will to power that brings them to a halt before the saint. Nietzsche ends the section on a playful note by not finishing his sentence: "they had to ask him." The most likely conclusion Nietzsche wants his readers to infer is the lesson of the will to power: the powerful ones lacked a proper psychology and could not infer what we are now able to, namely, that the "meaning" of the saint resides not in the external will of a transcendent power (God) but in life conceived as will to power and which is able to assume spiritual forms as it becomes sublimated.

Section 49 contrasts Greek religiosity with Christianity: where the former is a religion of gratitude the latter is a religion of fear. In section 52, Nietzsche contrasts the Old and New Testaments and sees the latter as more to the taste of modern Christians (it was also Schopenhauer's preferred text), whereas his taste, so the hint is given, is for the former. The Old Testament is Jewish and a book of divine justice. It is a monument to what humanity was once capable of, containing speeches "in so grand a style that Greek and Indian literature have nothing to compare with it." We can only stand in reverential awe, even terror, before it. The New Testament, the book of grace, by contrast appeals to the taste of us "tame, domestic pets" of modern-day Europe. Given this fundamental contrast between the two books, Nietzsche asks, was it not a great literary sin to have put them together in the one Bible?

In section 53, a short section, Nietzsche asks, "why atheism today?" and responds in essence by suggesting that it is because the human, all too human qualities of God, as that which we have bestowed on him, have been refuted: God the father, the judge, the rewarder, and so on. In addition, Nietzsche notes—a point he had already made in *D*—God is notoriously unclear in his communication (we simply don't know what he wants or what his intentions and plans are) (see *D* 91). God does not hear our pleas to him and even if he did hear he would not know how to help: there is a huge chasm between us and this distant God. However, at the end of the section Nietzsche claims that the religious instinct in man is far from diminishing as a result of the rise of atheism; on the contrary, it is growing powerfully even though the "theistic satisfaction" is refused with a deep suspicion. What exactly does Nietzsche mean in making this complex point? On the one hand, he might be referring to the fact that although atheism is in the ascendancy, our ways of thinking still remain in the grip of morality and metaphysics, in short, the "prejudices" he sought to expose in part I of the book. On the other hand, he may be referring to his "religious" satisfaction, which is about to come to the fore in section 56, in which the will to power and affirmation of life are to be subject to a kind of deification and eternalization. This suggests that the religious instinct is not only a religious neurosis as seems to be stated in section 47 but rather that it can assume both neurotic and healthy forms as a kind of god-forming and worshipping instinct, such as the expression of gratitude to life.[7] In this respect, atheism is something of a modern disaster for Nietzsche simply because humankind is left empty, unable to satisfy its religious instinct and devotes all its energies to an entirely secular culture with no aspiration to anything higher or superior to itself.[8]

In section 54 Nietzsche focuses on modern philosophy as a form of epistemological skepticism and that is, "overtly or covertly," anti-Christian but not anti-religious (and as stated in the previous section). The attempt has been made to get rid of the old concept of the "soul." Hitherto the soul was believed in as one believed naively in grammar and the grammatical subject, as in Descartes's famous proposition about the cogito: "I think, therefore I am," in which "I" is the subject and thinking is the predicate: "thinking is an activity," Nietzsche says, that supplies the subject as the cause of thinking. Nietzsche then talks about how Kant refined and criticized this proposition by making the "I" the effect of a synthetic unity of apperception necessary for thinking but in which neither subject nor object can be proved as such. Rather, they enjoy a merely apparent existence in the sense that they are not substantial entities but formal ones: they are empirically real but not metaphysically foundational.[9] When we speak of substances and faculties—the Ego, the Will, and so on—we are engaged in fabrication. We are distorting and simplifying processes and events that are much more complex than our categories and established modes of thinking enable us to appreciate. Nietzsche wishes us to be on guard against this tendency to substantialize entities, including ourselves, in this way, and this is why he is sympathetic to Kant's critique of the paralogisms of pure reason in his *Critique of Pure Reason* (1781/7) since the positing of the transcendental unity of apperception does not allow us to make any knowledge claims about the subject as a substance. In this respect, Nietzsche notes, modern European philosophy appears to be is moving toward a position on the "I" and the soul held by Vedanta philosophy and that formed part of its tremendous power (see also *GM* III:27 on this philosophy).

In section 55 Nietzsche writes of a "great ladder" of religious cruelty composed of numerous rungs, and singles out what he takes to be the three most important (a) the sacrifice of human beings in a pre-moral period to one's god, such as one's most loved ones or of the first born in prehistoric religions; (b) the sacrifice, "in the moral period" he says, of one's strongest instincts to one's god, and which centers on the cruel eyes of the ascetic and enthusiast of the "anti-natural"; (c) finally, the sacrifice of God himself and, as a piece of self-cruelty, in favor of the worship of the nonhuman (stone, gravity, fate) and the nothing. It is this final sacrifice, Nietzsche says, that is reserved for the generation now coming into existence. This final sacrifice contains a "paradoxical mystery," since it sacrifices those things for the sake of which the other sacrifices of humanity were made and that hitherto consoled it, such as "all hope, all faith in hidden harmony, in future blisses and justices . . ." This amounts to a nihilistic sacrifice.

ETERNAL RECURRENCE

In *EH* Nietzsche recounts the story of Zarathustra and mentions how the basic conception of the work, the idea of eternal recurrence, offered as the highest formula of affirmation attainable, "came" to him. He tells us that the idea belongs to August of 1881, and was jotted down on a piece of paper with the inscription "6000 feet beyond man and time." He was walking through the woods beside the lake of Silvaplana in Sils Maria when he stopped beside a mighty pyramidal block of stone: "Then this idea came to me." In his unpublished notebooks, dating from August 1881, Nietzsche presents the eternal recurrence variously as a cosmological hypothesis, a new center of gravity with respect to existence, an existential challenge, and a new mode of being ethical (of any action I propose to undertake I can ask myself, "do I want to do this *again and again*?").[10] In the first published presentation of the thought in *GS* 341 Nietzsche employs the thought to bring the text to a climatic denouement, providing an affirmation of life in its sternest and most troubling forms and as a counter-doctrine to the famous dying words of Socrates ("I owe Asclepius a cock"), which Nietzsche reads as expressing a desire to escape from life since it is but one long illness (*GS* 340). The original 1882 edition of the text concludes with an aphorism that introduces the figure of Zarathustra into Nietzsche's writings for the first time and in which, it is stated, "the tragedy begins" (*GS* 342). In *GS* 341 the thought centers on a demon that steals into our existence and the hour of most solitary solitude and presents us with the challenge of the thought that asks us if we are prepared to live over again and again this existence in the same sequence and succession. How well-disposed toward ourselves and life, it is asked, would we have to become to want nothing more ardently than this ultimate and eternal confirmation and seal? That is, how could we transform such a burdensome thought ("the greatest weight") into something joyful? It is only in the notebooks that Nietzsche works out various sketches for a cosmological "proof" of the thought. For Nietzsche, then, it is a hypothesis—he considers it to be the *most scientific* of all hypotheses, and one that is appropriate for a totally godless universe in which there are no end goals or final purposes at all—and one that he challenges himself to hold: he thinks he has the earned the right to hold it on the basis of his having worked his way through, but also beyond, Schopenhauer's pessimism. In essence, Nietzsche depicts a world of forces that suffers no diminution and no cessation, it is a world that never reaches equilibrium, so that whatever state this world can achieve, it must have achieved not only once but innumerable times. Let us take this very moment, Nietzsche says: has it not already been here once before, and many times, and will it not recur as it is? Is it not the same with the moment that gave birth to this one and with the moment that will be its child? He then turns to address humanity in this way. The whole of one's life turns again and again like an hourglass, including every pain and every pleasure, every friend and foe, every hope and every error—"the entire nexus of all things." Nietzsche adds: "This ring, in which you are a grain, shines again and again." He concludes with the decisive insight: "In every ring of human existence there is always an hour in which the most powerful thought surfaces, first for one, then for many, then for all, that of the eternal recurrence of all things—it is each time for humanity the hour of *midday*" (*KSA* 9:11[148]).[11]

In section 56 Nietzsche presents eternal recurrence as expressive of an *ideal* of a superhuman well-being: "the ideal of the most audacious, lively, and world-affirming human being." To be capable of holding to this view one needs to have become supremely well-disposed toward oneself and life, and this is why the affirmation of the thought implies or requires entitlement. Here it works in the context of working through the world-weary pessimism of Schopenhauer's denial of the will to life, and takes Schopenhauer's pessimism into dimensions of life it did not have the courage to go.[12] In section 56 he writes of seeing a drama or hearing musical performance and declaring loudly "de capo" (from the beginning), which we don't just say to ourselves but to the whole drama of which we are a part and which requires our existence for its completion and perfection. To say "yes" in Nietzsche's sense (highest formula of affirmation attainable) is to include the repetition of the "yes" ("I want it again and again"). It is this "again and again," the repetition, that confirms and seals. In a note of 1881 he writes:

> We always want to experience a work of art over and over again! One's life should also be fashioned in this way, so that one has the same wish as regards each of its parts. This is the main idea! Only at the end will the teaching be presented of the repetition of everything that has been, once the tendency has first been planted, so as to *create* something, which can *flourish* a hundred times more strongly in the sunshine of this teaching! (*KSA* 9:11[165])

With regards to this section in the chapter, attention should be paid to the following: (a) Nietzsche is attempting to think pessimism down to its depths and to liberate it from the narrowness and simplicity ("half-Christian" and "half-German") in which it has presented itself to us in the nineteenth century, notably the philosophy of Schopenhauer; (b) Nietzsche is attempting to think and work through pessimism "beyond good and evil" and free of "morality," with an "Asiatic and supra-Asiatic eye" (the reference is clearly to Nietzsche's appropriation of the historical and fateful figure of Zarathustra)[13]; (c) that this attempt *may* lead, without intending it and just possibly, to an inverse or opposite ideal (*umgekehrte Ideal*); (d) and, finally, that the affirmation contained in the thought makes both the spectacle necessary and the affirmer himself necessary; would this not be, Nietzsche ends by saying, "a vicious circle made god?". It seems clear here that (a) the "god" in question is not the God of Christianity but Dionysus (see also *BGE* 295), and (b) Dionysus provides a personification of cosmic eternal recurrence.[14] If this is right it cannot be the case, then, that merely an erotic necessity is at work for Nietzsche; rather, the "necessity" in question must be of stronger kind, namely, a physical or cosmological one (though we can imagine human beings coming to *love* this necessity as in Nietzsche's doctrine of *amor fati*, *GS* 276; *EH* "Clever" 10).[15]

With the thought of eternal recurrence, to what extent is Nietzsche offering a religion of the future to supplement or complement his philosophy of the future?[16] This thought, he says, contains more than all religions that teach us to despise this life as something merely fleeting and to focus our gaze on an indeterminate other life (*KSA* 9:11[159]). It is an experiment designed for new modes of living. This "powerful thought" uses the energy that has hitherto been at the command of other aims. It has a transforming effect, not through the creation of any new energy but simply by creating new laws of movement for energy. It is in this sense that it holds for Nietzsche the possibility of determining and ordering individual human beings and their affects differently (*KSA* 9:11[220]). For Nietzsche the eternal return is "the hardest thought" (*der schwerste Gedanke*). He stresses it can only be endured through a revaluation of all values: "No longer joy in certainty but in uncertainty; no longer 'cause and effect' but the continually creative; no longer will to preservation but power; no longer the humble expression, 'everything is *merely* subjective,' but 'it is also *our* work!—Let us be proud of it!'" (*KSA* 11:26[284]; *WP* 1059). In order to endure the thought of return one needs freedom from morality, new means against the fact of pain, and enjoyment of all kinds of uncertainty and experimentalism as a counterweight to extreme fatalism. It is this "greatest elevation of the consciousness of strength of human beings" that comes into being as the over-human or superhuman is created (*KSA* 11:26 [283]; *WP* 1060). We should not be on the lookout for unknown felicities or bestowals of grace; rather, we should make the effort to live in such a way that we wish to live this life again and like this for "eternity."

In one note from 1887 Nietzsche speaks of his "fundamental innovations," saying in place of moral values he posits purely naturalistic values; in place of society the culture complex; in place of epistemology a perspectival theory of the affects; and in place of metaphysics and religion the theory of eternal recurrence (as a means a breeding and selection) (*KSA* 12:9[8]; *WP* 462). Nietzsche will treat religions as means of cultivation/breeding and education later in this chapter of *BGE*. Eternal recurrence has an affinity with religion in that it is a doctrine of (Dionysian) faith (*TI* "What I Owe the Ancients": 4–5). But it is a faith concentrated on life, on the this-worldly character of the actual world, not otherworldliness. Nietzsche conceived the cultivation of the teaching in terms of a slow sinking in: "whole generations must build upon it and become fruitful so that it will become a large tree, which would overshadow all humanity to come" (*KSA* 9:11[158]). Like religion, it must provide a response to pain and suffering since these are what lead people to embrace metaphysics and religion in the first place. This explains why Nietzsche says that to endure the thought of return, one needs various things such as freedom from morality (in the sense of the eternal peace of the transcendent, the purity of the good), new means against the fact of pain, and the enjoyment of all kinds of uncertainty and experimentalism.

What would be the new means against pain and suffering? For Nietzsche it is not suffering per se that is a problem for human beings but rather senseless suffering. As Nietzsche says in *GM*, human beings can welcome suffering provided there is a meaning to it or that can be credited to it. He further notes in this text that suffering was not senseless for either human beings of ancient or primeval times or for Christians; it is only becoming such for us moderns and for obvious reasons. The naïve humans of ancient times saw suffering as a spectacle and created festivals of cruelty devoted to this spectacle; the Christian sees in suffering an entire hidden machinery of salvation. So, how will we atheistic moderns now approach questions of pain and suffering? At the moment, Nietzsche thinks we are responding to this by relying upon or trusting the gay science—life as a riddle or life as a problem of knowledge (*GM* II:7). This is our hope and eternal recurrence is our consolation. But it is not without ground: the pessimist of strength finds "senseless ills" the most interesting; they are entirely natural and stripped of evil (*KSA* 12:10[21]; *WP* 1019). Nietzsche does have a worry about this and it informs his analysis of the ascetic ideal in *GM* III. The danger is that we will remain "idealists of knowledge" when we need more than this idealism. That is, knowledge is only of value if it transforms us. This is why Nietzsche's great question is (from 1881–1882): "to what extent truth and knowledge stand or endure incorporation?" (see *GS* 110, for example). By truth and knowledge here he means the truth and knowledge that go against the heart's desire and can generate new life, new values. A critic might say of those embarked on this search that they are disappointed idealists or children that have had their hands burnt. Nietzsche, however, thinks we can conceive of ourselves differently, namely, as those who take delight in the boundless or the free as such (the new open sea of *GS* 343):

> an almost Epicurean bent for knowledge develops that will not easily let go of the questionable character of things; an aversion to big moral words and gestures, a taste that rejects all crude, four-square opposites . . . we still ride mad and fiery horses, and when we hesitate [as we do] it is least of all danger that makes us hesitate. (*GS* 375)

Eternal recurrence is not a religion if we understand religion to denote a teaching or doctrine that brings and binds people together in the form of a community in which they can recognize each other.[17] The "new" for Nietzsche cannot come from community. He does value friendship and perhaps this is the model he use to think how new individuals would relate to one another. He envisages "solitaries" who have seceded from society, but it is not clear if he thinks this is a temporary measure or expedient, or a necessary act in a transitional phase and that at some point in the future a new society will, or could be, constituted. Nietzsche writes perceptively of founders of religion

(*GS* 353), but stresses in *EH* that he is no such founder. In his notebooks of the mid 1880s Nietzsche writes of the need for a doctrine that would be powerful enough to work as a cultivating or breeding agent, in which the strong would be even further strengthened (those who can live without extreme articles of faith and are not fanatics) and the world-weary would be paralyzed or even destroyed (see, for example, *KSA* 11:25[211]; *WP* 862).

Nietzsche makes some further points on eternal recurrence as a practice: we make no claim to being "holy" when we practice it (we are far too modest for this); and the thought is an "innocent" one in the sense that it neither apportions blame to those who are overwhelmed or crushed by it, nor merit to those who are able to be equal to it. Eternal recurrence, to conclude, is a religious thought where this entails living a conscientious life and one that is dedicated to the affirmation of life "beyond good and evil." It is a thought that sanctifies life "as it is and was" and wants this repeated to eternity. The thought carries with it an affirmation of "necessity" without assuming an imperative form. Nietzsche does not expect that everyone will prove equal to the thought and be able to "will" it, and there is no idea of an "ought" attached to it. One might suggest that the thought—and as articulated in *BGE* 56 with the "vicious circle become god"—is designed to replace the psychical function of a god and, as such, is intended as a kind of theogony.

FREE THINKING

Section 57 is a playful section in which Nietzsche speaks of man's "spiritual eye" enlarging the space around him so that his world becomes ever more profound with "ever new stars" and "ever new riddles" becoming visible. Perhaps, Nietzsche wonders, what the spirit's eye has exercised its attention on was but an occasion for this exercise, "a playful matter" and "something for children and those who are childish." Perhaps again we can imagine a future when such portentous and dreadful concepts as "God" and "sin" will seem to us as nothing more than a child's toy and a child's pain appear to an old man; and then would this old person still be in need of another toy and another pain, "still child enough, an eternal child!" Nietzsche here may both be alerting us to a religious "fact" of human nature—the need for fantastical conceptions and projections of reality—and lamenting the fact that mankind is so caught up in childish fantasies and unable to attain maturity. However, the reference to the "eternal child" recalls Heraclitus's image of eternity (aeon) as a child playing the dice game of existence, which so appealed to Nietzsche (see *Philosophy in the Tragic Age of the Greeks*, section 7). So, although we might experience distress in the face of the human need for childish fantasy, including fantastical concepts such as "God" and "'sin," the child is ultimately for Nietzsche an image of liberation and joy and in our constructions and ideals we will be "eternal" children. This conception of the child is signaled at various points in his writings: it indicates a capacity for playful inventiveness and innocence with respect to "earthly seriousness" to date (*GS* 382), and Nietzsche provides the "ideal" of a new kind of spirit that can play "naively" (with overflowing power and abundance) "with all that has hitherto been called holy, good, untouchable, divine" (ibid.). Thus, even those who have freed themselves from the dogmas— and toys—of the past remain in need of new toys and different pains as part of the necessary stimuli of life. In "Of the Great Longing" in *Z* Nietzsche writes of the giving of "new names and many-coloured toys"[18] (on the child as a figure of "innocence" and play see *Z* I: "Of the Three Metamorphoses"). Of course, for Nietzsche the new thinkers of the future will, in their construction of ideals, endeavor to remain true to earth and in this respect their implication in the "eternal child" will be quite different in character from the religious and metaphysical teachers of the past who have taught humankind to despise the earth and seek escape from the human and the humanly conceivable and palpable.

PHILOSOPHY AND RELIGION

The chapter on religion concludes with two quite long and important sections on the relation between philosophy and religion. Nietzsche begins section 61 by stating what the philosopher is for "we free spirits," namely, the one who has "the most comprehensive responsibility" and the "conscience for the overall development of the human being," and, as such, he will exploit religions for the ends of cultivation or breeding and education in the same way he exploits the political and economic circumstances of his time. This section is important since it indicates that Nietzsche's concern is not with the fate of a specific social class or elite group of individuals but rather has a "generic orientation" toward humankind as such: What is humankind to become? What is its fate? Contra the democratic Enlightenment, which is centered on herd-animal existence and equalization of all, Nietzsche's "new Enlightenment" focuses on what is excluded by the herd and concerns all of us: "the self-overcoming of the human" (i.e., its enhancement and perfection).[19] Nietzsche now enumerates the uses of religion, which include: as means for overcoming resistances and the ability to rule (it creates a bond between rulers and subjects); it is a means for obtaining peace or serenity from the "noise" of cruder forms of government, as well as purity from the "*necessary* dirt" of politics. Nietzsche gives the example of the Brahmins to illustrate the latter point. In addition, religion can give to a portion of the ruled instruction in how to prepare themselves for future ruling and obeying, walking the path to a higher spirituality and so having opportunities to test out the feelings of self-overcoming, silence, and solitude. Here, Nietzsche says, asceticism and Puritanism are indispensable means for educating and ennobling a race seeking to become master over its origins among the rabble and working its way toward future governance. Finally, for ordinary human beings or the great majority who exist for service, religion provides invaluable contentment with their station in life and their type of existence, in short, ennobling obedience: "Religion and religious significance spread the splendour of the sun over such ever-toiling human beings and make their own sight tolerable to them." Nietzsche compares the effect of religion on the majority to that exerted by Epicurean philosophy on sufferers of a higher rank, such as certain kinds of philosophical types: it refreshes, soothes, and refines and even sanctifies and justifies suffering. Both Christianity and Buddhism can be respected in this regard as religions that have taught the lowliest how, through piety, to place themselves in a higher order of things, no matter how illusory, and so maintaining their contentment with the real order in which their lives are hard (and necessarily so, Nietzsche adds in conclusion).

In section 62, the final section, Nietzsche turns his attention to the other side of this reckoning of religions for life, and in an effort to expose their dangerous character. The essential danger lies when religions seek to establish themselves as sovereign in life, no longer serving as a means of education and cultivation in the hands of the philosopher. His chief concern is with the fate of the higher types of human being and how religions endanger their flourishing. His concern centers on two "facts" as he sees them: (a) as in the rest of the animal kingdom there is among humans an excess of failures (the sick, the degenerating, the infirm); (b) the successful among humans are always the exception and their complicated conditions of life can only be "calculated" with great subtlety and difficulty. As far as the "economy of mankind" is concerned it is ruled over by the accidental and a law of absurdity.

Nietzsche now asks the question: what is the attitude of the aforementioned religious toward this excess of cases that do not turn out right? His answer is that both seek to, above all, preserve life, "to preserve alive whatever can possibly be preserved." In short, they are religions for those who suffer from life. While they can receive credit—"the very highest credit"—for their preserving care, the danger is that such religions, when they exist as sovereign, are among the principal causes that keep the type "man" on a lower rung of the ladder of life. Or, as Nietzsche perhaps dangerously puts it, "they have preserved too much of *what ought to perish.*" Nietzsche immediately goes on to express gratitude toward these religions, noting what the spiritual human beings of Christianity have achieved in Europe. But he reiterates his main point: this has been at the cost of worsening "*the European race*" and standing all valuations on their head, for example, breaking the strong, casting suspicion on joy in beauty, turning the instincts of the strong, domineering, and turned-out well types into uncertainty, agony of conscience, and self-destruction: "invert all love of the earthly and of dominion over the earth into hatred of the earth and the earthly." Has not an attempt been made to apply "a single will" over Europe for 18 centuries with the aim of turning man into a "*sublime miscarriage*" (*sublime Missgeburt*)? Such a "monster" is interesting and of a higher, refined kind (hence the word "sublime"), but nevertheless, Nietzsche thinks, it is a miscarriage of what *could* be bred and educated under different circumstances. With respect to these tasks, then, Nietzsche holds Christianity to be the most presumptuous religion to date, as well as the most calamitous. What has been bred, and whose hegemony now needs contesting, is man as "the herd animal." This phenomenon is what Nietzsche returns to focus his attention on in part V on morals after his section on epigrams and interludes, which provides a pause and perhaps some necessary relief after this consideration of such serious matters.

CHAPTER 6

PART IV: "EPIGRAMS AND INTERLUDES"

The fourth part of Nietzsche's *BGE* provides significant insight to the organization and structure of the book and its project. It follows three broad-ranging parts that provide an overview of the book as a whole: the question of the value of truth and its evidence in the prejudices of philosophers, anticipation of liberation from at least some of those prejudices (or the *grip* of such prejudices), and analyses of current and possible future spirituality, broadly conceived. Up to this point, Nietzsche's text breathlessly builds expectations concerning the urgency and necessity of this development.

Part IV follows the depiction of awesome yet terrifying images of the "philosopher of the most comprehensive responsibility," who "will make use of religions for his own project of cultivation and education, just as he will make use of whatever political and economic states are at hand" (§61), and the "'spiritual men' of Christianity" who are responsible for having "invert[ed] all love of the earth and earthly [. . .] until [. . .] 'becoming unworldly,' 'unsensual,' and 'higher men' were fused into a single feeling." [*Ein Gefühl zusammenschmoltzen*] (§62). What is identified here as "fusion" in Nietzsche's text refers to the organization and coordination of the various constituents of the "order of rank" human beings are. What seems to be particularly impressive and utterly fascinating to Nietzsche is how in the "primeval forest" (§45) of the human spirit the governing drive binds together certain things to coordinate and direct its form of life. This is explored throughout the book with morality identified as one of the most powerful forces in effecting such a process. As we shall see, particularly in parts VIII and IX, Nietzsche anticipates what it might take to break that bond and create a different fusion.

At the end of part III, Nietzsche presents two responses to the pathetic and gruesome amalgamation that constitutes modern humanity. Catching sight of modern human beings could inspire either divine laughter or destructive rage. Hesitating to enact either of these responses just yet in his psycho-philosophical drama, Nietzsche provides "Sprüche und Zwischenspiele," or "epigrams and interludes."[1]

Throughout, we have noted the fact that Nietzsche regarded *BGE* as having a special relationship to his *Z*, which he ultimately completed just prior to *BGE*.[2] *Beyond Good and Evil* is supposed to convey the same ideas as *Z*, just expressed very differently. But *BGE* does not simply originate as *Z*'s afterbirth. Near the physical center of the text, these "Sprüche und Zwischenspiele" are intimately and historically related to the core of the whole project. In 1882, Nietzsche drafted a set of 445 aphorisms that he considered adding to *D* (originally published in 1881),[3] with a suggested title of "Jenseits von gut und böse: Sentenzen-Buch." Thus, *BGE* had a rather different conception for its form in its earlier beginning.

Most of part IV is drawn directly from this earlier material, and part of what it aims to do is provoke different feelings, possibly a new *Ein Gefühl zusammenschmoltzen*. For example, included in the original set is a "Sentenz" that contrasts feeling grateful (*dankbar*) with the feeling of vengeance (*rachsüchtig*). Great obligations lead not to gratitude, as we might currently expect, but rather to vengeance (*KSA* 10:3[1].206) for the binds they create become unbearable.[4] We see this idea developed explicitly later on in *GM*, where in the second essay, Nietzsche discusses the development of moral concepts from those originally in circulation in an economy of debt. In *BGE*, we have already been introduced to the topic of "gratitude," although it has not yet been developed as a theme. In the section that ends part II (§44), the "we" that claims entitlement to the name "free spirits" indicates its *gratitude* for "need and vacillating sickness" and gratitude "to god devil, sheep, and worm in us." Gratitude also comes up at the end of part III (§62), where Nietzsche (again using "we," but this time more generally) expresses gratitude for those "spiritual men" just mentioned, who stretched the soul in incomparable ways even though the "sovereign religions" (among which Christianity numbers) preserved what really "ought to have perished": "What we have to thank them for is inestimable; and who could be rich enough in gratitude not to be impoverished in view of all that the 'spiritual men' of Christianity, for example, have so far done for Europe!" An ethos of gratitude, plenitude, and overflowing seems to be the antidote, anticipated in *Z*, to the ascetic economy of guilt and debt analyzed in *GM*.[5]

One way to approach this curious collection of aphorisms could be to identify themes that account for their particular organization (e.g., Lampert's approach) and show how the aphorisms are abbreviations and condensations of themes addressed elsewhere in the book (e.g., Burnham's). These are valuable perspectives. Our focus is on the context of the material, why it appears in the book at all, its specific place *within* the text, and what this indicates about Nietzsche's overall aims. Yet, we offer at least one general observation about the thematic content of the lot. Nearly every other "saying" in part IV makes reference to some form of love or to some effect love has on us,[6] whether it heightens and ennobles, or how our capacity for love exemplifies gratitude and plentitude (relative degrees of strength). Very many of the "sayings" treat precisely and positively affirm the perspective Nietzsche advanced as the ("real and only") basic motives of human existence, particularly "hunger, sexual lust, and vanity" (§26). These *Sprüche* Nietzsche offers are expressive of the perspective he thinks is buried and transmogrified by Christian morality; they work in concert with his ultimate effort, discussed below, to affirm life. See, for example, "hunger" treated in sections 83, 141, and 143; "sexual lust" mentioned in sections 75, 114, and 123; and self-love in the form of "vanity" mentioned in sections 73a, 111, 122, 170, and 176. In the end, as we discuss in the chapters on parts VIII and IX, Nietzsche anticipates the overcoming of the morality of pity and selflessness in a form of amorous spirituality. There is a good deal of further analysis that informed readers might engage, which we hope to facilitate with this chapter.

We can approach a better understanding of the purpose of this part through an initial analysis of its title: We have *Sprüche*—which Nietzsche discusses directly elsewhere in the text and in other places in his writings—and *Zwischenspiele*—which is a term evocative of specific parts and functions of artistic works, particularly musical compositions and theatrical works. Part IV is distinctive among Nietzsche's writings as a collection of aphorisms presented *as* a collection within the book.[7] They are true to a style Nietzsche exhibited in earlier works, as for example, in his *HH* volumes and *D*. He makes use of what could be identified as aphorisms in other places in *BGE*, two groups of which we will focus on in later chapters (the "Sieben Weibs-Sprüchlein" in "Our Virtues" and sections 275–87 in the concluding part, "What is noble?"). We can relate these to several important themes, including how Nietzsche thinks about aphorisms more generally as they relate to activities of reading and interpretation, their relation to prior discussions of taste and the creation of a desirable future, and how their designation as *Zwischenspiele* indicates Nietzsche's engagement with certain musical ideas that suggest an effective function of cultivating certain powers of attention and listening that are important for the audience he is trying to create and reach. The remainder of this chapter is devoted to considering each of these terms in turn.

SPRÜCHE

"Sprüche" might be translated as "sayings" or "epigrams," and sometimes Nietzsche uses the term synonymously with "aphorisms" (he also occasionally uses the term "aphorism"). Famously, Nietzsche comments directly on aphorisms and what they require of readers: "An aphorism, properly stamped and molded, has not been 'deciphered' when it has simply been read; rather, one has then to begin its *exegesis*, for which is required an art of exegesis" (*GM* P:8). He then goes on to claim that he provides an elaborate example of the kind of activity he is talking about in *GM* III, which begins with an epigraph. The whole of *GM* III, it seems, is supposed to be an exegesis of that initial epigraph. Divergent and extravagant explications of this appear in the scholarly literature.[8]

Nietzsche mentions exegesis (*Auslegen*) several times in the course of *BGE*. He refers to physics as "an interpretation and exegesis of the world" (§15) and claims logic is dependent on "*interpretation* of the process [which] does not belong to the process itself" (§17); he sees his own project as "putting his finger on bad modes of interpretation" (§22); and he notes a lack of philology as what enables the disabling thinking of "the religious neurosis" and its faith in "the immediate succession of opposites" (§47). He eventually comes to see all of morality as an interpretation of the meaning and significance of human existence, which partially accounts for its inventiveness and thus its artificiality (discussed in part IX).

The activity of interpretation Nietzsche seeks to cultivate is clearly linked with identifying what it takes to *read* him well, a subject to which he periodically turns in his works. This has temporal dimensions—*reading slowly*—and taps some of the same critical capacities that are supposed to eventually develop among coming philosophers Nietzsche imagines in "We Scholars" (§210).

As to how aphorisms, specifically, play a role in exegesis, we can look ahead to section 235: "There are expressions and bull's-eyes of the spirit, there are epigrams, a little handful of words in which a whole culture, a whole society is suddenly crystallized." A distinguishing feature of aphorisms is that they can *crystallize*, instantly capturing and conveying the spirit of a whole culture. The efficiency, immediacy, and vivacity of this phenomenon are particularly interesting to Nietzsche, and he endeavors to do this with his own thoughts, both here in part IV and later in part IX. Moreover, as a self-proclaimed work in "psychology," or study of human psychic constitutions (*metaphorically* "souls"), characterizations of the "spirit" that animate cultures or make forms of life possible are inherent to Nietzsche's project (§23). Collecting these is clearly part of providing a "typology of morals," as Nietzsche describes his task in the next part (§186): "to collect material, to conceptualize and arrange a vast realm of subtle feelings of value and differences of value [. . .]." Further, Nietzsche thinks, these forms are expressive of feelings, "which are alive, grow, beget, and perish—and perhaps attempts to present vividly some of the more frequent and recurring forms of such living crystallizations" (§186). In seeing values *live*, we can perhaps better understand how they *animate* forms of life, how such feelings make a difference in the organizations that constitute individual and social organisms.

Yet, the aphorism, for Nietzsche, potentially does more than simply reflect or display something. Another key feature of aphorisms is that they can be effective, they can *do* something other than just saying or asserting.[9] This is suggested later in section 246: describing a "master in the art of prose," Nietzsche claims he "handles his language like a flexible rapier, feeling from his arm down to his toes the dangerous delight of the quivering, over-sharp blade that desires to 'bite, hiss, cut.—'"

But aphorisms do not simply have aggressive, corrective, or critical functions. The affective dimensions of reading and writing, the tempo and musicality of language, and "reading with one's ears" are of significant interest to Nietzsche throughout his works, interests expressed directly and quite clearly from at least Z onward. In this respect aphorisms can also have therapeutic effects. Marsden points out Nietzsche's interest in the relation between understanding (how we make sense of the world; *Sinn*) and sensation (*Sinne*);[10] this theme recurs in GS and elsewhere. Nietzsche's aphorisms also appear to have a practical, therapeutic purpose of retraining the senses, facilitating different ways of listening and hearing, new forms of seeing and understanding. "We have to learn to think differently—in order at last, perhaps very late on, to achieve even more, *to feel differently*" (D 103).

Finally, the aphorism has the ability to condense thought and draw the reader into processes of thought that make them their own. "He who writes in blood and aphorisms does not want to be read, he wants to be learned by heart. In the mountains the shortest route is from peak to peak, but for that you must have long legs. Aphorisms should be peaks, and those to whom they are spoken should be big and tall of stature" (Z:I "Of Reading and Writing"). As to whom such persons are, Nietzsche at times seems to think they do not yet exist; they belong to the future (though this notion is challenged by his thought of eternal recurrence, mentioned below). If this is the case, part of his task seems to involve preparation for this future, cultivating some of the powers that the free spirits and future philosophers might possess. One of these capabilities is a different kind of listening that will enable them to "hear what is spoken." Nietzsche's *Zwischenspiele*, we suggest, at least partially have this function, and this is consonant with his attentive regard for music, the musical qualities of language, and the appeal to Dionysus, god of music and wine, at the end of the book.

ZWISCHENSPIELE AND THE LISTENER OF THE FUTURE

The introduction of the "Epigrams and Interludes" following the dramatic conclusions of parts II and III certainly affects the tempo of the entire book. As we have already noted in the chapter on part II, Nietzsche is interested in the relation between tempo and thought and the rhythmic, temporal, and musical qualities of languages.[11] Throughout the book, Nietzsche discusses the misrecognition, misunderstanding, and mischaracterization, which typify human quests for knowledge and perfection. In section 27 Nietzsche remarks that one reason for such misunderstanding is the difference in tempo of thinking and living. Those who think at the pace and intensity of the current of the river Ganges, for example, are hardly recognizable by those who think and act at the pace of tortoises, or walk like frogs. To make communication possible, some "subtlety in interpretation" is necessary. In the same passage, Nietzsche uses Sanskrit words to convey the terms of contrast, and in the following section (§28), he remarks that "what is most difficult to render from one language into another is the *tempo* of its style, which has its basis in the character of the race, or to speak more physiologically, in the average *tempo* of its metabolism" (§28). "Tempo of metabolism," or the speed and meter that characterize the intensity and expression of *will to power* can be indicative of a general disposition toward life. This is not simply a matter of personal or individual preference but is embedded in cultural practices, most fundamentally in language. And languages have their general rhythm, cadence, and measure, which affect not only *how* one speaks but also *what* one can say.[12] In this section, Nietzsche makes use of four different languages: German, Italian (specifically musical terms), Latin, and French.

The significance of Nietzsche's discussions of tempo and language is heightened in part VIII, where he explores the European inheritance and resources (and liabilities) it might offer for the future. Nietzsche's *BGE* exhibits dramatic qualities, which include both the melodrama and foreboding and the even the "mood" of what he discusses (as for example, the pursuit of pessimism, or cheerfulness) as well as the pacing of ideas and their expression. The appearance of the collection of aphorisms that constitutes part IV significantly impacts the tempo of the work and serves to explicitly highlight and heighten its dramatic qualities.

The term "Zwischenspiele" refers to a period between main acts of a play (or opera) or between movements in a musical work. Such interludes have the functional purpose of lending time for set and costume changes, providing both actors and audience members with a break, and facilitating transitions. One of Wagner's innovations was what he called the "art of transition,"[13] the perfection of which aimed at sustaining continuous music. Indeed, Wagner claimed that what distinguished him from his contemporaries and predecessors was that he departed from modern arrangements "into arias, duets, finales, etc., and instead relate[d] the legend in a single breath."[14] Nietzsche himself mentions the significance of what can be said in a single breath in section 247.

The passage reflects Nietzsche's concern with both listening and speaking. In the section immediately preceding it, he writes, "there is *art* in every good sentence—art that must be figured out if the sentence is to be understood! A misunderstanding about its tempo, for example—and the sentence itself is misunderstood. That one must not be in doubt about the rhythmically decisive syllables [. . .] that one lends a subtle and patient ear to every *staccato* and every *rubato* [. . .] who among book-reading Germans has enough good will to acknowledge such duties and demands and to listen to that much art and purpose in language? In the end one simply does not have 'the ear for that'" (§246). In part V, Nietzsche writes: "Hearing something new is embarrassing and difficult for the ear; foreign music we do not hear well. When we hear another language we try involuntarily to form the sounds we hear into words that sound more familiar and more like home to us" (§192).

Nietzsche claims later that his *Z* inaugurates "a rebirth in the art of hearing" (*EH Z*:1) and can be regarded as music.[15] Yet in *EH*, he acknowledges that while *Z* might be likened to music and requires a new "art of hearing," it nevertheless *has not* been heard: "My *Zarathustra*, for example, is still looking for those [with good ears]—alas, it will have to keep looking for a long time yet!—One must be worthy of hearing him" (*EH* "Books" 4).[16] He continues, "the art of the *great* rhythm, the *great* style of long periods to express a tremendous up and down of sublime, of superhuman passion, was discovered only by me" in the dithyramb of the third book of *Z*. We suggest this is what Nietzsche endeavors to prepare his reader for with his *Zwischenspiele*. He is training the ear, cultivating and educating his listener of the future.

Wagner, who is immensely important in the upcoming part VIII, was adamant that during his own *Zwischenspiele* the theatre should be dark, no image should be visible, not even that of the orchestra. This furthered the aim of allowing music itself to play a dramatic role. Wagner saw his own role as educating the audience, teaching them *how* to experience not only his own work but also music as such. He regarded the *Zwischenspiele* as teaching his audience how to listen, how to pay attention only to the music so that they could and would experience it differently during the main acts. The similarity between Wagner's interest and innovation in the *Zwischenspiele* and Nietzsche's is more than mere coincidence or even an obscure and passing personal reference. It is an expression of how Nietzsche viewed himself connected with Wagner and aspects of the project Nietzsche ultimately thought Wagner betrayed.

To see this, we can look "cautiously before and aft" (*and* "with reservations, with doors left open"), as Nietzsche writes about the art of reading well in *D* P:5. Looking ahead, we see Nietzsche identify the "fundamental conception" of *Z* and his major intellectual and *personal* achievement in the thought of eternal recurrence. At a minimum, this idea represents for him the overcoming of pessimism and the ultimate affirmation—love rather than hatred of life, life affirmation as opposed to the pessimism and anti-naturalism he finds in the ascetic priestly ideal analyzed in *GM*. As previously discussed, Nietzsche describes his thought of eternal recurrence in section 56 as, "the ideal of the most high-spirited, alive, and world-affirming human being."[17] In the book that immediately precedes *Z*, Nietzsche describes such affirmation in terms of love, *amor fati* (*GS* 276), which at the same time is "the greatest weight" (*GS* 341). Eternal recurrence is the ultimate expression of the love of life insofar as one "wants to have *what was and is* repeated into all eternity" (§56).

Nietzsche reports that what predates his insight of eternal recurrence in August 1881,[18] and serves as an "omen" is "a sudden and profoundly decisive change in [his] taste, especially in music."[19] He links this moment of rebirth with the "sudden birth that occurred in February 1883," which is the culmination of his *Z*. And this, he claims was completed "exactly in that sacred hour in which Richard Wagner died in Venice" (*EH Z*: 1). Noticing that his period between conception and birth has a duration of eighteen months, Nietzsche remarks that this "might suggest, at least to Buddhists, that [he is] really a female elephant." These associations of eternal recurrence, Wagner, rebirth, and Buddhism, recall Wagner's own account[20] of a major turning point in his life when he received news of the death of Beethoven. Klaus Kropfinger gathers evidence for the view that Wagner's depiction of his experience of Beethoven's death draws on his views of metempsychosis (transmigration of the souls, *Seelenwanderung*), which he adopted from Schopenhauer.[21] On this basis, Wagner at least partially stakes his claim as heir to Beethoven's artistic genius insofar as he literally embodies it. The same appears true for Nietzsche's experience of Wagner's death (and perhaps is related to what appears to be Nietzsche's suggestion that insofar as he also seeks to be a *Zwischen-Begebnis* like Beethoven, *he*—Nietzsche—is the inheritor of Beethoven's spiritual resources, as discussed in the chapter on part VIII). Nietzsche's book *Zarathustra* is finally born in the moment of Wagner's death; the Buddhist allusion suggests Nietzsche intended the implication that Wagner, too, was reborn at this time and in Nietzsche's creative act.

The key idea of eternal recurrence is found not only in the explicit restatement in section 56 but also in the original materials for *BGE*, which predate *Z* and were written shortly after Nietzsche's alleged fateful insight "6000 feet beyond man and time" at Surlei (*EH Z*: 1). Among the 445 aphorisms Nietzsche wrote as part of his plan for the *Sentenzen-Buch* "Beyond Good and Evil" is one that draws a connection between love and eternity: "The love of life is nearly the opposite of the love of long living. All love thinks of the moment and eternity—but never of 'the length.'"[22] When Nietzsche writes that *BGE* says the same thing as his *Z* only differently, we should see it not simply as a *subsequent* restatement of those same ideas but also their *anticipation* in which at least portions of *BGE* capture ideas that shared the gestation process of *Z* but were not directly expressed in that work. This set of relationships, then, might provoke us to think further about the subtitle of *BGE*: "Vorspiel einer Zukunftsphilosophie." It plays out the aspirations of Wagner's artwork of the future, embodied in a work of art that chronologically predates this expression, but which also challenges our conception of the future itself insofar as eternal recurrence unites the moment and eternity and thus stands outside of time conceived as duration.[23] In this book Nietzsche anticipates what it would mean for the love of life (taken to the greatest extreme in the thought of eternal recurrence) to rule as supreme and give shape to a new sense of nobility.

We previously mentioned the connection between taste and orders of rank of souls. It is not simply that a "more noble" type (whatever that may be) has more refined taste by virtue of some sense of entitlement, or that because he is so rare, he loves only whatever else is also rare. Tastes can distinguish orders of soul because they are indicative of what rules and what commands in an individual, what such a person wants, his or her "heart's desire" (*BGE* 5). And we have seen in the context of our discussions of the *Republic*, how tastes are associated with loves insofar as they are evidence of what is actually wanted, desired, and sought. Moreover, the tastes we acquire pull the various desires that make up our constitutions in different relations, thereby creating different orders. In addition to continuing to watch for how taste is explored as relevant to doing philosophy, engaging in creativity, or being constitutionally strong or weak, we can observe that Nietzsche is also (for the same reasons) interested in love: both its objects and the forms it can take.

Some of the aphorisms collected here appear to have a performative character in terms of shifting from one set of tastes (which he considers base) to another (which has *prospects* for nobility). If we read the entire book as preparatory for asking the title question of the final part—*What is noble?*—then this feature of part IV is highly significant and not simply a diversion from the main purpose of the text, as might be suggested by Nietzsche's playful title of "Zwischenspiele." Rather than seeing Nietzsche's fourth part as a mere a play between acts of the more weighty parts before and after, we regard these "interludes" as preparatory for appreciating Nietzsche's later discussions of passages between tastes—the tastes of and for Wagner being most illustrative—and part IX, which anticipates a rank ordering of taste, and the cultivation of new tastes, on account of the multiplicity of latent desires bundled up in the "semi-barbarous" and "hybrid" creatures modern human beings, and particularly Europeans, are (e.g., §§153, 159, 168, 180, and 184). Standing "between," having an intermediary role in a transition from one taste and constitution that has such needs and preferences to another, is part of how Nietzsche ultimately regards his own position—*Zwischen*—in later parts. The *Zwischenspiele* are an important part of his ultimate task.

CHAPTER 7

PART V: "NATURAL HISTORY OF MORALITY"

To see *and to* show *the problem of morality—that seems to me the new principal task. I deny that it has been done in previous moral philosophy.* (Nietzsche, May–July 1885, *KSA* 11:35[30]; *WP* 263)

The title of this chapter, *Naturgeschichte der Moral*, announces the way Nietzsche wants to approach the topic of "morality." It has been recognized for some time now that Nietzsche "revolutionized" ethics and this chapter gives a good indication of the kinds of questions and concerns with which he is occupied.[1] Nietzsche examines the problem of morality the way the natural historian studies the development of living forms, focusing on conditions of emergence, growth, and evolution (see also §23 on "morphological" development, that is, the study of forms of growth; cf., *GM* P:3). His approach stands in marked contrast to his predecessors in German philosophy who either insisted upon a strict separation of theoretical reason and practical reason (the domain of ethics), as in Kant, or sought to define ethics in an essentialist manner, as in Schopenhauer.[2] The title may have been inspired in part by W. H. Lecky's *History of European Morals*, which opens with a chapter on "The Natural History of Morals."[3] This work was first published in 1869, and we know that Nietzsche read and studied Lecky (1838–1903) in 1881 and 1883.[4] In a note from May–July of 1885, Nietzsche flags what he regards as the deplorable condition of literature on morality in today's Europe and then reviews contributions in the area from England, France, and Germany. He singles out for special praise Jean-Marie Guyau's *Sketch of Morality without Obligation or Sanction* (1885) along with Paul Rée's *The Origin of Moral Sensations* (1877) and W. H. Rolph's *Biological Problems* (1881). He regards these three texts as the strongest in contemporary ethics (*KSA* 11:35[34]).[5]

To illuminate just what the "problem of morality" means for Nietzsche, we focus on sections 186–8 and 197–203. It should be noted that although Nietzsche focuses on "morality" in this chapter he already offered one definition of it in the opening chapter—"as the doctrine of the relations of supremacy under which the phenomenon of 'life' comes to be" (§19)—and treated aspects of it in several sections, such as sections 32 and 33. The object of his critique of morality is stated succinctly in section 33: "There is no other way: the feelings of devotion, self-sacrifice for one's neighbor, the whole morality of self-denial must be questioned mercilessly and taken to court." He will continue to address morality and its topics in later parts of the book, notably parts VII and IX.

MORALITY ON A RATIONAL FOUNDATION

The opening section of the chapter is noteworthy for at least two reasons:

(a) Nietzsche claims there is now coming into being a "science of morality" (*Wissenschaft der Moral*), which he regards as being at a crude level of development; he himself, he reveals, prefers "more modest terms."[6] This appeal to "modesty" is, in fact, a notable feature of the main task Nietzsche proposes with respect to "morality," namely its "self-overcoming" (see especially *D* Preface: 4).

(b) Nietzsche regards the effort on the part of philosophers to supply "a *rational foundation* for morality" (*Begründung der Moral*) as misguided. He provides the example of Schopenhauer's view that the real or genuine foundation, for which people have been looking for thousands of years like the philosopher's stone, is to be located in the proposition, "Harm no one, on the contrary, help everyone as much as you can."[7] Nietzsche regards this principle of ethics as "false and sentimental," especially in a world characterized by the will to power. It is clear he is opposed to any and all attempts to provide ethics or morality with a "rational foundation." We need to inquire why he holds to this view.

The "modest" approach to the phenomenon of morality Nietzsche proposes stands in marked contrast to what he thinks philosophers have accustomed themselves to doing in the study of it, namely, demanding from themselves something "exalted, presumptuous, and solemn." In wanting to supply morality with a "rational foundation" they have taken morality as "given." Nietzsche holds philosophers have been speaking about morality from a very limited realm of experience and knowledge; they have not been conscientious enough in their understanding of it. He mentions this regarding philosophers espousing certain "facts" of morality on the basis of their environment, their class and their church, and their climate and particular part of the world. This results in a largely uncritical perspective on morality. Indeed, Nietzsche goes so far as to claim that what has hitherto been lacking in the science of morality is the *problem of morality* itself and the suspicion that there might be something problematic at stake here. He then expresses his main worry about the attempt to supply morality with a so-called "rational foundation," namely, that it might be little more than a "scholarly variation of the common *faith* in the prevalent morality" and a new means of expressing this faith. If it is this, then it has to be seen as little more than another fact within one particular morality.

Nietzsche proposes an alternative approach which centers on what he calls preparing a "*typology* of morality" (*Typenlehre der Moral*). This consists in collecting material, conceptualizing and arranging "a vast realm of subtle feelings of value and differences of value," as well as possibly attempting to present in vivid terms, "some of the more frequent and recurring forms of such a living crystallizations."[8] In short, the approach Nietzsche proposes is historical and sensitive to particularity but also open to the view that certain forms of morality, such as master and slave types perhaps, "recur" and "crystallize" within history and thus enable us to speak of "types" of morality.

What reasons does Nietzsche have for opposing this effort on the part of philosophers to supply morality with a "rational foundation?" The answer is that such an approach is far too simple-minded and results in a reification of the phenomenon of morality, in the sense that it is being abstracted from its conditions of existence, which are on the one hand conditions of natural human life and on the other hand conditions relative to specific historical contexts. Once morality is abstracted in this way, it acquires a monstrous-like autonomous existence and seduces us into thinking that there is something essential we can call "morality." But this overlooks the fact that there are numerous moralities and that morality encompasses an enormous array of things. Additionally, privileging some principle of morality, as that which enables us to give it an essence, runs the risk of turning morality into something fanatical and into something that cannot do justice to the rich diversity of human action and the complexity of our ethical life. In this respect Nietzsche's approach to morality is reminiscent of Wittgenstein's approach to language in his *Philosophical Investigations*.[9]

Nietzsche is worried that to locate the criterion of moral action in, say, its disinterestedness and its universal validity, as we find in Kant, is to engage in "armchair philosophizing" (*KSA* 12:7[4]; *WP* 261). In place of this the moral philosopher should study different peoples to see what the criterion is in every case and what is expressed by it, including conditions of existence. He then discovers that forms of ethical life have their basis in specific conditions of a people's existence. In part, this explains why Nietzsche expresses dissatisfaction with Socrates and what he sees as his denaturalization of moral values. When moral judgments are severed from their conditionality—a form of life that would give them a meaning—they are denaturalized under the pretense of sublimation. Notions of the "good" and the "just" become liberated as "ideas" and become objects of dialectic in which we look for truth in them by taking them for entities or signs of entities. This procedure gives us only a set of abstractions such as "the good man," "the wise man," or "the happy man" (*KSA* 13:14[111]; *WP* 430; see also §§190–1 on Plato and Socrates).

In section 187, Nietzsche takes as an example Kant's positing of a categorical imperative, which states that one should posit a maxim of action in such a fashion that it can be made the basis for a universal law.[10] Nietzsche immediately asks what a claim of this kind tells us about the human being, in this case a philosopher, who makes it: "There are moralities which are meant to justify their creator before others. Other moralities are meant to calm him and lead him to be satisfied with himself." Nietzsche gives further examples, and his main point is that, at least on one level, moralities can be considered to be "a *sign language of the affects*." In making this claim he undercuts the abstract, rationalist pretensions of morality as defined by various moral philosophers, notably Kant. For Kant, to be a moral agent is to be an agent subject to the moral law that one freely imposes upon oneself. While the aspiration toward a form of autonomy is one that Nietzsche shares,[11] in Kant it can only be achieved by the subject severing all its attachments to natural life or what he calls the domain of heteronomy, including the desires, the inclinations, and the affects, and which are to be regarded as having a "pathological" interest (for Kant our performance of duty should be "pure"). In this section Nietzsche suggests the affects might be local and relative to a person's class, gender, culture, and so on, and he is inviting us to be suspicious of a morality's claims to universality. The next section is crucially important for understanding and evaluating Nietzsche's relation to Kant and his overall position on morality.

He begins section 188 by noting that because it is a form or system of discipline—whether this discipline is imposed on oneself voluntarily or through the internalization of social norms—every morality can be viewed as a piece of tyranny against "nature" and also "reason." For Nietzsche, this would be no objection to morality because many fruitful and creative modes of expression, such as language with its metrical compulsion of rhyme and rhythm, are made possible by subjection to a long compulsion. Here Nietzsche is taking to task what he calls the attitude of "*laisser aller*" (letting it go) one might find adhered to by libertarian-minded people such as anarchists, namely, the view that creative freedom can only be enjoyed where there is the absence of constraint and discipline. Nietzsche maintains the opposite view, noting that what has been attained in freedom—he mentions, "subtlety," "boldness," "dance," and "masterly sureness"—whether in thought itself, in rhetoric, or in government, in the arts and in ethics is the result of the "tyranny" of "capricious laws." In other words, there is a need of discipline and constraint and, moreover, history shows that such laws have not developed simply in accordance with rational standards but often arbitrarily and unconsciously. This suggests "nature" contains its own complex intelligence and "intelligent" behavior, such as we find in artistic creation or ethical self-discipline, consists in subjecting oneself to nature's laws. The artist allows himself to obey "thousandfold laws" so complex in terms of their determination that they defy formulation through concepts. Indeed, he notes this is the problem with the concept: it has great difficulty in recognizing fluctuation, variability, multiplicity, and ambiguity. Nietzsche writes in praise of "obedience" and, from our misguided perspective as so-called super rational agents, its "irrational" character. His point returns us to the opening sentence of this part, where he notes that we moderns have grown refined and subtle in nature and yet our "science" of morality is crude and raw. It is as if he is "reversing" perspectives and in so doing challenging our most dearly held assumptions about ourselves as cultivated rational agents. If we look into the past of mankind in the way he is suggesting, we will discover that what is to be valued in this history is "the long *unfreedom* of the spirit" (our emphasis). What has "*educated* the spirit" is a "rigorous and grandiose stupidity," that is, the tyranny and caprice of laws which by our modern rational standards seem lacking in refinement, civilization, and rationality. We have become disciplined, and hence free and creative, through various means and forms of enslavement.

The view Nietzsche is espousing concerning self-discipline could not be more different from Kant's conception of ethics in accordance with the rational moral law. The lesson Nietzsche wants his readers to derive from the kind of exploration he is undertaking in this section is that nature is "intelligent" in its "stupidity" since it implants in us, "the need for limited horizons and the nearest tasks—teaching the *narrowing of our perspective*, and thus in a certain sense stupidity, as a condition of life and growth." He concludes the section by engaging in an explicit dialogue with Kant on this very point. In contrast to Kant's rational categorical imperative, he posits a hypothetical imperative of nature itself, " 'You shall obey—someone and for a long time: *else* you will perish and lose the last respect for yourself.' " Nietzsche regards this imperative of nature as applying not simply to the individual but to "the whole human animal, to *man*." The imperative is "hypothetical" because it has conditions, namely, the quite natural and empirical value of self-respect.

HERD MORALITY

In section 197 Nietzsche opens up a number of questions about morality that he says he will treat in a chapter entitled "Morality as Timidity" (*Furchtsamkeit*, literally "fearfulness") within a future work. He returns to this theme in sections 198 and 201. In section 197 he questions why it is that moral philosophers seem to only know the "temperate zones" of moral action and valuation and are either unfamiliar with the "tropics" or can see in it only something to be despised and hated. Once again he is revealing his "taste," which is a taste for the exceptions over the norm (in this case Cesare Borgia), and which his opponents approach as something pathological. In section 198 he notes what is crude and coarse about civilized forms of morality. Each one will address itself to the individual and have its alleged happiness in view. In effect, these moralities are "counsels of behavior" concerned to guide and regulate how the individual lives with itself (Nietzsche notes the dangerous nature of the maturation process by which the individual develops), and also "recipes" directed at the passions, the good and bad inclinations, "insofar as they have the will to power and want to play the master" and so on. Nietzsche notes that these systems of ethical training and discipline are "baroque and unreasonable in form" because they address themselves to all and generalize where it is a fateful mistake to do so. Moralities, then, which bring with them the authority of the "unconditional," are insensitive to individual differences and variation. Nietzsche challenges the idea that such moralities represent "science," much less "wisdom"; in point of fact, he argues, they operate on the level of prudence. He then takes to task how various intellectual systems have sought to administer the care of the affects, including Stoicism, Spinoza's ethics, and the "Aristotelianism of morals." In all of these systems of ethical training the idea is that they are something dangerous and in need of taming or even extirpation and destruction, so they too will form part of the chapter on "Morality as Timidity."

In sections 199 and 201–3 Nietzsche focuses his attention on a topic he knows his readers will certainly be provoked by and more than likely be offended by, namely, the existence of the "herd" and the phenomenon of "herd animal morality."[12] In section 199 he notes a prevailing fact of human existence: that for almost all human history there have been "herds" of human beings—he mentions clans, communities, tribes, peoples, states, and churches—and thus for the most part people who have felt the need to obey. By contrast those who command others are much rarer and are fewer in number. Obedience, we might say, has become a dominant instinct in human beings and Nietzsche even wonders whether it has not now become an innate need in the average human being where it can be conceived as a kind of "formal conscience," that is, a conscience without any specific content and having only the form of a command to obey, as in, "'thou shalt unconditionally do something, unconditionally not do something else.'" This formal conscience is what Nietzsche will analyze in much greater detail and depth in the second essay of his next major text, *GM*. The need for this conscience is one that seeks to satisfy itself and to fill its form with some content, "it seizes upon things as a rude appetite, rather indiscriminately, and accepts whatever is shouted into its ears by someone who issues commands," be it parents, teachers, laws, class prejudices, or public opinions. In effect, what Nietzsche is unpacking here is something very strange and should disturb us: a need within the human being to be commanded and which suggests most human beings are so docile and lacking in genuine autonomy that they will respond to any issuing of a command so as to fill up this formal conscience. In section 188 Nietzsche draws the reader's attention to the secret wisdom contained within constraint and discipline, no matter how arbitrarily it was produced. Here he is alerting us to the dangerous side of such discipline in obedience. Such an insight is picked up on by Henri Bergson (1859–1941), who in his *Two Sources of Morality and Religion* argues, perhaps shockingly, that an absolutely categorical imperative—a purely formal command in need of content—"is instinctive or somnambulistic, enacted as such in a normal state."[13] Nietzsche's key point is that this "appetite" to be commanded is "rude" and "indiscriminate," in short, it is lacking in taste or discernment. It is a profoundly unsettling feature of human behavior that Nietzsche and Bergson are drawing our attention to.

Nietzsche then goes on in section 199 to address what he calls "the strange limits of human development," noting that its curious rhythm (it moves in circles, he says), is owing to the fact that the human inherits this herd instinct of obedience best, but does so at the expense of "the art of commanding." Nietzsche may think he is approaching this "development" in the manner of a natural historian but it is clear it contains a value judgment on history and supposes an interpretation, even a selection, of "facts." It enables him to appraise something like the herd instinct, to esteem the exceptional cases, and to assume that there are tendencies of, and possibilities of, human development, including the production of "higher" and "nobler" modes of human existence. Nietzsche is worried by the "herd" development because he thinks it can reach an excessive point where even those who hold positions of authority and leadership can be corrupted by it. He notes that this is the situation in Europe today where leaders protect themselves against their bad conscience by posing as executors of ancient or higher commands such as ancestors, the constitution, or even God; even worse, they borrow "herd maxims" such as "servants of the people" or "instruments of the common weal." Nietzsche objects to the "herd" existence in Europe because he think it takes itself to be "the only permissible kind of man" and praises those attributes conducive to the flourishing of the herd such as public spirit, benevolence, consideration, compassion, and so on. He concludes the section by appealing to Napoleon, who for him is another instance of the exceptional human being and one of his heroes (see also *GS* 362).[14]

After a consideration of "late cultures" in section 200 Nietzsche returns to the topic of the herd in sections 201 and 202. Section 201 is striking insofar as Nietzsche contests what can form the basis of a morality of neighborly love. He argues that there can be no such love so long as the utility that reigns in moral value judgments is allowed to be only the utility of the herd. This is because what is primary in the relation between different communities and societies is fear of one's neighbor. Once the structure of society as a whole has become fixed and made secure against external dangers then it is the fear of the neighbor that will now be the focus of moral valuations. The process involves the sacrifice of some drives, including those that previously served to consolidate society, in favor of others. Strong and dangerous drives such as foolhardiness, vengefulness, and craftiness, which had to be cultivated to become great, are now experienced as doubly dangerous since the channels by which they could be diverted are lacking and they are branded as "immoral." What now receives moral honor are the opposite drives: it is now a question of what will harm and endanger the community and existence of the herd, so once again, Nietzsche says, "fear is the mother of morals." What he calls a "high and independent spirituality" and "the will to stand alone" are now viewed as evils and dangers (see also *GS* 143).[15] As society develops in this fashion the mores and manners of the herd become hardened, giving rise to a submissive and conforming mentality and a mediocrity of desires: "the 'lamb,' even more the 'sheep,' gains in respect." The tendency of the "herd" kind of society is toward ever greater softness and tenderness and for Nietzsche this is developing in European societies to the point of pathology. He gives the example of our dislike of punishing criminals.[16] Europe considers itself to be on the path of moral progress in which one day, it hopes, there will no longer be anything to be afraid of.

The tone of Nietzsche's distress over this development becomes more strident and his argument more polemical in the closing two sections of this chapter. In section 202 he flatly declares that *"Morality in Europe today is herd animal morality."* He goes on to explain that by this he means it is just one type of morality, not the whole of morality, even if this is how it wishes to understand itself; and many other types, especially *"higher* moralities" ought to be possible even if herd morality resists such a possibility and such an "ought." Herd morality thinks it is morality in and for itself, and that nothing else, or no other way of looking at life and its flourishing, represents morality. With the assistance of a religion that flatters "the most sublime (*sublimsten*) herd animal desires" we have reached in Europe today, he contends, a situation where our social and political institutions are completely ruled by this attitude, so that: "the *democratic movement is the heir of the Christian movement.*" Here Nietzsche is clearly hinting at our modern obsession with the equal rank of all human beings as a formal morality. He goes on in the rest of the section to draw attention to what he sees as the ludicrous positions upheld by "anarchist dogs" and by socialists who dream of a "free society." Nietzsche ironically and bitingly calls this the society of the "*autonomous* herd," and his view is that genuine autonomy can only be attained by breaking with the values of the herd. He scoffs at the idea of "equal rights"—"for once all are equal nobody needs 'rights' anymore." Perhaps worst of all for him, among these developments, is the cultivation within social existence of a "religion of compassion" (*Mitleid*).[17] He worries that Europe is developing its own Buddhism in which suffering is seen as an objection to existence and human beings can no longer tolerate, so "feminine" are they becoming, the spectacle of seeing someone suffer (Nietzsche develops these insights at greater length in *GM*, especially the second essay). The supposition of we moderns is that shared compassion is "morality in itself" and the actual "*attained* height of man, the sole hope of the future" as well as "the great absolution from all former guilt." Nietzsche makes it clear in *GM* that he considers this development to amount to nihilism: "the sight of man now makes us tired—what is nihilism today if it is not *that*? . . . We are tired of *man*" (*GM* I:12).

TOWARD NEW PHILOSOPHERS

In section 203 Nietzsche turns his attention, and as way of drawing this chapter to a dramatic conclusion, to an alternative conception of the future of the human that rests on a different "faith." Nietzsche stresses "faith" and not "knowledge" is at work here simply because it concerns the future, which, by definition, is unknown, so one can only have belief in it and based on insights gained from one's knowledge of history, which discloses that the human is an animal of *possibilities*, including possibilities that have been aborted or ruined and ones also not yet actualized. Man is the "unfixed" animal despite the fact that modern morality seeks to "fix" him once and for all (§62). Nietzsche thus now looks toward "*new philosophers*" who will provide the "stimuli" for different, even opposing, valuations and so "revalue and invert 'eternal values'" and constrain the forces of human life and "the will of millennia upon *new* tracks." These philosophers teach the human that its future rests on its will, that is, on a conscious and deliberate decision concerning what it wants to become and willing the means to it—once, that is, such consideration has liberated itself from the totalizing perspective of the present (e.g., the idea that there is a single morality valid for "all"). Furthermore, these philosophers will prepare experiments and modes of discipline (*Zucht*) and breeding or cultivation (*Züchtung*) as a way of "putting an end to that gruesome dominion of nonsense and accident that has so far been called 'history'" (*Geschichte*). Breeding for Nietzsche is a means of storing up the tremendous forces of mankind so that the generations can build upon the work of their forefathers and provide, he thinks, some guarantee of perfection (*KSA* 13:15[65]; *WP* 398).[18] Of course, the rule of chance will not come to an end, since total control of the forces of life is an impossible goal to achieve and even undesirable. Rather, it is the "nonsense" of history to date Nietzsche wishes to see overturned: the future is too important to be left to accident. His main contention is that modern morality does not, in fact, allow for the future, it wants history to end in a universal reign of comfortableness and green pastures of happiness with no more longing, desiring, and suffering. As already stated, for Nietzsche this is nihilism. It also rests on a delusion: how can life not continue to grow? Would not the realization of a perfect "free society" have to cut off its own roots and thus become anti-life?[19] This final section of the book appears to be addressed to fellow free spirits and Nietzsche wonders whether, even to these kindred spirits, he has to speak out loud and make it clear that what is needed to bring about this different future, one in which there is a future for further enhancement of the human and not merely a wish for its terminal point, is the necessity of new leaders. It is no small task, he stresses in the rest of the section, to prepare for such leaders and yet there is perhaps no greater and sublime task facing the free spirits. Nietzsche concludes by making clear his opposition to modern ideas about the human and the human future. Modern ideas suffer from an "absurd guilelessness and blind confidence."

Nietzsche makes it explicit at the start of section 202 that he is now speaking of "our truths," that is, the truths of the new kind of free spirits he is appealing to throughout the book and who have a "taste" that is different to the "democratic taste" that prevails in the modern age (see especially §44). Immediately after speaking of these "truths" he acknowledges that it will be considered an affront to speak of the human being in the terms he has been using in this chapter, namely, counting man among the animals and using expressions such as the "herd" and "herd instincts," and using them "unadorned and without metaphor." Nietzsche is well versed in the art and knowledge of metaphor, so the fact that he now speaks like this suggests that he wishes to make his criticism of modernity an emphatic one and to be heard loud and clear. We moderns, he thinks, assume we know what Socrates confessed he did not know, that is, we think we know what morality is and that it is one thing and its history has one true destination, to end up being the morality of the herd and the unegoistic. This may be a good place to pause and reflect a little more widely on Nietzsche's insights into, and concerns about, "morality."

NIETZSCHE AND THE PROBLEM OF MORALITY

In the preface to *GM* Nietzsche says that his "will to knowledge" has led him to a focus and concentration on "morality" as a *fundamental* problem (preface 2). It is important that we try to be clear on what this problem is for him. In large part this involves understanding what he means by "morality" and the various labels he gives to his interrogation of it, such as the "self-overcoming" of morality and the "critique" of morality. Failure to appreciate what "morality" is for Nietzsche leads to all the misconceptions of his philosophy that circulate in the popular domain.

In a note for the preface to *D*, Nietzsche writes of the need to think about morality without falling under its spell; there is a need to resist the seductive character of its beautiful gestures and glances (*KSA* 12:2[165]; *WP* 253). He distinguishes himself from modern German philosophy, notably Kant and Hegel, and what he regards as half-hearted attempts at "critique." In these two cases criticism, he contends, is directed only at the problem (how morality is to be demonstrated, whether as noumenon or as self-revealing spirit) but never at the "ideal." In the actual preface to *D* Nietzsche claims that morality is the greatest of all mistresses of seduction and that all philosophers from Plato to Kant have been building "majestic moral structures" under its seduction (*D* P:3). Kant, he says, was really a pessimist who believed in morality despite the fact that neither nature nor history testify to it and in fact continually contradict it.

"Critique" is conceived as a preparatory task of revaluation and has several aspects (*KSA* 12:1[53]): (a) grasping and ascertaining the manner in which moral appraisal of human types and actions predominates at the present time; (b) showing that the moral code of an era is a symptom, a means of self-admiration or dissatisfaction or hypocrisy, in which the character of a morality is to be not only ascertained but also interpreted (otherwise it's ambiguous); (c) providing a critique of the method of judging at present: how strong is it? What does it aim at? What will become of the human being under its spell? Which forces does it nurture, which does it suppress? Does it make human beings more healthy or more sick, more courageous and more subtle, or more compliant and docile? In the preface to *GM* Nietzsche says there is a need for a "*critique* of moral values," which will examine the "*value of these values*"; it is necessary to develop a knowledge of the conditions and circumstances under which values grew up, developed, and changed (*GM* P:6).

Curiously perhaps, the insistence on a critique of morality is now to be regarded as our present form of morality and as an outgrowth of the sense of "honesty" (*Redlichkeit*) cultivated by Christianity and morality.[20] It now needs to be inspired by a sublime probity:

> These are the demands I make of you . . . that you subject the moral valuations themselves to a critique. That you curb the impulse of moral feeling, which here insists on submission and *not* criticism, with the question: "Why submission?" That you view this insistence on a "Why?", on a critique of morality, as being your *present* form of morality itself, as the most sublime kind of probity (*die sublimste Art von Rechtschaffenheit*), which does honor to you and your age (*KSA* 12:2[191]; see also *GS* 345).

Nietzsche, then, is drawing upon the virtues cultivated by "morality" as a way of conquering and overcoming its stranglehold on questions of life. He does this because he fully appreciates the fact that they have yielded a profit in our appreciation and judgment of things, such as "finesse (*das Raffinement*) of *interpretation*, of moral vivisection, the pangs of conscience (*Gewissensbiss*) . . ." (*KSA* 12:2[197]). Our spiritual subtlety, which we are now deploying in the emergent field of a "science of morality," was achieved essentially through vivisection of the conscience (KSA 12:2[207]). We have been educated and trained by morality; this training now leads us to say "no" to morality (to blind compulsion, dogma, the heart's desire, God).

Morality, Nietzsche contends, is frequently made the subject of outlandish claims, for example:

(a) It is supposed that morality must have a universally binding character in which there is a single morality valid for all in all circumstances and for all occasions. Morality expects a person to be dutiful, obedient, self-sacrificing in their core and at all times: this demands ascetic self-denial and is a form of refined cruelty.

(b) Ethicists such as Kant and Schopenhauer suppose it provides us with insight into the true, metaphysical character of the world and existence. For example, in Schopenhauer virtue is "practical mysticism," which is said to spring from the same knowledge that constitutes the essence of all mysticism. For Schopenhauer, therefore, "metaphysics is virtue translated into action" and proceeds from the immediate and intuitive knowledge of the identity of all beings. Compassion is "the great mystery of ethics."[21]

(c) It is supposed we have an adequate understanding of moral agency, for example, that we have properly identified moral motives and located the sources of moral agency. The opposite for Nietzsche is, in fact, the case: we almost entirely lack knowledge in moral matters.

(d) It is supposed we can make a clear separation between good virtues and evil vices but for Nietzsche the two are reciprocally conditioning: all good things have arisen out of dark roots through sublimation and spiritualization and they continue to feed off such roots (see §23).

(e) Moral values claim independence for themselves from nature and history and in order to win dominion they must be assisted by "immoral" forces and affects. It is in this sense that morality is the "work of error" and self-contradictory (*KSA* 12:7[6], p. 276; *WP* 266).

(f) Finally, once morality has attained dominion "all biological phenomena" are then measured and judged by moral values and an opposition between life and morality is established. Morality seeks to set the highest phenomena of life, as expressed in certain human modes of being, such as greatness, at variance with itself (ibid.).

Nietzsche calls for a "moral naturalism" in which we translate moral values that have acquired the appearance of being emancipated and without nature back into their "natural immorality," that is, the conditions of life conceived in terms of its full economy of affects (*KSA* 12:9[86]; *WP* 299). This is essentially what he means by translating the human back into nature (§230): "Homo natura: The will to power" (*KSA* 12:2[131], p. 132; *WP* 391; see also *BGE* 230). Nietzsche wishes to demonstrate that in the history of morality a will to power finds expression and that mankind's supreme values to date are in fact a special case of the will to power.

Nietzsche continues to affirm the need for morality when it is conceived as the practice of "continual self-command and self-overcoming . . . in great things and in the smallest" (*WS* 45; 212). Morality survives and has a future for Nietzsche, then, in at least two main senses: (a) as techniques of physical-spiritual discipline (*KSA* 12:10[68]; *WP* 981); and (b) as an instinct for education and breeding (*KSA* 12:1[33]; *WP* 720). Regarding (b), his attention is focused on the new form this might take in the future. He wants this "unconscious instinct" to be placed in the service of autonomous or sovereign individuals and not, as we have he thinks now, that of "the power-instinct of the herd." "My idea," he says, in a note from 1886/7, is that "goals are lacking and these must be *individuals!* We observe how things are everywhere: every individual is sacrificed and serves as a tool. Go into the street and you encounter lots of 'slaves.' Whither? For what?" (*KSA* 12:7[6]; *WP* 269).[22] In a note from 1887, Nietzsche once again speaks of the need for "strong individuals" and names them "*les souverains*" (KSA 12:9[85]; *WP* 284). He also states in a note of 1886/7 that his philosophy does not aim at an "individualistic morality" but wants an ordering of rank in which the ideas of the herd should rule in herd and not reach out beyond it (*KSA* 12:7[6], p. 280; *WP* 287).[23] There is no incompatibility here between Nietzsche positing "strong individuals" as the end of physical-spiritual discipline and his rejection of an "individualistic morality." For Nietzsche the latter is fully compatible with egalitarianism, which he opposes; an "individual" gains its value for him depending on whether it is part of an ascending or a descending mode of life (see also §262).

In the preface to *GM* Nietzsche makes it clear that it is the value of the unegoistic instincts that he wants to place at the center of his critique and of the revaluation project. He thinks we need to become suspicious over the unegoistic for a number of reasons. One main concern he has is that we become so caught in our fictions and projections of ourselves as good and pure that we become blind to the dangerously simple-minded view of ourselves we have created. We need to be suspicious of the "moral miracle" the unegoistic allegedly performs, transforming us from amoral animals into saintly humans. Nietzsche takes this self-image to task in section 47: "What? The 'miracle' merely a mistake of interpretation? A lack of philology?"

Morality makes a claim to knowledge it is not entitled to, since it is based on a failure to rigorously and soberly examine moral actions and feelings. The study of morality is thus lacking in genuine psychological insight and intellectual probity: "What is the *counterfeiting* aspect of morality?—It pretends to *know* something, namely what 'good and evil' is" (*KSA* 13:12[1]; *WP* 337). Morality's pretension to knowledge encourages fanaticism. The danger here is twofold: (a) first, supposing the good can grow only out of the good and upon the basis of the good; (b) second, holding there is a pure realm of morality where we disentangle the nonegoistic and egoistic drives and affects. The esteem we moderns accord to "the good man and the "will to good" rests on a dangerously naïve understanding of life and of the needs of the human animal. On the basis of an erroneous and inadequate analysis of morality a false ethics gets erected, buttressed by religion and metaphysical monsters, and "the shadow of these dismal spirits in the end falls across even physics and the entire perception of the world" (*HH* 37). If we examine what is often taken to be the summit of the moral in philosophy—the mastery of the affects—we find there is pleasure to be taken in this mastery. We can impress ourselves by what we can deny, defer, resist, and so on. Through this mastery we grow and develop. And yet morality, as we moderns have come to understand it, would have to give this ethical self-mastery a bad conscience. If we take as our criterion of the moral to be self-sacrificing resolution and self-denial, we would have to say, if being honest, that such acts are not performed strictly for the sake of others, since our own fulfillment and pride are at work. There are no moral actions if we assume two things: (a) only those actions performed for the sake of another can be called moral; and (b) only those actions performed out of free will can be called moral (*D* 148; here Nietzsche is supposing free will in the sense of some miraculous act of self-causation; see also *BGE* 21). If we liberate ourselves from these errors a revaluation can take place in which we discover that we have overestimated the value and importance of free and non-egoistic actions at the expense of unfree and egoistic ones (see also *D* 164).

When employed as a term of scientific knowledge "morality" denotes for Nietzsche the doctrine of the order of rank and of human valuations in respect of everything human. Most moral philosophers, he contends, only deal with the present order of rank that rules now. On the one hand, they display a lack of historical sense, and, on the other hand, show that they are ruled by the morality which says that what rules now is eternally valid. There is no comparison and no criticism, only unconditional belief (*KSA* 11:35[5]). In this respect moral philosophy is anti-scientific. The present age has one single conception and definition of morality ("the unegoistic") which it takes to be of suprahistorical validity. This morality is what Nietzsche also calls "herd-animal morality," "which strives with all its force for a universal green-pasture happiness of earth, namely, security, harmlessness, comfort, easy living . . ." (*KSA* 11:37[8]; cf. §44).[24] If we suppose that belief in God has now disappeared from the human horizon, Nietzsche asks, then "who" is it that now speaks in us? Nietzsche provides an answer not from "metaphysics," he says, but from "animal physiology": "*the herd instinct speaks*" and wants to be master. It allows value to be given to the individual only from the perspective of the whole and hates those who detach themselves (*KSA* 12:7[6], p. 279; *WP* 275). This "herd instinct" considers the middle and the mean as the most valuable and the place where the "majority" finds itself. It is thus "an opponent of all orders of rank, it sees an ascent from beneath to above as a descent from the majority to the minority"

(*KSA* 12:10[39]; *WP* 280). Nietzsche objects to this "herd tendency" because it "is directed toward standstill and preservation, there is nothing creative in it" (*KSA* 11:27[17]; *WP* 285). The kind of morality that Nietzsche is keen to promote is what he calls the "legislative" type, which contains the means for fashioning out of human beings the desires of a creative will or a will to the future. We see legislative moralities in operation, he claims, wherever an artistic will of the highest rank holds power and can assert itself over long periods of time, in the shape of laws, religions, and customs. Today, however, he holds that creative human beings are largely absent. The present morality needs attacking and criticizing precisely because it is a hostile force and obstacle to any hope that they might come into existence. "Morality," to repeat, wants to fix the human animal, which up to now has been the "unfixed animal" (§62). The philosopher of the future, by contrast, does not want the human animal to be something comfortable and mediocre but to breed "future *masters of the earth*" (*KSA* 11:37[8]; *WP* 957), conceived as human beings of the highest spirituality and strength of will. For Nietzsche it is the free spirit, not the free thinker, who thinks about this problem. He detects in the present a conspiracy against everything that is shepherd, beast of prey, hermit, and Caesar. The task will be to make use of the democratic movement as a way of cultivating a new spiritual tyranny: "the time is coming when we will learn to think differently about politics" (*BGE* 208). The aim is to allow individuals to be free to work on themselves as artist-tyrants (*KSA* 12:2[57]). He adds an important qualification: "Not merely a master-race, whose task would be limited to governing, but a race or people with *its own sphere of life* [. . .] a hothouse for strange and exquisite plants"(KSA 12:9[153]). The concept for this non-average type of human being is "the superhuman" (KSA 12:10[17]; *WP* 866). If morality for the greater part of human history has served the need of preservation, the morality of the future will be an "experimental" one in which the chief task is, "to *give* oneself a goal" (*KSA* 10:24[15], p. 653; *WP* 260; see also *BGE* 210, 262).

This part of *BGE* offers an important resource for gaining an understanding of Nietzsche on morality as a problem. By dissecting this problem in the manner he does, Nietzsche thought he distinguished himself as a philosopher, providing new and far-reaching suspicions about it. No doubt, he exaggerated his contribution—one thinks of the important contributions to naturalizing ethics we find in Hume, Spinoza, and Jean-Marie Guyau, for example. Much of Nietzsche's analysis remains at an impressionistic level and detailed historical insights are lacking (though he attempts to provide more detail in his next book, *GM*, intended as a supplement and clarification of *BGE*). In truth, what he is doing in this part of *BGE* is outlining a research program more than actually carrying out the necessary research. His approach to ethics is notable for its attempt to uncover a multiplicity of moralities and its concern with the "plant" and "animal," "man" and its cultivation and enhancement. Although he is critical of the "science of morality" and regards it as being at a crude level of development, it is clear that his sympathies lie with the approach of science. However, whether a science of morality could ever lay claim to being in possession of the kind of knowledge he wants and seeks with respect to human enhancement, and which would then sanction or permit the future legislation (rank ordering) of values, is a moot point—though much of Nietzsche's pretension as the kind of philosopher he wishes to be rests on securing this knowledge and being entitled to it.

Of the remaining sections of this part of the book they cover the following topics: 189: how a drive purifies and sharpens itself, including the sublimation of the sex drive into love; 190: how Plato is really too noble for Socratism and employed Socrates for his own "masks and multiplicities"; 191: on what is false about Socrates as the "great ironist"; 192: an important set of reflections on "lying" and "falsification" in which Nietzsche wants to show that we are much more of an artist than we commonly suppose; 193: on dreams; 194: on "possession"; 195: on the Jews as "a people born for slavery" according to Tacitus and who carry out the "miraculous feat of an inversion of values"; 196: a parable on reading "signs" and "inference"; 200: on "late cultures."

CHAPTER 8

PART VI: "WE SCHOLARS"

I have set up the most difficult ideal of the philosopher. Learning is not enough! The scholar is the herd animal in the realm of knowledge. (Nietzsche 1884, *KSA* 11:26[13]; *WP* 421)

The new philosopher can only arise in conjunction with a ruling caste, as its highest spiritualization. Great politics, rule over the earth, are at hand; complete lack of the principles that are needed. (Nietzsche 1885, *KSA* 11:35[47]; *WP* 978)

The core concerns Nietzsche expresses in this part of the book—the nature and fate of philosophy, the problem of the scholar, the possibility of greatness—are longstanding ones in his work. In his early writings Nietzsche conceives philosophy as "name-giving" that elevates (*erhebt*) the human being with origins in the legislation of morality (*Gesetzgebung der Moral*) (*KSA* 7:19[83]). Nietzsche returns to this lofty conception of philosophy in his late writings after having demoted philosophy in significance, relative to science, in the first book of his free spirit trilogy, *HH*. In *BGE*, for example, philosophy is defined as "spiritual perception" (or vision) (§252), which in *TI* is clarified as, "the *power* [*Macht*] of philosophical vision [*Blick*]" that is able to judge in all the most important matters and does not hide under the mask of objectivity (*TI* "Skirmishes of an Untimely Man": 3). The young Nietzsche notes that while philosophical thinking is of the same kind as scientific thinking, it differs from it in that it directs itself "toward *great* things and possibilities." He duly notes that the concept of greatness is amorphous, partly aesthetic and partly moral. For Nietzsche "greatness" departs from the normal and the familiar: "We venerate what is *great*. To be sure, that is also the *abnormal*" (*KSA* 7:19[80]). We can add to this several other things of value to Nietzsche, including: liberation of human beings from inferior modes of existence based on neediness, mere self-preservation, the lust for the moment, sense-less animal striving, the creation of a greater human freedom through broadening parochial perspectives, the education of the individual human being so that it becomes its own lawgiver, and *amor fati*. In this part, "greatness" emerges as a key theme and it seems appropriate that Nietzsche simultaneously presents his conception of "great politics."

SCHOLARS AND THE FATE OF PHILOSOPHY

Part VI is the most essay-like of the nine parts of *BGE*[1] and in this chapter we shall treat its ten sections together.

In his early writings Nietzsche is heavily preoccupied with the problem of the scholar. The problem for our age is the esteem accorded to the scholar since the scholar shows no awareness of the goals of genuine culture (the production of genius or esteem-ing what is rare, unique, and singular). In relation to science, philosophy draws attention to its barbarizing effects, that is, the fact that it so easily loses itself in the service of practical inter-ests. The *"laisser aller"* (let it go) attitude of the science of his day resembles, as he sees it, the dogmas of laissez-faire political economy: it has a naïve faith in an absolutely beneficial result (*SE* 2). In addition, philosophy employs artistic powers in an effort to break the unlimited knowledge-drive and in order to produce a unity of knowledge. The primary concern of philo-sophy, however, is with the question of the value of existence, with what is to be revered and esteemed. "For science there is nothing great and nothing small—but for philosophy! The value of science is measured in terms of this statement" (*KSA* 7:19[33]).

In the opening section, that is, section 204, Nietzsche speaks out, "at the risk of moralizing," against a shift he sees taking place in his time in the respective ranks of science and philo-sophy, one which is in the process of becoming established with a good conscience. As Kaufmann notes, *Wissenschaft* could just as well be rendered as "scholarship," and the German word does not have the primary or sole reference to the natural sciences that it does in English. What we are witnessing in the present age, according to Nietzsche, is the growing independence of the scholar and his emancipation from philosophy. He regards this as "one of the more refined effects of the democratic order," in which freedom from all masters is sought and which, he says, is the "rabble instinct" par excellence. Once science liberates itself from theology, whose handmaiden it once was, it seeks to play master over philosophy and lay down laws for it. However, the title of this part of the book is intriguing and can be read as a sign that Nietzsche wishes to enlist scholarship in the service of the noble ends of genuine philosophy as he sees it while at the same time acknowledging, of course, his own training as a scholar: he is speaking from experience. Moreover, we should not overlook the challenge Nietzsche presented to philosophy in the opening chapter of the book and his portrayal of psychology as the queen of the sciences that opens the path to the truly fundamental problems (§23). Traditionally, and typically, philosophy valorizes the mind or soul over the body, the intellect over the drives, and consciousness over the unconscious. For Nietzsche all of this is to be overturned and philosophy needs to incorporate psychology in its practice as a way of effecting this change. At the same time, philosophy is to be valued as a mode of "spiritual perception" (§252) and as a practice that has legislative tasks (§211); in addition, its peculiar and specific concern is with the "over-all development" of the human (§61).

Along with this declaration of independence with respect to philosophy, Nietzsche thinks he observes a disdain toward it on the part of scholars and scientists. A utility principle on the part of modern scholarship may make it blind to the value of philosophy, with the result that philosophy is seen as little more than a series of "*refuted* systems" and a "prodigal effort" that benefits nobody. Or, Nietzsche speculates, the lack of respect shown to philosophy today might be the result of the bad after-effect of some philosophers, and he gives the example of Schopenhauer. In his early writings Nietzsche had heaped praise on Schopenhauer as his special educator and as a genuinely untimely philosopher. Schopenhauer provides the lesson needed of achieving independence in relation to the present age (*SE* 3). Schopenhauer purified himself of the opinions and valuations of his age and made himself unfashionable. Schopenhauer's greatness consists in the fact that he deals with "the picture of life as a whole in order to interpret it as a whole," and he does so without letting himself become entangled in a web of conceptual scholasticisms (ibid.). He can serve as a model in spite of his scars and flaws. Nietzsche freely acknowledged the dangers of Schopenhauer's philosophizing, which consist in his pessimism and his disgust with becoming. In *BGE*, however, Schopenhauer is criticized for his "unintelligent wrath" against Hegel, which only succeeded in removing Germans out of the context of German culture and its employment of the subtle historical sense.

Nietzsche goes on in section 204 to note a deeper reason for philosophy's woeful state in the present age, and this is to do with its own self-image and practice where it has become timid, reduced to the "theory of knowledge."[2] When it has allowed itself to become little more than a timid enterprise through the dominance of epistemology this may be taken as a signal that philosophy is in its last throes. Nietzsche thinks it has today certainly lost the will to be master, that is, the will to direct other inquiries and surmounting them by determining the "whither" or "where to?" of humanity. In this section he reminds readers of philosophy's past glories; he mentions three figures in particular, each one a "royal hermit of the spirit": Heraclitus, Plato, and Empedocles. He contrasts these hermits with today's "hodgepodge philosophers" who call themselves positivists and philosophers of reality and who embody today's "*unbelief* in the masterly task and masterfulness of philosophy." In the mid-nineteenth-century context, positivism was a progressive force, which held out the promise of a radical secularization of knowledge, countering the fog of metaphysical dogmatism on the one hand and religion on the other.[3] The term "positivism" was first used by Auguste Comte (1798–1857) to denote a philosophy based on the positive facts of experience and avoiding metaphysical hypotheses (on Comte see §48). As one commentator notes, it was applied to any view that privileged the empirical sciences over metaphysical thought.[4] In its classical expression in the work of Comte, positivism also offered a grand narrative of human development from a theological phase (the age of gods or of God) through a metaphysical phase (the age of metaphysical abstractions) to that of positive scientific knowledge in which human maturity is reached with the abandonment of ultimate explanatory causes. With the arrival of positivism the human mind contents itself with focusing on observed facts, which it subsumes under general descriptive laws such as the law of gravitation. Knowledge is relative, not absolute, in the sense that we do not know the whole universe but only as it appears to us, and we relinquish concern with absolutes and ultimate causes.[5] Nietzsche fails to mention the memory of his own positivist phase in which he had championed the rights of science over art, metaphysics, religion, and even philosophy itself, which is especially evident in the texts of his middle period, notably *HH*, where Nietzsche announces his farewell to "metaphysical philosophy" and embraces what he calls "historical philosophizing" that shows the extent to which everything in the world, including the faculty of cognition, has become (*HH* 1–2).

In this opening section Nietzsche makes it clear he is speaking from his own memory as someone who was trained as a scholar. An old philologist, he has the experience of the scholar's training, and philologists are said to be the most learned and most conceited of all scholars. The scholar is trained to be a specialist and "nook dweller," an educated person who must resist "any kind of synthetic enterprise and talent" (§204). Two critical questions are significant for our engagement with the rest of this chapter: (a) What would a synthetic enterprise of knowledge amount to and especially for a new project of philosophy today? (b) How is philosophy to be restored to its former glorious role as master and how can Nietzsche avoid the charge of atavism in advocating that philosophy return to its ancient roots, if this is indeed what he is doing?[6]

In section 205 Nietzsche focuses his attention on the current dangers facing the development and maturation of the philosopher. He notes they are so manifold that it is far from clear such a fruit can ripen. For example, there is the fact that the construction of the various sciences has grown to an enormous size, and this may make the philosopher weary during his apprenticeship and he may choose to become a specialist. When this happens the philosopher does not attain what Nietzsche calls his "proper level," which he construes as, "the height for a comprehensive look" or vision. Or, if he does attain it he attains it too late when his most favorable time and strength are spent; or he could be delayed on account of the severity of his intellectual conscience and such is his fear of becoming a dilettante, "an insect with a thousand antennae." If the philosopher loses his former self-respect (the importance of this respect in general has been touched on in §188), he knows it is impossible for him to lead and to command in the realm of knowledge—unless, Nietzsche notes, he is willing "to become a great actor, a philosophical Cagliostro and pied piper, in short, a seducer." Nietzsche notes here that ultimately it is a question of taste even if it is not solely a question of conscience, that is, much depends on what one wants and desires, what one prefers and esteems. For Nietzsche one of the problems that afflict modern human beings in general is their need to become actors. In *GS* 361 he notes that the problem of the actor is one that has bothered him the longest. For him Wagner embodies this problem as a musician and artist. When addressing the problem of the actor Nietzsche often has the case of Wagner in mind. Wagner is "theatrical" to his core who wants his audience to delight in the "gesture hocus-pocus of the actor . . ." (*GS* 368). As one commentator notes, how to honor taste and yet be a pied piper of minds is part of the problem addressed in the final chapter of the book, "What is Noble?" and which culminates, as does the book itself as a whole, in a divinization of the tempter Dionysus.[7] It is the second reference to Cagliostro Nietzsche makes in the book—see also section 194—who stands for the archetype of a human being whose power and influence is founded on deception. Count Alessandro di Cagliostro was the alias for Giuseppe Balsamo (1743–1795), an Italian adventurer, occultist, and forger.

The focus in this part is on the philosopher and in this section at least Nietzsche has a sober appraisal of the chances of the fruit of the philosopher ripening. A further problem he notes is that the philosopher demands from himself a judgment, a Yes or a No, not about the sciences but about the value of life, and yet he is reluctant to believe that has such a right, or even a duty, to such a lofty judgment, if not the loftiest of judgments it is possible to conceive. The path to such a judgment, based on experiences, is perilous and the philosopher frequently hesitates and doubts, and may even lapse into silence. It is perhaps not surprising, Nietzsche notes, that the crowd misjudges and mistakes the philosopher, taking him for an ideal scholar or religiously elevated and enthusiast of God or the divine. Is not "wisdom" a detachment from life and a form of escape? Nietzsche responds by declaring the "genuine philosopher" to be a person who lives unwisely and imprudently, since he constantly puts himself at risk by playing "the wicked game" (*das schlimme Spiel*). This is very similar to how Nietzsche construes "the great health," which is constantly put to the test by being lost and won again (*GS* 382).[8] In the note for this, Nietzsche states that the philosopher, being an experimenter, cannot live a life of "timid virtuousness" (*KSA* 11:35[24]). The "wicked game" refers to this experimental life and experiencing its necessary disturbances and hazards: the word "schlimm" can mean bad or ugly, and there is a similar point being made here to what Nietzsche has said about the "necessary dirt" of politics in section 61.[9]

In sections 206 and 207 Nietzsche takes a closer look at the scholar and the "objective spirit" (what he says here can be instructively compared with the long list of attributes he credits the scholar with in *SE* 6, commencing with the scholar's "integrity" [*Biederkeit*]; see also *BGE* 244).[10] Nietzsche wants to know what *type* of human being the scientific human is. He claims the scholar is not a "noble" type but rather implicated in a "Jesuitism of mediocrity, which instinctively works at the annihilation of the uncommon man and tries to break every bent bow or, preferably, to unbend it," and which is done, he further contends, with "familiar compassion" (§206). We should note here the reference to the "bent bow," which connects with something vitally important Nietzsche has prefigured in his preface to the book. In section 207 Nietzsche notes that there are good reasons to welcome up to a point a spirit that weds itself to objectivity. The danger comes when we exaggerate the importance of the depersonalization of the spirit as if this was the goal of existence or what is most real and most important. The objective spirit sees itself as a mirror of reality, simply submitting before whatever it is that is to be known and providing a mirror to it. The scholar allows himself to be used as an "instrument" and seeks to do everything possible to remove what is accidental and arbitrary from its perception of the world. Nietzsche notes there is a high price to be paid for this depersonalization of the human being for the sake of attaining the ideal scholar: one loses seriousness for oneself. The scholar may be cheerful but this is not owing to a lack of distress but rather a lack of fingers for his own needs. The scholar has a "dangerous unconcern about Yes and No." The irony of the scholar's taste is that it results in lack of concern with the need for (discriminating) taste and judgment (the need for the Yes and No). The scholar thinks he can only attain authenticity by being strictly objective, and if love and hate are wanted from him he will do what he can and give what he can—but it won't be much, but rather, "inauthentic, fragile, questionable, and worm-eaten." Nietzsche contrasts the scholar with the philosopher whom he describes in this section as "the Caesarian cultivator [or breeder] and cultural dynamo." The objective man is a pure instrument and, as such, "the most sublime (*sublimste*) type of slave" who weds himself to a cause (objectivity) that has no aim or goal other than detachment from life. Such a human being is a *formal* man, "without substance and content," a " 'selfless' man" (compare what Nietzsche says about the "formal conscience" in the previous part of the book and his earlier discussions of "independence" in part II). Nietzsche argues that this curious type of human is neither a begetter nor a conclusion and sunrise, "no complementary man in whom the *rest* of existence is justified." This question of existence standing in need of "justification" (*Rechtfertigung*) is something that occupies Nietzsche's mind from the beginning of his intellectual career, for example, in his first published book, *BT*, where he spoke of existence being justified "to eternity" only as "an aesthetic phenomenon" (*BT* 5). Justification in this sense constitutes a reckoning before what we valued most of all. It is indicative of what we ultimately value and represents the true test of our beliefs.

We can also note his deep preoccupation, evident in several of his notes from the middle to the late 1880s, with the problem of training and education of different types of minds. His intention is not simply to devalue the scholar. In a note from 1887–1888, for example, he states that one of the tasks of a higher schooling is to show that one's duty can be found in "objective" activity. This task of learning that pleasure and duty are altogether different things is, he argues, one of the main reasons why the philologist is an educator: "his activity provides the model of sublime monotony in action" (*KSA* 12:10[11]; *WP* 888). The task of this kind of education is to make a human being useful and approximate him "to an infallible machine" (ibid.). For some types, then, the "mechanical form of existence" will be the "most venerable form of existence" (ibid.).

Nietzsche's psychological analysis of the scholar is extraordinarily perceptive and, like most of his psychological analyses, it has disturbing aspects. The scholar's life is afflicted but the affliction—which is "our" affliction since "we" *are* scholars— may not be recognized. The scholar ensures, for all his admirable virtues, that as a result of his attachment to objectivity, life suffers for life demands the Yes and the No and yet it is precisely this that the scholar cannot give. The scholar is important; the philosopher has a greater importance and assumes the risk of judgment, of the Yes and the No.[11]

Sections 208 and 209 consider the philosopher's relation to skepticism and kinds of skepticism. Section 208 also outlines an important conception of "great politics" in Nietzsche's work. We might begin by asking: is Nietzsche not a great skeptic? Does he not teach, as something decisive, skepticism about "morality?"[12] The analysis of skepticism in section 208 follows on from what Nietzsche has said about the objective spirit in section 207. The skeptic is said to be a "delicate creature" whose conscience "is trained to quiver at every No; indeed even at a Yes that is decisive and hard." The skeptic has an army of excuses to marshal against anyone who would demand a judgment (a Yes and No) from it, ranging from noble abstinence to Socratic wisdom and the wisdom of time itself. In truth, however, such a skeptic, Nietzsche avers, suffers from a paralysis of the will that has physiological conditions, including "nervous exhaustion and sickliness." Nietzsche refers to the "radical mixture of classes and races" as a feature of modern Europe to account for widespread skepticism, claiming that what becomes sick with the emergence of such hybrids is the will to make independent decisions. Where races have been crossed we find that many inherited valuations struggle with each other and hinder each other's growth. Later in the book he will attempt to imagine how it might be possible to make a virtue of this fact of modern existence (see our discussion of parts VIII and IX). He admits to making a diagnosis of what he takes to be a peculiarly modern situation in which objectivity, being scientific, art for art's sake, and pure knowledge liberated from the will, are taken as signs of progress but which, in truth, amount to "merely dressed up skepticism and paralysis of the will."[13] Such disease of the will, he further notes, is distributed unevenly over Europe: France is the most skeptical nation, while the strength of will is greater in Germany and even stronger in England, Spain, and Corsica (the birthplace of Napoleon, of course), while Italy is said to be too young to know what it wants. It is strongest, he then contends, in Russia, and it is in the context of reflecting upon the fate of Russia and Europe as a whole that Nietzsche evinces his notion of "great politics." The Russian "will" is "waiting menacingly to be discharged," and for this to be confronted may require Europe to become equally menacing, "*to acquire one will* by means of a new caste that would rule over Europe." Here Nietzsche is envisaging a united will of Europe that could set itself long-term aims and goals and for which its division into "splinter states" and "democratic splinter wills" would prove insufficient and so in need of overcoming. Nietzsche ends section 208 by declaring that the "time for petty politics" is over and that the next century will bring with it "the fight for the dominion of the earth" and so "the *compulsion* to great politics." Exactly what Nietzsche envisages and commits himself to will be examined at the end of the chapter.

One thing he has in mind is a "new warlike age," which he mentions at the start of section 209 where he also notes this may bring with it a different and stronger type of skepticism, what he also calls a "virile scepticism."[14] He says he will comment on it in the form of a parable and which is said especially for German ears since it concerns German history and especially the phenomenon of "Frederickianism." What interests Nietzsche most about this "*German*" form of skepticism is not so much its imperial qualities but rather the fact that it has sublimated itself spiritually into a warlike distrust of soft and beautiful feelings, for example, in the "strong and tough virility of the great German philologists and critical historians" who present "a *new* concept of the German spirit" and do so "in spite of all romanticism in music and philosophy."[15] This gives such a spirit the courage of analysis and readiness to undertake "dangerous journeys of exploration." Perhaps he is speaking of himself and his own generation here. Nietzsche ends this section by referencing Napoleon's reaction to Goethe: he expected a German and found a man. Goethe, of course, is one of Nietzsche's greatest intellectual heroes (see *TI* Skirmishes:49).

Sections 210–12 present some of Nietzsche's most important insights into the philosophers of the future. Section 210 notes that these philosophers might have to be skeptics in the sense covered in the previous section but also "critics" and "men of experiments." They have a "passion for knowledge" that compels them to go further with experiments than the "effeminate taste of a democratic century" approves of.[16] These coming philosophers have a number of traits, including genuine independence in relation to prevailing valuations and opinions—they are untimely and unfashionable. Throughout his writings Nietzsche stresses the need for the thinker to gain distance from his time in order to truly address it, to be out of sync with his time to the point where his birth will be posthumous (*EH* "Why I Write Such Good Books":1). Nietzsche's untimeliness consists in not paying obeisance to the sovereignty of popular opinion as an arbiter of taste, valuation, and truth. He who follows public opinion is always timely. In some key respects the later writings such as *BGE* represent a return to the style of the early Nietzsche, being polemical and unmodern. He conceives *BGE* precisely in these terms in the entry on it in *EH*: as a book that is in search of a noble, yes-saying type of being it seeks to be as unmodern as possible. In section 212 Nietzsche stresses that for him the philosopher is "*of necessity* a man of tomorrow and the day after tomorrow" and is compelled to find himself in contradiction to his today: his voice is not the voice of "today." Indeed, the "greatness" of the philosopher's task requires he assume the guise of the bad conscience of his age. Nietzsche is keen to specify the sense in which he conceives philosophy: not as the theory of knowledge but rather as that knowing and creative activity that directs the future development of humanity. Perhaps necessarily, then, the philosopher is at odds with his own time and appears foolish, dangerous, incomprehensible, and disagreeable.

In section 210 Nietzsche focuses on the critical and negating qualities of future philosophers who have "a pleasure in saying No and in taking things apart." By the standards of humaneness they necessarily will be judged to be hard, and this is especially the case in their conception of the practice of truth: for them "truth" is not something that will please, elevate (*erhebe*), or inspire. In short, dedication to "truth" is so severe that it will have little truck with our feelings, enthusiasms, and idealism since the chief task is to aim for "cleanliness and severity in matters of the spirit" (Nietzsche will return to this "hardness" in later sections of the book such as section 227—on "we last Stoics"— and section 230—on the need to translate man back into nature).[17] Feelings, including and especially feelings of elevation and delight, are not to serve as measures of whether or not something is part of "truth": we are, then, to think against ourselves and our inherited humanity. Despite this cultivation of "critical discipline" Nietzsche does not wish philosophers of the future to be labeled *mere* critics who draw boundaries and establish the limits of knowledge. Critics, including great ones such as Kant, are important but serve primarily as instruments of the philosopher. Nietzsche once again takes issue with positivist-minded philosophers for whom the label "critic" would be perhaps the highest sign of the philosopher's strength and nobility.

Section 211 builds on this treatment of the philosopher as critic. Taking further issue with positivists Nietzsche regards it as fatal if philosophical laborers and scientific men are confused with philosophers. The task of the true philosopher is to "*create* values," and although to attain this he may have to pass through the entire range of human values and value feelings, being at different turns in time critic, skeptic, dogmatist, historian, poet, and solver of riddles so as to attain the requisite level of comprehensiveness, all these identities are for him merely "preconditions of his task." On the one hand, we have the philosophical laborers—Nietzsche speaks of Kant and Hegel as noble models of this type—who "press into formulas . . . some great data of valuations" or "former *positings* of values." This task is an important one since it enables us to conquer the past: everything long, including time itself, is abbreviated and rendered serviceable for life, including our digestion and comprehension. On the other hand, however, there are the true philosophers who are "*commanders and legislators*" since they declare of things and existence, "*thus it shall be!*" With the preliminary labor of the philosophical workers at their disposal the true philosophers are able to determine "The Whither and For What of man." Famously, Nietzsche writes, the "knowing" of such philosophers is a "*creating*, their creating is a legislation, their will to truth is—*will to power*"' (recall the end of §9, where philosophy is said to be a "tyrannical drive" and "the most spiritual will to power").[18]

Section 212 focuses on the concept of "greatness." Although Kaufmann notes that Aristotle's treatment of "greatness of soul" exerted an influence on Nietzsche's thinking on this topic, Schopenhauer and Burckhardt are its main sources. Nietzsche follows Schopenhauer in construing the "great" or "greatness" as "that sublime predicate" and which for Schopenhauer is reserved for genius.[19] Nietzsche is also inspired by Burckhardt's lengthy consideration of greatness in his *Reflections on World History*, lectures Nietzsche attended at Basel, which left their mark on him.[20] Nietzsche's view in section 212 that the philosophers apply the knife vivisectionally to the chest of the virtues of their time—and note the signal to the next part of the book on "Our Virtues"—so as to learn of "a *new* greatness of man" and a "new untrodden way to his enhancement," is a clear echo of Burckhardt's judgment that our starting-point might be modern selves, taken as "jejune, perfunctory, many-minded," in which we discover that "Greatness is all that we are *not*."[21] In contrast to "a world of 'modern ideas,'" which seeks to ensure that every person is a "specialty" and a little corner, Nietzsche holds that the philosopher, supposing the concept of him can exist today, wishes to find greatness in man's "range and multiplicity," that is, the fact that he is whole only to the extent that he is multiple: "He would even determine value and rank in accordance with how much and how many things one could bear and take upon himself, how *far* one could extend his responsibility." The "taste of the time" today, however, is in favor of weakness of the will. This means that for the ideal of the philosopher what belongs to the concept of greatness can only be a "capacity for long-range decisions." Moreover, in the face of the war that modern ideology is waging on behalf of "equality of rights" and hence against everything "that is rare, strange, privileged," including the "higher" duties and responsibilities held by higher types of man, the concept of greatness needs to entail, "being noble, wanting to be different, wanting to be by oneself . . . standing alone," and so on. Nietzsche closes the section by offering a definition of greatness—it consists in being "beyond good and evil," master of one's virtues, and overrich in will—and then posing the question whether this greatness is possible today. Aspects of Nietzsche's conception of "greatness" seem to echo his definition of "life" in section 9: not "indifferent nature" but rather "estimating, preferring, being unjust, being limited, wanting to be different."

Section 213 is important because in it Nietzsche expresses his unfashionable view that to have "a right to philosophy" it is necessary to be "cultivated" or bred for it. As a critical genealogist he refers to the importance of origins, ancestors, and blood—all these taken in their metaphorical sense because the breeding Nietzsche has in mind is as much cultural as it is biological or genetic. Nietzsche places stress on the rarity of the genuine philosopher and the need for it to be cultivated because he wants to uphold the (again) unfashionable view that there is an order of rank among states of the soul and of problems that accords with this. Not everyone is predestined to deal with truly great problems and tremendous tasks. Nietzsche is in favor of a plurality of philosophical types. The available resources for this enterprise, our *inheritance*, are explored in parts VIII and IX and draw heavily on the analyses of human development Nietzsche offers in the chapters on religion, morality, scholarship, and virtue. What he doesn't want us to lose sight of is the need of genuine philosophers and yet because the modern taste and ambition is in danger of becoming purely "plebeian" this is indeed what we are losing sight of.

PHILOSOPHICAL CREATORS

As Kaufmann notes, Nietzsche's distinction between philosophical laborers and creators is questionable. He gives examples of thinkers in the history of philosophy who carry out both analyses and make normative suggestions, such as Plato and Aristotle, Spinoza, and Kant. However, Nietzsche distinguishes himself from Kant owing to what he sees as Kant's attachment to the "heart's desire" and lack of intellectual integrity. Nietzsche has no truck with Kant's attempt to deny knowledge in order to make room for faith, seeing in this only a half-hearted attempt at a true "critique." Kant is simply not "hard" enough for what Nietzsche sees as the philosopher's taste: Kant invents "a special type of reason [practical reason] so that people would not have to worry about it when morality, when the sublime (*erhabne*) command 'thou shalt,' is heard" (*A* 12). Spinoza is a good example to focus on, not simply because Nietzsche thought he had found a precursor in him,[22] but also because he is a thinker, one might argue, who disconnected truth from pleasant feelings and elevation in the way Nietzsche stipulates as being necessary for the dedicated work of philosophy. One might also venture the suggestion that Spinoza is a creator of concepts, which for Nietzsche is one of the hallmarks of the true philosopher.[23] And yet Nietzsche makes critical observations in his late writings, including *BGE* (5, 25, and 198) and book five of *GS* added in 1887 (*GS* 372). We think something else is at work for Nietzsche, which Kaufmann does not address: the difference between Nietzsche and his precursors and forerunners is that he is profoundly anti-modern; he does not write for the benefit of humaneness or humanity, at least not how these are conceived in the democratic language and values of the modern period. This comes out strongly in the drafts he prepared for many of the sections of *BGE*, including sections of this part. For example, in a note from 1885 on the search for new philosophers Nietzsche says he is looking in the direction "where a noble mode of thought is dominant" and he adds, "such as believes in slavery and in many degrees of bondage as the precondition of every higher culture" (see also on slavery §§242, 257–8). Where a "*creative* mode of thought dominates," he goes on, it will not posit "the happiness of repose" as a goal for the world and honors in peace only "the means to new wars." A mode of thinking seeking to prescribe "laws for the future" will be "harsh and tyrannical toward itself" and "all things of the present." This will be a "reckless, 'immoral' of thought" that recognizes the need "to develop both the good and the bad qualities in man to their fullest extent" and because "it feels it has the strength to put both in their right place" (*KSA* 11:37[14]; *WP* 464). Once again the distinction between the "free thinker," with his democratic taste, and the free spirit is crucial for understanding how Nietzsche conceives the philosophers of the future. The present age, he notes, possesses the "*reverse* instincts" since it wants above all "comfort . . . publicity and that great actors' hubbub, that great drum banging that appeals to its funfair tastes," and it wants "that everyone should fall on his face in the profoundest subjection before the greatest of all lies—it is called 'equality of human beings'—and honor exclusively those virtues that *level* and *equalize*" (ibid.; see also from 1885 *KSA* 11:37[8]; *WP* 957).

Two critical points are worth making on the issue of the new philosophers. First, it cannot be a question of Nietzsche making a straightforward and naïve appeal to "nature" to justify his vision of the future. In his reading of this part of the book Lampert argues that for Nietzsche the ultimate ground for philosophy's right to be master "is given in nature and human nature."[24] This is difficult to square with Nietzsche's emphasis on "life" as the domain par excellence of "wanting to be different" and on the philosopher as one who seeks difference and independence. Moreover, even if we suppose Nietzsche seeks to ground his conception of the future, including the sovereignty of philosopher-legislators, in a conception of nature it is difficult to know what could sanction this: why should human beings obey or conform to what nature dictates? Indeed, there have been philosophers of the twentieth century from Bergson to Gianni Vattimo who place value on democracy and democratic virtues precisely because they are *anti-natural*.[25] It is by no means clear that Nietzsche thinks his "radical aristocratism" can find its basis and sanction in nature. For Nietzsche the realization of genuine personality and individuality is something extremely rare and difficult to attain. He says that it is almost something "anti-natural" (*KSA* 12:10[59]; *WP* 886); this is why he favors protecting the strong from the weak (*GM* III:14). The solitary type of species has against it the instincts of the herd and the tradition of values and they themselves may be lacking in strong protective instincts and dependent on chance for so many things. In a note from 1887 he expresses the worry that the class struggle that aims at equality of rights will wage a war against the solitary personality. On the other hand, though, he wonders whether the solitary species can best maintain and develop himself most easily in democratic society simply because of the habits of order, honesty, justice, and trust it is based on (*KSA* 12:10[61]; *WP* 887). Despite the impression sometimes given by Nietzsche, his thinking on the future is more speculative and open-ended than it might appear.

Second, for all his talk of creating new values it is abundantly clear that the ethico-political values Nietzsche prizes are ones taken from the past, namely, Greek and Roman antiquity and the Renaissance. The reader of *BGE* needs to look hard to find evidence of what precisely is "new" about the new values that Nietzsche thinks the coming philosophers will create and forge. Although it is clear that Nietzsche holds a return to past aristocracies is impossible and even undesirable, and he speaks explicitly of the need for a "new aristocracy," his principal attachment is to the aristocratic "enhancement" of the human (§257) and many passages, published and unpublished, indicate he thinks some form of "slavery," albeit of a "sublime" kind, is necessary to achieve this end.[26] This is an issue we shall return to in our discussion of part IX of the book.

GREAT POLITICS

The German term "great politics" was a term in vogue in the 1870s and 1880s and referred to the then fashionable conviction of the primacy of foreign policy conceived as a higher form of politics that addressed European world power conflicts in contradistinction to lesser forms of politics dealing with internal affairs.[27] Nietzsche first employs the term in *HH* 481 entitled "Great Politics and Its Drawbacks." Here he notes the political growth of a nation entails an intellectual impoverishment and lassitude, resulting in diminished capacities for the execution of works requiring great concentration and specialization.[28] As Bergmann notes, and as something typical of Nietzsche's many reformulations of the term over course of the next decade, Nietzsche "interjects a seesaw theory, an either-or choice, between politicization and cultural flowering" that challenges the widely held conviction that cultural flourishing necessarily and eagerly follows on from military conquests and success.[29] It is this kind of "great politics" that Nietzsche puts to work in *TI* (1888) where he uses it more in the sense of macro-politics or *Realpolitik*: ". . . the whole of Europe already has a notion of it—great politics deceives no one . . . Germany is being seen more and more as Europe's *flatland*"[30] (*TI* "What the Germans Lack":3; see also *TI* "Morality as Anti-Nature":3). In his final text, *EH*, the notion acquires a more apocalyptic meaning: ". . . I am necessarily a man of impending disaster . . . when truth squares up to the lie of millennia, we shall have upheavals . . . such as have never been dreamed of. The notion of politics will then completely dissolve into a spiritual war (*Geisterkrieg*), and

all configurations of power from the old society will be exploded
. . . there will be wars such as there have never yet been on earth.
Only since I arrived on the scene has there been *great politics* on
earth—" (*EH* "Why I am a Destiny":1). From initially mocking
the notion—the politics of the new Reich amount in fact to a
"petty politics," Nietzsche jabbed ironically—he ends up appropriating it for the ends of his own prophetic mission. We should
also bear in mind that the years 1884–1885, that is, the same
time as the drafting of material for *BGE*, witness Bismarck's
acquisition of colonies such as the Cameroons, German East
Africa, and New Guinea. It is not too far-fetched to suggest this
is on Nietzsche's mind when he conceives "great politics" in the
mid-1880s in terms of the coming "mastery of the earth." The
concept was one he was keen to appropriate and make use of.
His very final notebook, in fact, begins with a section entitled
"Die Grosse Politik" (*KSA* 13:25[1]).

The precise meaning of Nietzsche's positive deployment of
"great politics" has exercised many of his commentators: just
what kind of wars does he have in mind? And what exactly
would be a "spiritual war?"[31] Is Nietzsche thinking "war" independently of violence and slaughter, or is he tying these to
higher and nobler ends? What would these ends be? In section
208 the focus is on "the dominion of the earth" and the need for
Europe to forge "one will" in response to the alleged menace
of Russia. Nietzsche certainly envisaged a "tragic age" for the
future of Europe but whether this entails violent conflict as
something unavoidable is difficult to say with certainty. Evidence
suggests Nietzsche favored the end of bloody, nationalist wars
and was an advocate of peace.[32] He conceives his idea of "great
politics" in opposition to the power politics of his time and
dynastic, democratic and nationalist fragmentation. He did not
envisage a central power such as Germany dominating rest of
Europe; rather, the good European (§§254 and 256) is contra the
"nationalist nonsense." Nietzsche thought the economic unity
of Europe must come (*KSA* 13:11[235]) and this would lead to a
united Europe.[33] His "party of Life" (*EH BT*:4) would operate
outside the terms of power politics and would not be a political
party based on class, race, or nationalism, but would be international in scope seeking the guardianship of the entire culture
of the earth and, ultimately, universal peace.

CHAPTER 9

PART VII: "OUR VIRTUES"

In this chapter Nietzsche continues his dissection of morality and focuses on the question of virtues. He also deals importantly with the "order of rank." There are interesting links between many of the sections that compose it, and the chapter reaches a climax with section 230 on the "fundamental will of the spirit." Section 231 provides a pause for the reader and then sections 232–9 present Nietzsche's notorious "truths" about woman. One task is to work out why this treatment of woman appears, in this concentrated form, at this particular point in the book.

Aristotle is perhaps the most influential classical source for a moral philosophy of virtues in which a fulfilled life is one lived in accordance with virtue, that is, one in which specifically human capacities are put to their best use. Aristotle groups virtues into two main classes: virtues of character (moral virtues) and virtues of the mind (intellectual virtues). At the start of the second book of his *Ethics* Aristotle makes it clear that moral goodness is the result of habit (it is connected to the word *ethos*) and that none of the moral virtues are engendered in us by nature. We cannot train a stone to rise or fire to burn downwards. Although we are constituted to receive moral virtues by nature, their full and actual development is due to habit. With the title of his chapter Nietzsche is making it clear he wishes to address what, if any, are the specific virtues of modern Europeans. Do we have virtues? If we do, what are they? And if the question is a complex one for us to address as moderns why is this? In fact, it becomes clear as the chapter unfolds that the "our" in Nietzsche's title refers to two groups: the free spirits and modern Europeans.

OUR LABYRINTH

Section 214 begins by immediately signaling the difficulty we face in considering the question of our virtues. Nietzsche concedes "it is probable" we still have our virtues but they don't have the character of our forebears, specifically they are not "simpleminded and four-square." We hold our forebears in honor for their simpleminded virtues but also at arm's length. We cannot be like them. This is because of what modern Europeans are: dangerously curious, multiple with an "art of disguises," and with a mellow and sweetened cruelty in spirit and senses. So, if it turns out that we have virtues they will be those qualities or attributes—dispositions and habits—which are congruent with our "most secret and cordial inclinations" and our "most ardent needs." We will find them in our labyrinth. For Nietzsche, then, we moderns live a labyrinthine existence, an image conjured at the beginning of part III and with which the book ends. Already in *D* Nietzsche had noted that in comparison with earlier cultures and ages, such as the Greeks, our souls are labyrinthine: "If we desired and dared an architecture corresponding to the nature of *our* soul . . . our model would have to be the labyrinth!" (*D* 169). Section 215 uses the example of the astronomical discovery of a planet's orbit being under the guidance of two suns, in which it enjoys suns of different colors shining on it, to indicate that modern human beings are complex creatures: we do not think, feel, and act under the influence of "one" morality but rather of different moralities. Nietzsche makes a witty reference to Kant's moral law when he refers to the "complicated mechanics of our 'starry sky'" (Kant held that two things fill the human mind with awe and wonder, the starry heavens above and the moral law within). For moderns, he is suggesting, the moral law cannot be univocal or simpleminded; for a start, Nietzsche will argue in part IX, each modern human being is a synthesis of master and slave moralities (§260). We become comprehensible to ourselves only when we admit this complexity.[1]

Several of the sections that now follow are designed to invert our typical understanding of the exercise of moral judgment. In section 216 Nietzsche suggests that we have learned how to love our enemies and, in fact, have done something higher and more sublime (*Sublimere*): we learn to despise when we love and even and especially when we love best. We now do this without noise and pomp and with a modesty and concealed goodness that does not allow itself "virtue formulas." This is because today "morality as a pose—offends our taste." In section 217 Nietzsche advises us to beware of a person we would expect him to admire and esteem, namely, the person who displays moral tact and subtlety in making moral distinctions. The suggestion seems to be that we can never be subtle enough in our exercise of moral judgment and, moreover, that such a person hides the fanaticism of a moral being, which comes to the surface once they make a mistake either in front of us or against us—"they become instinctive slanderers and detractors." In short, the fact that we become offended by our errors of judgment shows we can be too enamored of our own our virtuousness. This is why Nietzsche ends this section with a paean to the forgetful since they are at least able to get over their stupidities. In section 218 Nietzsche suggests as a new task for psychologists the observation of the norm in its battle against the exception, and this question of the norm and what is outside or beyond it becomes a theme of the part with its overriding concern with morality and the order of rank.

THE ORDER OF RANK

Section 219 argues for an order of rank where the merely moral human being wants there to be none but only equal agreement and the acceptance of one set of standards, namely, the standard of equality. Here Nietzsche argues that judgments and condemnations are: a form of revenge of the spiritually limited against the less limited, a compensation for having been ill-favored by nature, and an opportunity for acquiring spirit and becoming refined, that is, being able to practice judgment and discernment (he calls this spiritualized malice). Some of these will strike the reader as more speculative than others, for example, the argument on compensation. Such types gain the pleasure of feeling that there are standards before which those other types that overflow with the privileges of spirit become their equals (such types fight for the doctrine of the equality of all souls before God and need such a faith). Nietzsche then turns his focus to the notion of "high spirituality" and contends that such spirituality, which entails highly developed capacities of judgment and discernment, for example, the judgment of ages and epochs as eras of decline or ascent, of the value of different human types, cannot be compared with the solidity and respectability of the "merely moral human being." Such a proposition, Nietzsche imagines, enrages the merely moral person and he wishes to avoid doing this since they have enough of the spirit of revenge and resentment in them as it is. Instead he chooses to flatter them by arguing that high spirituality is in fact a product and synthesis of moral qualities and owes its existence to a long discipline and exercise, for example, as in the case of the spiritualization of justice. Ultimately, this process leads to a justice that recognizes the chief task of the spiritual philosopher: "to maintain the *order of rank* in the world, among things themselves—and not only among men." The order of rank concerns making distinctions of value as they concern different human types in different ages and epochs, and so on. But why does Nietzsche also refer to "things themselves"? Do justice and the order of rank also concern themselves with non-human things and the "world"? It is not clear just what Nietzsche has in mind (some commentators have read him as referring to some natural order of rank in the world).[2] Although Nietzsche chooses to flatter the moral person, what he says about the order of rank is deeply revealing since it indicates that for him its expression is not without conditions of existence and emergence.

For Nietzsche we moderns are almost naturally antipathetic to the idea of an order of rank because "it undermines the modern sense of individuality in which every person is a unique, completely independent source of value."[3] As he puts it at an earlier point in his writings: "One no longer has class-rank! One is an 'individual'!" (*D* 203). Nietzsche's great worry, in *BGE* and other texts, is that this means we no longer know how to properly value anything, be it ourselves as creatures who fashion ends for ourselves, or things in the world itself—and this is largely because we forbid ourselves the right to make value distinctions and shape the value of things in terms of some rank ordering. For Nietzsche the "order of rank" is not primarily a substantive notion; it is rather that he "is interested in the availability of normative authority rather than prescribing any specific hierarchy,"[4] such as some fixed aristocratic kind (he favors "aristocracy" as an ideal because it allows for distinctions of rank—between types of people and things in the world—to be made possible). As Robert Guay has correctly noted, Nietzsche's normative attention is never focused on a natural hierarchy, but rather on "life" as a transcendental condition of normative claims and moves. As Nietzsche puts it, "order of rank merely formulates the highest law of Life itself" (*A* 57). And, as Guay nicely glosses this: "order of rank makes possible the evaluative, self-relating activity distinctive of Life as such, not as a causal condition, but by contributing to the content by which persons distinguish themselves from the rest of nature."[5] This means that rank ordering in Nietzsche does not reflect some *pre-given* evaluative order—this is to commit the error of a naturalistic fallacy (deriving what ought to be the case from what is), which is so frequently but wrongly attributed to Nietzsche by both defenders and detractors of his philosophy alike. As Guay correctly stresses the point, Nietzsche presents the notion of an order of rank "not as reflecting a natural or mythic order, but as a condition for the availability of normative authority."[6] For Nietzsche, then, the rank ordering of values is fundamental to "Life," that is, to what lives and grows; it is this concern with value distinctions that makes "Life" for Nietzsche the primary category in his "bio-ethics" and "bio-politics," as opposed to "nature." Where life is guided by the priority of ends and goals, non-living nature is simply moved by external causes alone. This distinction between "life" and "nature" is crucial to Nietzsche's thinking and should not be lost sight of. He has emphatically stated, in *BGE* 9, for example, that life involves wanting to be different from nature and what is merely "natural" and that central to this difference is evaluation (having preferences, being unjust, being limited, etc).

Section 220 continues the theme of rank ordering by addressing the question of what interests and concerns different human beings. It begins with Nietzsche referring to the praise accorded in modern times to the notion of "disinterestedness," as found, for example, in the Kantian view of aesthetic appreciation as being a form of disinterested contemplation, and that was also taken up by Schopenhauer. Kant holds that when we experience something aesthetically we are in a unique relation to that thing: we do not, for example, make a logical judgment of it by asking after the class of objects to which it belongs, so we contemplate it without interest in this specific sense.[7] In the aesthetic mode of experience we are governed neither by the demands of theoretical cognition (I am not cognizing an object in the sense of needing to know what it is, be it a dog, a ball, or a chair) nor those of practical reason (the demands of moral action). Nietzsche overlooks these specifics in Kant's account and he perhaps does so in order to make the point he wants to (he seems to think that disinterestedness involves being dispassionate and impersonal but this is contestable).[8] Nietzsche notes that the things that will interest and attract "choosier and more refined tastes and every higher nature" will appear to the average or common human being as totally uninteresting: the tastes are different. The average human being may even consider the interests of the higher nature so beyond the norm that they appear to him as being of a "disinterested" character. Nietzsche contends this is an error of judgment since the "naked truth" of the matter is that what appeals to the higher nature in so-called "disinterested" actions is, for him, something exceedingly interesting. Nietzsche concludes the section by contesting a widespread assumption that love and the making of sacrifices don't involve the interested ego. In making a sacrifice one always expects something in return, some profitable experience, for example, and which often enables one to grow. The denouement to this section refers the reader back to the book's preface and its provocative claim that "supposing truth is a woman." Nietzsche wants us to infer that the pursuit of the "naked truth" about truth is neither boring nor disinterested either to truth (woman) itself or to truth's pursuer: truth cannot be bored by such questioning, only "violated."

THE UNEGOISTIC

The topic of the unegoistic occupies Nietzsche's attention in the next two sections. In the preface to *GM* he makes clear the "morality" he wishes to subject to critique is the morality of the unegoistic, that is, self-sacrifice, self-denial, and compassion. He does not explicitly address the question of whether unegoism is genuine or only a disguise, though there is much here and in his previous writings such as *D* to suggest that unegoism is neither what it appears to be not what it takes itself to be (e.g., "the mask of philanthropy" as he puts it here in §221). What remains the case is that it exists as something real in the form of an ideology actively promoted in society and social relations. In section 221 Nietzsche takes the unegoistic morality to task for presenting itself unconditionally. When it does so it violates taste—a superior taste would recognize and value difference—and, perhaps even more seriously, it injures the higher and rarer type by seducing them to neglect their own tasks, which are different from the norm. This is why Nietzsche insists that moralities must be forced "to bow . . . before the *order of rank*" and learn that it is "immoral," in the moralist's own language, to suppose that what is right for one (the dutiful herd type) is fair for the other (the higher and rarer type). We can note here Nietzsche's use of irony with reference to the "moralistic pedant" that is speaking in the section. Why does the pedant want to be so right in every instance? Should he not be laughed at and as part of a "good taste"?

In section 222 Nietzsche notes that compassion is becoming our "religion" today, not literally but in the form of society's self-image and raison dêtre. The German *Mitleid* is translated by Kaufmann as "pity" though "compassion" better reflects the German, which has the meaning of "suffering with." What the modern human being takes to be its core virtue, compassion, shows itself to be in fact a disguised form of self-contempt and may even be a vice: "He suffers and his vanity wants him to suffer only with others, to feel compassion." Nietzsche is keen to undermine the pretensions of this cult of compassion: it is fully interested, fully egoistic, and fully human, all too human (vain). For Schopenhauer the basis of *morality* resides in compassion (*Mitleid*), which he conceives as the "absence of all egoistic motivation" and "*the criterion of an action of moral worth.*"[9] In acting in accord with compassion it is not, for Schopenhauer, only a case of my elevating myself above my natural egoism and so becoming a moral agent; it is rather, that I am now acting in accord with the *metaphysical truth* of existence: namely, I have pierced the veil of Maya (illusion) and reached the real truth of being, namely, that individuation (plurality) is not real, all is One, and "this art thou." For Nietzsche, Schopenhauer's valuation is lacking in real psychological insight and intellectual integrity.[10] Nietzsche holds that in any given action multiple motives are in play, so the attempt to posit purely other-regarding affections as the basis of human morality does not withstand psychological scrutiny. For Nietzsche it is simply not the case that we ever act from single motive. If we wish to free ourselves from *our* suffering in acts of *Mitleid*, which is what he thinks is taking place, it is also the case, Nietzsche surmises, that with the same act we surrender to an impulse for pleasure, for example, in the thought of praise and gratitude which will come our way if we were to come to someone's aid. The performer of the act can thus take a delight in himself, for example, in the sensation that the action has put an end to an injustice that arouses one's indignation—the release of this indignation can have an invigorating effect. Nietzsche has several objections to compassion when it is esteemed as a virtue. For example, he thinks it can display a superficial understanding of another's suffering (see *D* 133), that it is often a question of the mental state of the agent and not the actual sufferer, and it fails to appreciate that in an individual's formation happiness and unhappiness grow up together as sisters, even twins (see *GS* 338). Moreover, he holds that the cult of the sympathetic affections, such as *Mitleid*, within modernity represents a tyrannical encroachment on the requirements of self-cultivation (see *D* 174).

THE HISTORICAL SENSE

The next two sections consider the modern historical sense and spirit. In the opening sections of *HH* Nietzsche called for "historical philosophizing" and with it the virtue of modesty: everything, including the faculty of cognition, has become and this insight can teach us modesty about things since we recognize they do not enjoy an eternal existence or truth. In *GM* II, Nietzsche deploys the will to power as a principle of "historical method" as a way of showing that only that which has no history can be semiotically defined: there is always everywhere an entanglement of "meanings." In these sections of *BGE* he is giving specific critical coloring to our appreciation of the historical sense. Section 223 notes that the modern European is hybrid in nature—"a tolerably ugly plebeian" for reasons soon to be disclosed—and finds itself in need of a costume simply because it has to cultivate a self-image in some way, an identity for itself even if, and perhaps especially if, it lacks a real or authentic identity. For such a spirit, history provides the storage room for costumes, although none fit him especially well and he keeps trying on new ones. What is peculiar to the modern age is the way in which it studies the costumes of the past and here the modern spirit finds its advantage, able to study new pieces of history (including prehistory) and foreign cultures, including their moralities, modes of belief, their taste in the arts, and so on. At the end of the section Nietzsche suggests, perhaps with a heavy dose of irony, that we moderns will find here our realm of "invention," where we can be "original," "as parodists of world history and God's buffoons," so that at least our laughter has a future if nothing else does.[11] Nietzsche's concern with history, and with the dangers its study presents to our being our own authors and original sources, goes back to his second untimely meditation of the uses and disadvantages of history (1874). In *BGE*, as evident in this section, Nietzsche's worry is whether the extent of our study of history signals, in fact, the end of history and the fact that we are no longer active agents in the world but merely passive consumers. Nietzsche's play-fulness may conceal a very serious concern he has and is subtly alerting us to.

In section 224 Nietzsche defines the "historical sense" as the capacity for quickly guessing the order of rank evident in the valuations according to which a people, a society, or even a human being has lived, and he claims that modern Europeans lay claim to it as a special sense, a kind of sixth sense, which has emerged from the "semi-barbarism" into which Europe has plunged as a result of the "democratic mingling of classes and races."[12] For the modern spirit the forms and ways of life of past ages and cultures lay next to and on top of each other and "our instincts now run back everywhere" to the point where we are in fact a kind of chaos.[13] Again, there is a great deal of irony in Nietzsche's analysis: how can one have *instincts* that run back? Although Nietzsche once again notes that the spirit can find advantage in this chaos that it is, the reader should not overlook his worry: modern human beings are living in the past, the future is perhaps no more for us (it appears not to be our concern, we are not "interested" in it). One advantage of our semi-barbarism is that it affords us access to things no noble age and spirit has had access to, including the labyrinths of unfinished cultures. The historical sense is fundamentally ignoble since it is willing to taste everything. It is thus devoid of a superior taste, which calls for discrimination and judgment. We who are ruled by a plebeian curiosity differ from a noble culture, which has a definite Yes and No and even a reserve toward everything foreign. By contrast we feel we can assimilate everything. An example of the modern "spirit" Nietzsche gives is Shakespeare, "that amazing Spanish-Moorish-Saxon synthesis of tastes" which is a complexity, he thinks, that would have all but killed with laughter or irritation an Athenian of the circle of Aeschylus. But it is among "our virtues" that we moderns accept such a wild abundance of colors and medley of attributes "with a secret familiarity and cordiality." Note here the connection to the opening sections of the chapter: if we can be this magnanimous in our appreciation of a dramatist such as Shakespeare may we not also have the wisdom to appreciate many different moralities and the need for an order of rank? If a rich and mature taste, including a taste for complexity, is one of our virtues then why can we not cultivate the taste for difference and the order of rank with respect to morality?

These questions concern Nietzsche in the second part of this long section. He notes that as human beings of the historical sense we do have our virtues, such as being modest, courageous, and full of self-overcoming and devotion, we are selfless, patient, and accommodating, and so on. But, he goes on to suggest, what may be our virtues are also our vices since what we lack with these virtues is the "good taste," even the "best" taste, that would allow us to grasp (and actually taste) the "perfection and ultimate maturity of every culture and art." In short, our virtues may be misplaced simply because while of value—for example, the tremendous value of self-overcoming—their attachment to the historical sense as our distinctive sense means that we find it virtually impossible to become "noble," that is, finding "halcyon self-sufficiency" and self-consummation. What is alien to us moderns who have such an extensive taste for the foreign is measure. We feel at home in the "thrill of the infinite, the unmeasured," for example, in our modern attraction to the sublime.[14] This may strike us as an odd insight: how can the modern historical spirit with its virtues of modesty and selflessness, so patient and accommodating, have a bent for the unmeasured and for placing itself now and again in peril? It may be that Nietzsche wants his readers to infer there is a link here: it is precisely because of our modest selflessness that we also have a need for the unmeasured and for danger.[15]

NIETZSCHE'S COMPASSION

In section 225 Nietzsche reveals, cautiously, what *his* compassion centers on. It is not compassion for social distress and society but something higher and more farsighted: it is compassion for the ways in which the human is made small. Social compassion seeks a state of affairs in which suffering has been abolished and this for Nietzsche amounts to nihilism (in *GM* I:12 he asks if this is what nihilism means for us today, namely, that we are tired of the human). Nietzsche needs to be read carefully on this question of suffering since he is not advocating a "cult of suffering." On the contrary, it is this cult that seeks suffering's removal from human existence since we cannot tolerate the sight of it (see §293). His key point is that it is the "discipline of great suffering" that has so far led to all enhancements of the human. He is slim in providing details of what exactly he has in mind here and the reader will find extensive relevant analyses in previous texts such as *D* and *GS*. Here he mentions how the tension of the soul in unhappiness cultivates strength such as an inventiveness and courage in enduring, interpreting, and exploiting suffering (see also *GS* 338). It is under these seemingly adverse and negative conditions that the human animal has acquired spirit, cunning, and greatness, in short, "virtues" that have enabled it to come to know life and affirm it. Nietzsche posits a distinction between creature and creator in the human, which are in fact united in it: on the one hand there is the human being as material, fragment, clay, dirt, nonsense, and chaos and on the other hand we also find the creator, form-giver, and hammer hardness. While we can well understand our compassion for the creature in the human, for what has to be formed, broken, and purified, can we also understand and have compassion for the need of creation and what this requires? We can have compassion for this other task because it does not always result in success or triumph. Nietzsche addresses the question of the identity of the "immoralists" in section 226 in the way he does because they concern themselves with the "creator" in the human, that is, they are concerned with and interested in the world (which they fear and love) of "invisible and inaudible . . . subtle commanding and obeying," that is, the world of will to power as it centers on the cultivation of the human animal. In this respect the so-called "immoralists"—since their concern is not with the world of mere morality—are humans of duty; they feel duty-bound to the tasks of the "secret hardness" of their destiny (*Geschick*) and on this front they have appearances against them—how on the understanding of the merely moral human being can "immoralists" experience duty? Nietzsche is inviting us to ask.

HONESTY

In section 227 Nietzsche addresses what is the specific virtue appropriate to the free spirits, which he names "honesty" (*Redlichkeit*). In *D* 456 Nietzsche already described this as our "youngest virtue," something immature and not yet aware of itself. He thinks both the antique conception of the unity of virtue and happiness and the Christian appeal to the kingdom of God have not been made with total honesty; rather, the supposition has held sway that where we are selfless we are somehow permitted to trouble ourselves less about truth and truthfulness. *Redlichkeit* may well be, he suggests in section 227, the only virtue left to such spirits, which they need to work on (with both love and malice) and not get tired of perfecting. Love and malice because of the complex psychology informing the drives and emotions (there is no such thing as a pure emotion for Nietzsche); and it may be the only virtue left to them because of its special character: it is the "virtue," which, if properly exercised, enables free spirits to enjoy their freedom, finding perfection in their imperfection and need to constantly perfect themselves ("perfecting" is in scare quotes signaling an ongoing task). One commentator astutely notes we cannot translate *Redlichkeit* as honesty (or probity or integrity) without rethinking the content of the word.[16] In being honest or "redlich" we are made aware there are different ways of seeing (a multiplicity of perspectives on a thing) and we can name differently (things have becoming, not "being"). Nietzsche goes on to argue that if our honesty should grow weary and we would like to have things easier and more tender, "like an agreeable vice," then we have to remain hard like "the last Stoics" we are. We are to cultivate a certain relation to this virtue of honesty as a way of keeping it something vital: Nietzsche refers to our "devilry," such as our courage and curiosity, and our most subtle and disguised spiritual will to power, including our overcoming of the world and that concerns the realms of the future. Part of our honesty as free spirits is that we speak of and to ourselves in such terms (acknowledging that we have our desires and our "devils"); as Nietzsche says in this section, "it is a matter of names" and of knowing one harbors a multiplicity of spirits. Free spirits, however, have to guard against this virtue becoming their vanity, limit, and stupidity. There is a real danger that through being so wedded to this virtue of honesty free spirits allow themselves to become saints and bores. Surely, Nietzsche suggests, life is too short for boredom! Honesty, then, is a "virtue" but one that is peculiar to and fitting for free spirits.

Some discussion of Nietzsche's reference to "we last Stoics" is merited since it is obvious from his writings that he is not a Stoic, at least not in any straightforward sense. The Stoic, for Nietzsche, is a type that prepares itself for the worst, training itself, for example, to swallow stones and worms, slivers of glass, and scorpions without nausea (*GS* 306). Nietzsche's conception of fate does not entail Stoic preparation for "petrifaction": "We are *not so badly off* that we have to be as badly off as Stoics" (*GS* 326). Stoicism enables one to conceal well what one lacks, donning a cloak of prudent silence, affability, and mildness, and this is the cloak of the idealist who, in reality, is an incurable self-despiser and deeply vain (*GS* 359). Might the philosopher's wisdom, including the Stoic's, be a screen behind which he hides from "spirit" (ibid.)? Given these stinging criticisms, why does Nietzsche refer to "we last Stoics" in section 227? He appeals to Stoicism in his late writings as a morality or ethical practice in which the instinct of health defends itself against incipient decadence. It is what he calls a "brake-shoe morality" that is "stoical, hard, tyrannical" (*KSA* 13:15[29]; *WP* 268). It denotes a union of will and knowledge that entails "respect for oneself" (*KSA* 13:11[297]; *WP* 342; see also 11[375]; *WP* 427). In short, self-control is required so as to prevent clumsiness and sloppiness with regards to the tasks that face the free spirit: "let us see to it that it [honesty] does not become our vanity, our finery and pomp, our limit, our stupidity" (§227). We must guard against falling in love with our Stoicism as it is a means in life and not an end in itself.

Section 228 continues the theme of boredom with Nietzsche declaring all moral philosophy to date to have been boring and a sedative. He thinks this because it has addressed the topics of moral philosophy in such a naïve and simple-minded manner. In modern Europe nobody dares to entertain the idea that thinking about morality could be dangerous and that a calamitous fate (*Verhängniss*) could be involved—simply because how we think about morality will be decisive for the future and our moral thinking may even sacrifice the future for the sake of some eternal present (see *GM* P). To illustrate his point Nietzsche gives the example of British utilitarianism, which regards general utility or the happiness of the greatest number as the correct way to virtue and that this is all that striving can consist in when reduced to its essence. Nietzsche contests the wisdom of this ethical system by addressing those who espouse it as "ponderous herd animals" who have "unquiet consciences." In short, he thinks it represents a lazy way of thinking about the ends to which morality can be put, such as the enhancement of the human. The "general welfare" is not, he contends, an ideal or a goal but only an "emetic." For Nietzsche utilitarianism represents a very good example of morality assuming univocal status, so again he states the need for an order of rank between human and human and between one morality and another.

TRANSLATING THE HUMAN BACK INTO NATURE

Sections 229 and 230 are closely knitted together. In section 229 Nietzsche begins by noting that late ages may be so proud of their humanity that they live in superstitious fear of the so-called savage, cruel beast that lies dormant within the human. He suggests to think this through we need to reconsider cruelty, and he invites us to reflect on the fact that nearly everything we hold in esteem as higher culture supposes a spiritualization— refinement, sublimation—of it. When we appreciate this insight we come to realize that the so-called "savage beast" indeed lives and flourishes in our midst and has simply become "divine." Even when we think we are completely removed from it or elevated above it, as in the examples Nietzsche gives of tragic pity and the sublime (*Erhabene*), as well as the most delicate heights of metaphysical thinking, cruelty is at work. A clumsy psychology of old times would have us believe that cruelty only comes into being at the sight of the suffering of others. Nietzsche suggests, however, there is an abundance of enjoyment to be had in one's own suffering and making oneself suffer (he mentions religious self-denial, voluntary subjection to certain ascetic practices, and vivisections of the conscience). The same is also true of the seeker after knowledge who forces himself to recognize things that go against the inclination of his spirit and the wishes of his heart, for example, saying No where he would like to say Yes. The human being of knowledge has to be considered, therefore, one of the artists and transfigurers of cruelty. Why does Nietzsche want us to know this? What are we to learn from it? The next section provides some answers.

At the end of section 229 Nietzsche refers to the "basic will of the spirit" as one that dwells naturally within the apparent and the superficial. This will of the spirit (or mind) forms the basis of the analysis of the first part of the long and intriguing section 230. Nietzsche argues that spirit (or mind) is: (a) led by a need for "mastery" (a will to synthesize and bind together, to simplification); and (b) can be compared to a stomach on account of the insight that its basic needs and capacities are the same as anything that lives, grows, and reproduces. Its "energy" in appropriating what is foreign to it expresses itself in simplification and reduction: it needs the familiar, it does not want the contradictory or too much ambiguity; anything new must be made to fit into old schemas or established ways of thinking and feeling. This is how spirit incorporates new experiences and undergoes growth or the feeling of increased power. This will is also served by an instinct that appears to be something opposite such as a decision in favor of ignorance, for arbitrary conclusions, a defensive posture against much potential knowledge, being content with un-enlightenment (a certain darkness), a limited horizon, and so on. When it is in this mode the mind allows itself to be deceived with a good or clear conscience, it is even capable of experiencing joy in uncertainty and ambiguity, even if it has the mischievous intuition that things are actually not this way or that but rather this is how the mind works and needs to work (it is limited in both time and space). The "spirit" (mind), then, has at its disposal many Protean arts that enable it to don multiple masks and which enable it to experience a self-satisfaction in the caprice or arbitrariness of all these expressions of power. The section is, in effect, a demonstration of the "will to power" of the human animal and what characterizes it: the need for mastery even in its craftiest and loftiest operations. When Nietzsche declares spirit to be a stomach this is a metaphor he is giving us, one designed to alter how we typically conceive the mind, for example, as enjoying a free-floating existence and that supposedly engages in pure, lifeless and automatic cognition.

In exposing the character of the "fundamental will" of the spirit or mind in this way Nietzsche is not simply arguing against it. In section 188 he argued in favor of the "limited horizon": "stupidity" is a precondition of life and its growth. In his preface to *GS* he speaks of what we can learn from the Greeks conceived as philosopher-artists: "They knew how to live. What is required for that is to stop courageously at the surface, the fold, the skin, to adore appearance, to believe in forms, tones, words, in the whole Olympus of appearance (*Schein*)" (*GS* P:4).

In the second part of the section Nietzsche moves on to discuss the nature of a counter tendency to this basic will of the spirit, which he calls "sublime" (*sublim*), and which is the will to knowledge and involves "a kind of cruelty of intellectual conscience" and of taste.[17] It seeks a different kind of mastery from the other will of the spirit discussed in the first part of the section. Its cruelty expresses itself in "severe discipline" and "severe words"; it is no longer attracted by the surface and skin of things but compelled toward the depths. Those who have this will to knowledge, the free spirits, would prefer not to speak of the "cruelty" of their conscience but rather of their attachment to "excessive honesty." But a free spirit must reject this ostentation of being honored with the title of a "hero of truthfulness" and a devotee of honesty, and so on. Instead, such a spirit practices a "hermit's conscience." This is perhaps the most extreme and severe form of the intellectual conscience we can imagine, one that perhaps comes into operation where the free spirit removes itself from all social bonds and superficial humanity. Intellectual conscience does not allow itself the "heart's desire" and indeed positively works against the heart. The praise of the free spirit must be rejected—by the conscience—simply because in it we can still detect the "pomp" and "junk" of unconscious human vanity (see also §289 on the hermit; and §295 on "venerable junk and pomp"). There then comes the crucial denouement to the section with Nietzsche calling for the human to be "translated back into nature" so that we may become master over the numerous *vain* and *overly enthusiastic* interpretations that have to date been "scrawled and painted over the eternal basic text of *homo natura.*" In this way the human stands before itself "hardened in the discipline of science" and "before the rest of nature." Science shows us that we are not something higher than the rest of nature or have a different origin or descent (*Herkunft*). What is under attack in section 230 in part is the desire of metaphysicians who want to teach the human animal that it is somehow different from the rest of nature and not subject to the same conditions and processes of life. We need to beware of human vanity and resist the temptation to over-idealize the human. When we do this we fail to develop knowledge of its nature or character, for example, that it is engaged in processes of selection, incorporation, and interpretation.

In this section Nietzsche speaks of "translating" man back into nature; he encourages us to recognize the "basic text" of "homo natura," and he writes twice of this basic text, once stating it to be "eternal." What is the character of these references to nature and to the natural? We would go wrong here if we supposed that Nietzsche was inviting us to find a "text" that was cut off from all interpretation, such as a "being in itself" or an ontological truth. A metaphysical reading of the world conceals the text as interpretation, so unmasking this metaphysical illusion cannot simply amount to "removing from the text a cloak veiling the truth." Rather, "it means showing the clothing which an apparent 'nakedness' conceals, it means doing away with the rags and replacing them with clothes of flesh and blood."[18] In short, it means reading the "basic text" as will to power (a mode of interpretation as we have seen). Our being in the world involves at its most basic or fundamental level processes that characterize organic life as such, and this is why Nietzsche likens spirit to a "stomach." In this section, then, Nietzsche is not positing an original text of being or truth that is independent of interpretations: interpretation, we might say, goes all the way down and is what "life" is. Thus, instead of thinking that Nietzsche is asking us to discover some original text of natural human life—a set of brute facts about it and that would serve to limit its nature—we would do better to read him as calling for psychological and philological probity when it comes to dealing with the many "vain" and "fanciful" interpretations that have been scrawled over the eternal basic text and which conceal their nature as such by masking the fact that the text, any text, is only what it is through interpretation. The "eternal" basic text is one of constituted meanings, not meanings that are simply ever "given."

"WOMAN AS SUCH"

On one level the sections on man and woman (§§232–8) can be read as continuing the basic theme of section 230 on the two opposing wills of the mind or spirit. As Lampert notes, the final theme of the chapter is the warfare between the sexes, and "expresses in the natural divisions of gender the two inclinations of the mind, the basic will of the mind to create and sustain artful surfaces and the renegade will to penetrate to true depths."[19] On another level the sections continue Nietzsche's attack on the basic assumptions of "the democratic Enlightenment," principally the modern presumption in favor of equality, including equality between the sexes. Against this modern movement Nietzsche seems to take pleasure in being decidedly "antimodern" in his thinking on gender and the relation between the sexes. For example, he regards the attempt on the part of women to enlighten men about "woman as such" as "one of the worst developments of the general *uglification* of Europe" (§232). Woman is said to have a great deal of reason for shame—she conceals much pedantry, superficiality, schoolmarmishness, and so on—and until recent times this has been repressed and kept under wraps by her "*fear* of man," which she is now unlearning (ibid.). Woman's art is said to reside in grace and taking things lightly, and she becomes boring when she unlearns her true role in life (ibid.). It is thus of the worst kind of taste "when woman sets about becoming scientific," imitating man and his search for knowledge (ibid.). Perhaps through enlightenment woman is seeking a new adornment for herself and seeking mastery, but Nietzsche also thinks that woman does not want truth since her great art is the lie and her highest concern is with appearance and beauty (ibid.). Nietzsche regards it as a sign of real shallowness on our part that we have gone so badly wrong on the "fundamental problem of 'man and woman,'" in which we deny "the most abysmal antagonism" between the sexes, "the necessity of an eternally hostile tension," and dream of equal rights, equal education, and equal entitlements and obligations (§238). A man that has depth in his spirit and desires needs to think of woman as the Orientals are said to do, namely, conceiving woman as a possession, "as property that can be locked, as something predestined for service and achieving perfection in that" (ibid.). Through "the democratic inclination and basic taste" the so-called "weaker sex," although now in our modern era being treated with more respect than ever before, is in danger of losing her own special taste, as well as her fear of man: "the woman who 'unlearns fear' surrenders her most womanly instincts" (§239). In defiance of modern assumptions Nietzsche claims that with the rise of "the industrial spirit," which has triumphed over the military and aristocratic spirit, woman is in fact "*retrogressing.*" He contends that since the French Revolution the influence of woman in Europe has fallen in proportion to the rise of her rights and entitlements. In the cause of the "emancipation of woman" he detects "an almost masculine stupidity" (ibid.). In these sections, then, Nietzsche continues his unfashionable criticism of modern "free thinkers" and free thought in general. He attacks the "scholarly asses of the male sex" who are advising woman to defeminize herself and imitate the stupidities of modern European manliness and which characterize its sickness: "they would like to reduce woman to the level of 'general education,' probably even of reading the newspapers and talking about politics. Here and there they even want to turn women into freethinkers and scribblers . . ." (ibid.). In contrast to this "freethinking" appreciation of woman Nietzsche celebrates what it is in her that, so he claims, inspires respect: her uneducability, the cunning suppleness of a beast of prey, the tiger's claw under the glove, the inner wildness, and "the incomprehensibility, scope, and movement of her desires and virtues" (ibid.).

On the face of it, it would seem that Nietzsche's views on women underwent a transformation in the course of his intellectual development. As a recent biographer notes, Nietzsche fought hard to have women admitted to Basel University, and many of his closest associates and admirers throughout his life were women, several of whom were highly independent-minded and inclined to supporting and promoting the feminist cause.[20]

In the texts of his middle period, such as *WS*, for example, Nietzsche is sympathetic to the burgeoning woman's movement with a sound grasp of how women suffer at the hands of a paternalist society: a male culture is one which forces women into devalued social and familial roles and women are just as intelligent as men, so their debarment from having opportunities to exercise this intelligence amounts to a tragic waste. For the Nietzsche of this so-called "positivist" period, the future society is one that can only be built on the basis of the admittance of female intelligence.[21]

Nietzsche's position in *BGE* appears to be different and he now seems keen to attack the movement for female emancipation. However, as Maudemarie Clark has sought to show, his misogyny is not the simple or straightforward matter it appears to be. Her argument is that Nietzsche exhibits his misogyny on the level not of belief but sentiment and that it is deployed by him to illuminate the points he is making about philosophy in general and the will to truth in particular. For her the comments on feminism do not, in fact, amount to a rejection of it but rather are designed to challenge feminists: "to exhibit virtues comparable to what Nietzsche exhibits in dealing with his misogyny."[22] His "truths" about women form a labyrinth in which, Clark holds, we are meant to locate the threads of his own virtue. This provides us with a valuable insight into why Nietzsche's "truths" about woman and her virtues appear at this point in the chapter and the text: through his examination of the woman question, as we might call it, Nietzsche is exposing his own stupidity and as part of his quest for self-knowledge. For example, the seven women's proverbs (§237) clearly require interpretation and, as Clark suggests, might be expressions of resentment disguised as beliefs: "Nietzsche's 'truths' about woman might serve to exhibit for us (and to express) his misogynistic feelings, even though he is honest enough to admit that the assertions these feelings inspire are not really true."[23] As she acknowledges, there is a danger here, namely, denying that Nietzsche means and believes what he says about woman and intends the challenge they are designed to present. What is required is that we read Nietzsche carefully or astutely, and distinguish between what he does assert and what the reader is inclined to conclude from these assertions. In particular we need to recognize that throughout these sections Nietzsche writes of "woman as such" and "the eternal feminine," and thus his truths about "woman" are about a construction and not individual women. As Clark notes, Nietzsche is writing about a social construction—some imputed female essence—and individual women may not exemplify this.

We must, then, not lose sight of the convoluted character of *BGE* and that it presents challenges to the reader seeking to know how to read it. Nothing could be more misguided than to read sections 232–8 at face value. In section 231 Nietzsche signals to the reader that his approach to the question of "woman" is to be a complicated affair. For a start there is the fact that he is going to speak about, as he tells us, "woman as such" (*Weib an sich*) and this is clearly a construction: he is enough of a non-essentialist to appreciate that no "essence" independent of culture and history can be attributed to anything, including "woman." Nietzsche writes of the "Eternal Feminine" (§239) but he surely knows this to be a mystification.[24] Secondly, Nietzsche will offer "truths" that are his, that is, that reflect something of his nature and exposure to life, they are not intended to be truths set in stone, a set of definitive or ultimate truths. Rather, they are intended to reveal something about what lies concealed beneath the process of learning, "some granite of spiritual *fatum*, of predetermined decision and answer to predetermined selected questions" (§231). Thus, whenever some truly important problem is being addressed we need to appreciate the extent to which prejudices abound in which we often only finish learning rather than relearn (we discover how something is "settled in us"). Note that Nietzsche then goes on to talk about finding certain solutions to problems that then inspire strong faith in us, which we then call our "convictions," and that this is part of the process of self-knowledge and taking initial steps on it. Such steps are in fact "signposts to the problem we *are*," moreover, "to the great stupidity we are" (e.g., our unteachable and hidden spiritual *fatum*). Nietzsche is thus exposing himself in this part of the book and as a necessary aspect of the philosopher's commitment to honesty and seeing things for what they nakedly are: assumptions, presuppositions, prejudices—often dressed up as eternal verities and pearls of wisdom. We can also note that the most explicitly misogynistic remarks in this part of the book belong to the self-contained "Seven Women's Proverbs" (Kaufmann has "Seven Epigrams on Women") are not necessarily attributable to Nietzsche as their author. Of course, this does not mean that what Nietzsche says in this part of the book is not meant to offer instruction to women and the women's movement. Sections 232 and 239 in particular seem designed to alert women—including his female feminist friends—of the dangers of seeking emancipation as a straightforward desire to be "equal" to, or the same as, men. Nietzsche's "truths" on woman are a complicated tangle of prejudices, limitations, warnings, and attempts at genuine unfashionable insight. There is a mixture of devilry and concealment informing the presentation of his "truths" about woman as such, and this is in accord with how Nietzsche thinks free spirits practice their honesty. It is the workings of this key virtue that he is trying to illustrate in the denouement to part VII of Nietzsche's book.

CHAPTER 10

PART VIII: "ON PEOPLES AND FATHERLANDS"

In part II on "The Free Spirit," Nietzsche associates himself with one who both tempts (lures) and seeks, playing on the senses of *Versucher* (§42). He often has recourse to the language of *enchantment* (*Bezauberung*). And we have already noted that part of Nietzsche's project seems to be to create a community of fellow travelers (not followers) who are "free spirits" with whom he contrasts the *Freidenker*. He attempts to *enact* this with intensity and focus in the final two parts of the book. In part VIII Nietzsche surveys the current conditions of modern Europeans, his target audience, to assess their constitutions and identify resources they might potentially tap. He considers conditions and examples of cultural passage in the form of potentially fruitful interludes (*Zwischenbegebnis*) from one taste to another. And he performs his analysis by challenging and engaging the dominant currencies of identification and change in his contemporary times, especially the vocabularies of nationalism and evolution.

TASTE, NATIONALISM, AND FUTURE HUMANITY

Nietzsche focuses on taste insofar as it is directly related to the problem of values at the core of his thought. *How does what we want shape our values? How do our values indicate what we really truly want?* Recall Nietzsche thinks philosophy amounts to a "desire of the heart that has been filtered and made abstract" (§5), and this is indicative of *what* masters the other drives that comprise him and "*who he is*—that is, in what order of rank the innermost drives of his nature stand in relation to each other" (§6). Also recall section 2 in which Nietzsche anticipates that "one really has to wait for the advent of a new species of philosophers, such as have somehow another and converse taste and propensity [*umgekehrten Geschmack und Hang*] from those we have known so far—." Nietzsche explores how wants expressed as values are shaped. And he considers whether the process of formation admits of evaluation, and whether it affects the quality of the resulting valuations. Finally, he asks whether and how such desires might be reformed and transformed.

Tastes are indicative of more general terms of evaluation brought to bear in judgments and estimations. Nietzsche thinks these provide the terms on which whole ways of life are organized. Nietzsche's chapter "On Peoples and Fatherlands" brings the concern of taste to the fore as prelude to his final interrogation of the question *what is noble?* with which the book ends. It is an analysis of current conditions and possibilities for forming new terms of identification, new preferences and priorities, new tastes and desires that might very well make new ways of life possible. In a nutshell, the riddle Nietzsche both seeks to draw out and then suggests ways to resolve turns on negotiating the great variety of tastes that characterize modern human beings, who are tremendous mixtures as the result of mass transportation of goods, people, currencies, and ideas, which they need to synthesize without necessarily extinguishing or subsuming differences. In short, modern human beings share a much greater variety of tastes than has ever been possible before because they encounter so many more ways of life and forms of organization. This makes modern human existence at once incredibly fertile and vulnerable, since the various ways in which they have attempted to distinguish themselves have had rather deleterious effects and resulted in a motley assortment of tastes.

One dimension of the problematic nature of hybrid modern human beings is that they are incapable of loving or desiring anything in particular. Thus, they are in some respects less free than if they were subject to a tyrannical desire. Nietzsche thinks this because he associates what today we might describe as "capabilities" with having a set of life goals and orientations. This does not have to be any particular set of goals, of course, although Nietzsche does in fact investigate various forms and objects of desire of this sort (various tastes) to see whether or not they are enabling or incapacitating. Freedom for Nietzsche, in some respects, seems to be being capable, enabled, and potent in this sense.

We have been primed for discussion of Nietzsche's anticipated rehabilitation of modern humanity in the preceding sections. The new taste Nietzsche anticipates is related to the kind of "independence" identified in *BGE* II, where he considers it in terms of *not remaining stuck* to people, fatherlands, pity, science, virtues, or even our own "detachment" [*Unabhängigkeit*] (§41). The "free spirits" he heralds exhibit *Unabhängigkeit*, non-attachment in any permanent sense, and they overcome the temptations of hospitality mentioned in *BGE* 41 (cf. §44).[1] This means that they do not readily or strictly adopt the perspectives and values of the various cultures they encounter and they resist nationalistic chauvinism. The point, as already discussed in our Chapter 4, is *not* that we should never form attachments. Independence is not being *free* of attachments: contrary to popular understanding of Nietzsche's individualism, his "free spirits" are not free of meaningful and important connections with others. Rather, independence in the sense Nietzsche associates with the free spirits entails *not remaining stuck* in those associations. Thus, one of the dangers of the free spirit is *Gastfreundschaft* (§41), hospitality—too readily feeling at home in a foreign place and thus tempted to not leave, too welcoming of others to linger when they should move on. The free spirit will have to cultivate a knack for traveling freely among the various places (including people and ideas) he might roam without being isolated and alone (§44; contrast §207), adopting such places as his own, and yet free to continue his travels and form new and further associations. This challenge of identification and distinction is similar to the constitutional challenges Nietzsche thinks characterize the modern condition.

Parts VI and VII explore how moderns are "sick and exhausted" owing to the fact that they are such an extreme "mixture of types" (§208), and thus they *lack the ability* and *fail to experience the pleasure* of willing anything in particular. If what characterizes a type is what one ultimately *wants*—the desire or set of desires that rule within—then a mixture of types could lack an organizational structure sufficient to focus with any intensity on a single goal or set of goals that could effectively direct individual pursuits and activities. Such beings could find themselves unable to express any particular distinguishing will, and would lack *style* that constitutes character in this special sense. Nietzsche thinks this is particularly true of modern human beings gripped by what he calls the democratic taste, which is not only a preference for the lack of rule (anarchism) but also hatred of any rule (*misarchism*) (*GM* II:12). Types mixed in this way are unable to say, "Yes" or "No," much like the "last men" of *Z*, who like the ass can merely say, "Yea-Ah" to everything. Modern human beings, in sum, are lacking in their ability to exercise *judgment*, a theme discussed at length in Chapter 3 of this book. In section 210 Nietzsche implies that future philosophers, rather than being a new "type" like the others he has analyzed in the chapter (and which he scrutinizes elsewhere), will be multi-faceted and multi-capacitated. They will somehow overcome the problem of hybridity that characterizes their fellows (§§212 and 223), which is a form of barbarism masquerading as refinement (§224). And it is *this* accomplishment that characterizes what Nietzsche identifies as a kind of "higher spirituality" (§219). How such hybridity is connected with a problem of taste (and tastes as reflective of our powers of judgment that inform our values and *capacity to create* values) is elaborated in section 224, and this point is further emphasized and illustrated here in part VIII.

Processes of social and cultural organization are fraught with tension as there are great mixtures of peoples and ideas, and yet each expresses a desire to cling to something distinctive and self-preserving. Nietzsche seriously struggles with the notion of the *potential* fecundity of multiplicity, which is rare and fragile on account of the devastating incapacitation and leveling that can come with hybridity, which often results from attempts to organize such different parts. The challenge is to harness all of that difference for a productive purpose, to utilize it catalytically like a bow that makes use of tension to shoot at the most distant goals, as Nietzsche describes the potentially productive struggle against Platonism and Christianity in the preface. A possible purpose is a new nobility, but this is still undefined, and *remains* undefined, merely scouted by Nietzsche. But Nietzsche's ideas about the process, or the harnessing, are clearer by the end of this part: it requires utilizing the abundance of cultural resources by means of a new taste, a new set of wants and desires. Part VIII surveys these resources and their connections with various desires.

Nietzsche is also clear that what is needed (elsewhere: "'das Eine, was noth thut'"[2]) is not something that can be taught; rather, it must be *acquired*, learned through a different means.[3] A dominant concern in his works is exploring whether and how one can acquire a taste (a love, a dominating and domineering desire) for *life* itself:[4] "The question is to what extent it is life-promoting [*lebenfördernd*], life-preserving [*lebenerhaltend*], species-preserving [*Art-erhaltend*], perhaps even species-cultivating [*Art-züchtend*]. [. . .] To recognize untruth as a condition of life— that certainly means resisting accustomed value feelings in a dangerous way; and a philosophy that risks this would by that token alone place itself beyond good and evil" (§4). Nietzsche prepares to ask the question "what is Art-züchtend?" in tempting his readers to think *beyond good and evil*. This is merely a preparatory transition rather than the accomplishment of transformation, which for a time Nietzsche thought Wagner might realize.

WAGNER'S PROBLEM AND PROMISE

Nietzsche mentions many people by name in this part, but three loom especially large: Wagner, discussion of whom provides the bookends for part VIII; Beethoven, a significant transitional figure; and Nietzsche himself, who announces in his title and examines in this part the possibility of providing a *Vorspiel einer Philosophie der Zukunft*. The latter takes form here in part VIII as a project whose task is to mark a *Zwischenakt* (§245).[5] Nietzsche surveys possibilities for achieving philosophically what he claims Beethoven accomplished musically, to become a *Zwischen-Begebnis*. This transitional quality and status is directly linked with the problem of modern taste and the need and challenge of synthesizing without destroying the many that "want to become one." The feat requires harnessing productive cultural resources from the rich diversity of European cultures to create a stronger, more resourceful, more resilient *new* form of human organization, which is more specifically anticipated in the next and final part of the book.

Nietzsche sees Wagner drawing on an immense wealth of resources, a great variety of possible tastes and expressive capabilities. Moreover, in Wagner's efforts to create the artwork of the future, he engaged (though ultimately failed to resolve) the very problem Nietzsche thinks moderns, particularly, face: he attempted to draw on the collecting forces of the arts and organize them into a significant whole.[6] Appreciating the nature of this challenge and its possibilities requires us to draw on several other important discussions of Wagner in Nietzsche's works, not the least of which is *BT*, of course. In fact, we might regard *BGE* VIII as recasting in more elaborate terms just what it was that he thought was Wagner's promise in the second half of *BT*. That he is not finished with understanding that problem, why and how Wagner failed to deliver, and why it matters *that* he failed, is evident in Nietzsche's relentless efforts to articulate and reframe the problem in his later writings, each of which has significant sections devoted to Wagner and his type.

In *BT*, Nietzsche extends the hope that Wagner's operas might achieve for modern Europeans what tragedy did for the ancient Greeks, which Nietzsche regarded not merely as a *product* of a culture already vibrant but rather as a vehicle for *producing* culture. Put another way, Nietzsche considered the ancient Greeks *as becoming Greeks*—as *becoming what they are*—in and through their creation of and participation in the tragedies. The tragedies were not simply representations of views about the significance of human beings and their relation to the gods; rather, participation in the tragic festivals *forged* those relations. And ultimately, Nietzsche thought these were maximally affirmative in terms of their judgments of the value of human existence despite all of the pain and suffering it entails. The evidence of this affirmation is a particular taste he thought the tragedies evinced—in short, they expressed a *taste for life* in rendering beautiful (through the tragedy as a whole) what was otherwise unbearable: the senseless sufferings of human beings. Nietzsche conceived this as redemptive—human existence was positively revalued—and in sharp contrast to the moral, particularly Christian, model of redemption that locates meaning and significance of human existence in relation to a supreme *otherworldly* giver of meaning. The terms of the latter are familiar: human life and worldly existence is fundamentally and irremediably base. Human significance is measured in relation to the amount of suffering and sacrifice offered for it by an external source (e.g., an almighty god, who is conveniently off the hook for creating the mess in the first place). The enormity of the sacrifice (permitting the murder of his own son, trading his "life" for that of all humankind), supremely enhances the value of human existence at the same time it generates an irreconcilable debt. Nietzsche's *BT* sought to comprehend the different logic of redemption that gave tragedies their culturally formative powers and the relation between those effects and individuals who experienced them.

Nietzsche's story about the dynamic relation between the artistic (world-creative) forces of the Apollinian and Dionysian is familiar, but a quick recap is in order to understand how this relates to the problem of Europe and its future, which is the main and overarching concern of Nietzsche's *BGE*. What Nietzsche calls the Apollinian and Dionysian, and particularly how he characterizes *their relation* in *BT*, can be regarded as mapping to (not strictly the same as) the relation between the dual tendencies of "the basic will of the spirit" as Nietzsche describes it in section 230. Recall that the names Apollo and Dionysus are used by the early Nietzsche to distinguish tendencies of giving form, creating images, making distinctions, and individualizing (Apollinian) from those that seek to dissolve distinctions, obliterate boundaries, and celebrate formlessness (Dionysian). Ordinarily directly opposed, these tendencies are engaged in a dynamic (which in *BT* is dialectical) struggle evident in the development of the arts and various other life processes of creation and destruction.

In *BGE*, a similar, though non-dialectical, dynamic is located in the "basic will of the spirit" in terms of a tendency to dominate, appropriate, and assimilate—to achieve a certain definite unity from out of the multiplicity of experience, which we might also associate with efforts to master nature through systematic projects to characterize and control it—and an opposing tendency, which Nietzsche loosely associates with willful ignorance in which one "merely accepts such and such a delight in all uncertainty and ambiguity, a jubilant self-enjoying in the arbitrary narrowness and secrecy of some nook [. . .] a self-enjoyment in the caprice of all these expressions of power." At first glance, it might appear that the first tendency identified is the same as the Apollinian, and that which takes delight in uncertainty and ambiguity the Dionysian, but strict identification is problematic.

We note a *resemblance to* rather than strict *correlation between* these two dynamics, since they do not seem to be identical and might well reflect a revision of Nietzsche's earlier account of these two basic tendencies. The will to ignorance is not the same as the Dionysian, for Nietzsche in section 230 also associates it with intentional deception and *form-giving* rather than dissolving. In *BT*, the Dionysian is explicitly what dissolves form. In *BGE*, what he calls a "will to appearance" (*Willen zum Schein*) includes a lack of regard, suspension of craving for plumbing the depths of existence, seeing existence *as* appearance rather than *behind or beneath* appearance; whereas in *BT*, the Apollinian is chiefly linked with the will to appearance, the "veil of Maya," which provides the illusion of individuation, and the Dionysian is linked with the perspective that sees behind appearance to recognize the basic character of existence in which the individual is mere illusion, a momentary and fleeting appearance from out of the churning chaos of the world. Beneath the veil, there is ceaseless striving, much like, though significantly different in its import, Schopenhauer's view of the world as will.[7] So, in *BGE*, that which seeks to appropriate and assimilate strives to *forge* or *create* a kind of unity out of multiplicity; in *BT* a primal unity is disclosed, discovered, glimpsed in the Dionysian perspective beyond the illusory images of the Apollinian. But in *BGE*, the opposing tendency, the *will to appearance* is not really Apollinian, for it denies there is anything beyond appearance, that there is appearance and nothing else, and it regards the real *as merely* apparent but suffers no loss or grief on this account.

Yet, the relation between the opposing tendencies—Apollinian and Dionysian, will to knowledge and will to ignorance—is quite similar: Nietzsche conceives both in agonistic terms in which opposing tendencies *potentially* further each other's ends rather than cancel or overcome them. For example, in section 230, Nietzsche couches this productive tension in terms analogous to digestion. Were it not for the fact that the will to ignorance "shuts its doors" and "says no," it would not be possible for the will to knowledge to have anything in particular to cling to, to distinguish from out of the flow of what is perceived; there could be no proper experience as distinct from this flow. Thus, the will to ignorance (in a dynamic reminiscent of the current view of neurological development) has a "pruning" effect on the reaches of the will to knowledge, and makes it possible for what is known, appropriated, and synthesized to stand out as something specific—this allows for a genuine unity distinguished from the chaotic multiplicity of which its components were once a part.

We see a similar dynamic at work in the cultural projects of *BT* and *BGE*: how is it that a multiplicity (of cultural characteristics: French, German, English; or creative possibilities) becomes united, becomes potent rather than dysfunctional? Nietzsche, of course, is not the first to ask this question, and arguably it is *the question* that is top of mind among his contemporary Europeans, though they grapple with it from somewhat different perspectives, such as *what is German? How do we unite the many fiefdoms and principalities that have characterized Germany and unite them in a nation state? What distinguishes the Germans from French, and how are they to be united?* Put another way, Nietzsche sees his fellow Germans (and English, and French, but particularly his German compatriots) asking the question, *How do we become what we are?* Nietzsche thinks there are better and worse ways to set about answering this ultimate question, and for the most part his contemporaries have failed, quite miserably.

Right from the start, the Germans have failed to understand that this question is fundamentally oriented toward the *future*. The answer does not lie in past origins; there is no specific and necessary historical destiny: it requires a measure of invention, and is not simply a matter of discovery. As a product of invention (recall the relation between finding, inventing, and discovering in §12; cf. §223), this will be a creative product that requires artistic resources (which might include *making a claim* to a particular destiny as a way of setting a goal), and just as significantly, a particular sense of taste. In fact, insofar as the question *What is German?* is about ways of living that follow from shared ideals and goals, conceptions of distinctive and definitive characteristics or types, it is fundamentally a matter of taste; thus, *becoming German* will turn on questions of style. But there is more, for one does not create ex nihilo, and projects of becoming and establishing those distinguishing qualities occur in a variety of ways. From early on, particularly in *BT*, where Nietzsche is specifically concerned with the fate of Germany rather than all of Europe as he is in *BGE*, he is critical of the project of establishing excellence simply on the basis of the achievement of military superiority (e.g., *UM* I). Successful demonstration of force alone does not establish *nobility*, and we clearly see Nietzsche circle back on this concern again in *BGE* where he considers the cultural resources and creative (as well as decadent) inheritances of European peoples. This concern is evident in his reflection on the significance and value of the achievements of Bismarck in passages discussed below; and in *BT*, it was the status of the German victory in the Franco-Prussian war that spurred Nietzsche's rumination of the questions of what *makes* a people (how is a social and cultural entity formed, on what basis does it become *one*) and how does it possibly become great—or, more precisely, how, in its formation, does it take on the goal of pursuing greatness? What does this entail? In *BGE*, Nietzsche considers this on a grander scale than he did in his first book. Wagner plays an important but different role in each of these accounts.

Wagner represents for Nietzsche great potential as a transitional figure, though Nietzsche expresses rather different impressions of this prospect from the perspectives of his early and later works; yet it is important to notice that the core challenge remains. In short, Nietzsche thinks Wagner nearly but ultimately failed to achieve a dynamic and productive synthesis harnessing and preserving the variety of human cultural and physiological inheritance. Nietzsche's own quasi-biographical *EH* illuminates this problem and his anticipated solution. In the chapter "Why I am so Wise," he focuses on the resources and liabilities he inherited from his parents. At the same time, he diminishes their role in determining him when he writes: "to be related to one's parents is the most typical sign of commonality. Higher types have their origins infinitely further back, on which at long last, an atavism must be unified, retained. Great individuals are the most ancient individuals."[8] This suggests the higher type Nietzsche conceives is someone who somehow accesses and taps other, ancient characteristics, and is perhaps distinguished by virtue of the depth and reach of ancestral resources. Indeed, this is how Nietzsche describes himself earlier in the same section when he writes, "But as a Pole I am also an uncanny atavism. One must go back centuries to discover in this noblest race of men pure instincts to the degree that I represent them."[9] There is a wealth of human resources, a trove belonging to humanity as such, to the "household of the soul" (§20), to recall the metaphorical social structure discussed earlier. Nietzsche explores whether and, if so, how one may tap, educe, activate, and bring them to life in the order one is.[10] Nietzsche's Wagner exemplifies a mixture characteristic of modern humanity that nearly became *synthetic* and *consummatory*: "What flavors and forces, what seasons and climes are not mixed here! It strikes us now as archaic, now as strange, tart, and too young, it is just as capricious as it is pompous-traditional, it is not infrequently saucy, still more often coarse and rude" (§240). It "has the pride of presupposing two centuries of music as still living, if it is to be understood." And yet, Wagner fails to achieve this synthesis or produce an artwork that would embody such unity. Instead, Wagner remains in Nietzsche's eyes primarily an actor rather than a musician insofar as his artistic effects are largely dramatic and the kind of unity his works exhibit is achieved artificially through the technical use of the *leitmotiv*, leaving his works with a superficial organization that resolves in a decadent, ultimately pessimistic form of redemption. The latter is particularly problematic because of the deformed conception of love it advances. It is here we clearly see the relation of Nietzsche's ideas about taste and loving life, the estimation of life as a basis for creative valuation and human productivity. What it would take and what is at stake in shaping such orientations—taste on a cultural rather than merely personal scale—occupies much of book VIII.

ORIENTING THE FUTURE: NATIONALISM AND TASTE

In section 241, an imagined dialogue between two old patriots conjures a specter of a statesman (Bismarck), who effectively shapes the will of the masses through a process that includes "making their spirit narrow [*eng*], their taste 'national.'" The two disagree over what constitutes greatness in a statesman— whether sheer might and force constitute greatness or whether something more is required. While it seems clear Nietzsche has sympathies with the patriot who challenges the conception of greatness defined in terms of raw power to shape in this way, the narrating voice of the observer of the dispute (Nietzsche?) rests assured that the strong (however defined) will soon be mastered by ones even stronger, and the spiritual "flattening" of a people will be recompensed by the deepening of another.

The next section makes it clear these are not necessarily separate peoples (i.e., nations); rather, the spiritual flattening (in §242 "leveling and mediocritization of man") is somehow preparatory for deepening the spirit more generally. In this part of the book, Nietzsche is more confident than he is earlier where the outcome of this process is less certain. These sections should be compared with the rather terrifying images in sections 61 and 62, where Nietzsche anticipates the "philosopher who will make use of religions for his cultivation and education just as he will make use of whatever political and economic states are at hand" (§61). Section 241 is particularly illuminating of Nietzsche's conception of strength as something other than raw power (political or spiritual), which simply seeks overcoming and is neither good nor evil (cf. §230). Furthermore, as discussed in the next chapter, Nietzsche's concern is with "nobility" (*Was ist Vornehm?*) rather than "greatness" (*Grösse*), reinforcing the distinctions suggested here.

Despite efforts to define and draw distinctions among the emergent modern European nations, Nietzsche thinks Europeans are physiologically becoming increasingly similar and "detached from the conditions under which races originate that are tied to some climate or class" (§242); thus they are more "independent [*Unabhängigkeit*] of any *determinate* milieu that would like to inscribe itself for centuries in body and soul with the same demands" (ibid.).[11] The result is an emerging new type of human being whose fate is not yet determined: it is at once free of national demands (*übernationalen*) and specific conditions of place[12]—it is nomadic—and has "a maximum of the art and power of its typical distinction" (§242).

Thus, the very same conditions that "level" potentially make possible the "birth" of "exceptional human beings of the most dangerous and attractive quality" (§242). Nietzsche's explanation for this is that the exercise of the adaptive power rendering people more pliable and subservient unintentionally provides conditions for the emergence of an opposite type: "stronger and richer than perhaps ever before" on account of their freedom from the prejudices of other forms of thought and social and political organization. When one is taught to obey only one master, there is only one object of resistance to be overcome (in contrast with the many influences of culture, place, and ancestry that might otherwise prejudice one's views). Moreover, such conditions provide the greatest resistance (produce a "so tense a bow" to "shoot for distant goals" *BGE* P). Potentially this results in a situation with significant possibilities for freedom. Nietzsche names this phenomenon *tyranny*,[13] which refers to a certain form of ruling, both politically, and spiritually (cf. §9 on philosophy as "*this tyrannical impulse itself* the most spiritual will to power, to the 'creation of the world,' to the *causa prima*"). Also notice how Nietzsche's characterization of the relation between democracy and tyranny nearly perfectly mirrors that of the Platonic Socrates in Plato's *Republic* book VIII, except that Nietzsche seems to think tyranny is *conducive* to the production of those who turn out well while Socrates thinks it is the worst form of rule of all, furthest from the best.

Section 244 provides a brief "vivisection" of the German soul, beginning with its construction or composition. It is essentially "manifold," Nietzsche claims, "of diverse origins, more put together and superimposed than actually built." Nietzsche's earlier suggestions for replacement conceptions of the atomistic model of the soul, including "soul as subjective multiplicity" (§12), are particularly apt in this case, for he thinks the Germans have "many souls," are *multi-souled* (§244) and are "the most monstrous mixture and medley of races." They thus *potentially* crystallize a problem of the future of Europe, which as Nietzsche sees it is to find a way to put together a soul (the likes of which has never been known) from the most productive and creative resources of the various European constituents. The language Nietzsche uses to describe this mixture is reminiscent of his account of Wagner at the opening of the part—"How disorderly and rich this whole psychic household is!"—and it becomes increasingly clearer throughout this chapter that Nietzsche is tracing the ancestral inheritances (*Herkunft*), including potencies and liabilities, of the "good Europeans" he anticipates. Nietzsche's goal is to locate the spiritual resources of the Europe that "wants to become one" (§256).[14]

The Germans allegedly love what is "unclear . . . unformed . . . blurred"; they thus embody one aspect of the creative dynamic Nietzsche identifies in the struggle between the will to knowledge and the will to ignorance in section 230 and the creative tension of the Apollinian and Dionysian discussed above.

As a multi-souled lover of what is unclear and unformed, the German is a model of becoming: "The German himself *is* not, he *becomes*, he 'develops'[;] 'Development' [*Entwicklung*] is therefore the truly German find and hit in the great realm of philosophical formulas." However, Nietzsche thinks this is currently poorly executed: Europe does not need to become German, but by tapping German resources, future Europeans could be produced on account of this native capacity to develop. Another significant feature of the Germans Nietzsche highlights is their "Widerspruchs-Natur": their contradictory nature, which is systematized by Hegel and "set to music by Richard Wagner." This will be an important resource and capacity that Nietzsche will want to exploit in the formation of future humanity, but he finds its current execution deficient, as discussed above.[15]

Nietzsche's discussion of the differences of taste in the period of the history of music between Mozart and Beethoven (§245) is key, since it provides important clues to how Nietzsche regards his own position and project as *between* states, propelled by conditioning a new taste. While Mozart consummates the end of a significant period of "European taste," Beethoven is "an interlude," intermediate and transitional, evincing conflicting and contradictory tendencies, "a style break": at once a "mellow old soul that constantly breaks and an over-young future soul that constantly *comes.*" Beethoven is a *Zwischenakt* of *European* rather than *merely German* taste. Recall that part IV is titled *Sprüche und Zwischenspiele*. We shall see in the following chapter that Nietzsche's description of his own thoughts and ideas, his own contributions (as *Vorspiel*) to the *Philosophie der Zukunft*, bears resemblance to this portrait of Beethoven. Yet Nietzsche hopes for a better fate than what he sees in the example of Beethoven who musically expressed and captured the spirit of Europe at a time when it "dreamed with Rousseau, danced around the freedom tree of the Revolution, and finally almost worshipped before Napoleon." But that feeling—and the degree to which it engendered a sense of shared future, sameness, oneness, or unity, but in a different sense from the egalitarianism of democracy—is nearly gone. We have *knowledge* of this feeling but are no longer able to actually *experience it*, to truly feel in that way.[16] What follows Beethoven is romanticism and its attendant ideals of democracy, "second rate" and evident of "small taste" as indicated in the decline toward *fatherlandishness*.

This section not only provides some insight into Nietzsche's possible self-conception as a break in taste and style and one who prepares the way for a legislator of a kind of taste that would *give* Europe a future, it also suggests what is problematic about fatherlandishness: it fails to articulate lofty and worthwhile goals, fails to claim a sense of nobility, and instead claims to *find* (rather than *invent* or *project*) already existing distinguishing characteristics of a group of people. At this point in the text it becomes clearer that Nietzsche is interested in the formation of a *public* rather than politics. In fact, it is politics, and the misdirection and perversions of passion that can go along with it, that Nietzsche thinks *prevents* the formation of the greater union he envisions. This makes Nietzsche's work similar to that of the Platonic Socrates, whose concern in the *Republic* is to ascertain how it is possible for a people to "all sing the same song together" (*Rep.* 432a,b). Nietzsche is interested in the mechanisms, procedures, and practices that make "mine-saying" possible, and the content of such values. Thus a "tyranny of the spirit" that shapes a people is quite different from a political boundary achieved militarily.

We see this notion recur throughout the chapter, as for example, in section 251, where Nietzsche is brutally dismissive of German nationalism and anti-Semitism and emphasizes cultural vitality as indicated by its ability to digest and incorporate difference in a process engaging the "great play and fight of forces" (§251). Such activity involves more than simply subduing or excluding opposition and difference (cf. the "hereditary art of commanding and obeying" with §19), insofar as it sees its opposition (and the activity of *opposing*) as a resource rather than something to be avoided or overcome. In this section, Nietzsche designates "the 'European problem'" as one of "cultivation of a new caste that will rule Europe." It becomes increasingly clear this is a *cultural* and *historical* problem rather than a *political* one, and that it requires organization and cultivation of *cultural* resources. In sum, it is a creative project. Thus Nietzsche's interests in style and taste stem directly from their relation to value and cultural productivity.

Following the section about the expression, creation, and invention of European taste, cultural identity and ideals in section 245, Nietzsche shifts in section 246 to discussion of the reception, appreciation, comprehension, and incorporation of style, as for example, in his reminder about the musicality of language, the extent to which the tempo of thought is related to *what* one can think, and the activities of reading and writing. Nietzsche discusses these matters earlier in the book (e.g., §28) and acts upon them throughout. For example, part IV's *Sentenzen* must be read in light of what Nietzsche writes here: "There is art in every good sentence (*Satze*)—art that must be figured out if the sentence is to be understood! A misunderstanding about its tempo, for example, and the sentence itself is misunderstood." Nietzsche endeavors to create a style that can be read and heard in the way he imagines as most likely to facilitate or realize the grand style he heralds in section 245.

Section 247 makes observations about the incorporation of style and the musicality of language, and the acts of reading, writing, and listening.[17] He discusses specific elements of style that make a difference, particularly the aural dimensions of literature, ideas he employs and practices in the *Sprüche* and *Sentenzen* of part IV: to create a style that can be heard and read in a new way.[18] He emphasizes the *public* expectations, anticipations, and comprehension of style. Drawing on his earlier work on ancient rhetoric and extending the emergent research in the physiology of sensation, Nietzsche notices that a period is not merely a convention for punctuation but also a "physiological unit [. . .] held together by a single breath." Nietzsche contrasts the public of the Roman forum with that of the pulpit in terms of what commands and what comprehends within those spheres. This sheds light on the particular way Nietzsche's discussion has *political* relevance, because it is not especially concerned with the micro-politics of the modern nation-states of Europe or the theoretical development and practical application of liberal democratic political theory. It is more consonant with the Platonic sense of concern for the *conditions for the possibility of a republic*, what allows a "'people'" to "say 'mine' and 'not mine'" about the same things (*Rep.* 432b). Nietzsche's concern is not merely with the *form* of this relation but with the *content* of what is affirmed, its character. Thus we find a contrast between unity achieved through military exploits, as in the case of Bismarck, and with the tyranny of the spirit, which Nietzsche finds in Napoleon, and the content of the values thus affirmed. So, style and how it leads to or produces a taste that is shared plays a significant role in Nietzsche's ruminations on future philosophy and the production of over-humanity (cf. §250 below). Of particular interest is the physicality of the style he anticipates: syllables and words *weigh*, sentences "strike, leap, plunge, run, run out."

CREATING THE FUTURE

Throughout his writings, Nietzsche characterizes cultural productivity in terms of tensions of opposed elements. He frequently cites sexual reproduction as exemplary and paradigmatic of broader creative cultural and historical forces. This is evident as early as *BT*, where the forces of the Apollinian and Dionysian "give birth" to tragic culture and all of the philosophical, artistic, and political achievements associated with it, and his further association of the characteristics of tendencies or forces as evident in various different cultures and as mapped to sexual characteristics. Thus, in *BT*, Nietzsche comments on the sexual agonistics at the roots of what he calls the "Aryan" myth of Prometheus and "Semitic" myth of the fall (*BT* 9). In both cases he finds a dynamic of opposition expressed in gendered relations. The Prometheus story of sacrilege is associated with a form of masculine activity whereas the myth of the fall revolves around succumbing to (ultimately *subjected* to, passively) feminine seduction or lust. We find throughout Nietzsche's writings that he takes sexual reproduction as a paradigm of creativity. This is a variation within a tradition that stretches back to the pre-Socratics and is clearly evident in Platonic philosophy, as for example, in the *Symposium*, and the Romantic tradition, for example, Goethe's projection of the Eternal Feminine.[19] Elsewhere, Nietzsche emphasizes the extent to which these tendencies are in opposition and contest, conflict. These ideas are clearly related to Nietzsche's controversial ideas about women and his concern that women not become just like men, that men and women potentially embody this dynamic, literally, both physically and culturally. Just as he does not want Europe to become one in the sense of unified on the basis of identity, he does not want humanity to become one sexually. For this reason, he is motivated to preserve, perhaps even heighten, the differences between men and women.

In section 248, sexual tension is generally cast in erotic terms involving love and lust, but Nietzsche also notes this same tendency is expressed in domineering situations, and he considers this tension as the root cause of misunderstanding (cf. §§85 and 238). This section reiterates the dynamic of power explored in section 230, discussed above, where Nietzsche characterizes a "'basic will of the spirit'" as a dynamic opposition of powers of appropriation and exclusion. This duality is a simplification and general characterization of the great play of forces Nietzsche regards as constitutive of "life," and the basis of the "social structure" of commanding and obeying forces contributing to the "synthetic concept 'I'" (§19). This further reinforces the idea of drawing on all of the capacities of Europe for creative productivity rather than simply pursuing *unity* as in the sense that "Europe wants to become one." Different conceptions of women and love (as they relate to the prospects of fecundity and the kind of creative tension and opposition necessary for productive fertilization) are found throughout Nietzsche's writings. This is crucial to Nietzsche's ultimate preference for Bizet's Carmen over Wagner's Kundry, as discussed below.

Section 249 underscores the difficulty of the task of *becoming*, both in terms of what it would take to become something greater and what it takes to engage in such a process of organization at all. It is not as simple as identifying some new worthwhile goal and then setting about pursuing it. In the context of producing future Europe, Nietzsche writes, our situation is such that "what is best in us we do not know—we cannot know." The point here is that our current virtues are not necessarily indicative of our greatest capacities. Nietzsche calls them "tartuffery," extravagant expressions of what we currently value, of our present tasks and preferences. Such stylings stand in contrast with the "grand style" in morality discussed in the next section. We might see the problem of European identity and its future becoming as similar to that of individual becoming; and both seem to be related to what Nietzsche calls *spiritual fatum* in section 231. In *EH*, Nietzsche describes the difficulty of "becoming what one is" when he writes, "to become what one is" requires "one must not have the faintest notion *what* one is" (*EH* "Clever" 9). This idea is a bit puzzling, particularly in light of the previously mentioned context of "giving style to one's character" (*GS* 290), which suggests something of a project that one aims to implement, some activity one deliberately pursues. But, considered in light of the relation between taste and forms of life, we can see that what Nietzsche has in mind is the realization of some sort of necessity, a way of life rather than a particular project one plans and executes. In other words, becoming what one is might be properly thought as an expressive activity rather than a projection that implies some gap between what one is and what one does or aims to be.

Nietzsche briefly treats what he calls "the grand style" in morality in section 250, and this provides an important indication of how he thinks problems of morality and valuation revolve around questions taste. The "grand style" engages a struggle with the infinite and sublime thereby bringing about a spiritual stretching and transformation much like the slave revolt in morality he identifies in *GM* I:6, where he claims that the "*essentially dangerous* form of human existence" that the priests realize provides the condition for the soul "in a higher sense" to "acquire depth." We can think of "the grand style" as a higher order value in the sense that it pertains to wholesale judgments of the estimation of life, and thereby influences the whole scope and orientation of values rather than just a particular value or set of values. And Nietzsche envisions the creation of a future community that draws together European resources and utilizes what he calls "spiritual perception" (§252), which selects and coordinates the various capacities to be tapped.[20] These capacities are further surveyed in sections 252–4, where Nietzsche claims that the English are more *pious* than the Germans insofar as they are "gloomier, more sensual, stronger in will, and more brutal" and "music-less."

The relation between Nietzsche's conception of the music of the future and the philosophy of the future becomes clearer when we recognize the relation between problems of taste and value as they relate to the value of truth (recall the opening of *BGE*), and the difference it potentially makes when this is scrutinized (arguably, the subject of at least *BGE* I–III). If we came to have different tastes, we might not only love (and value) different things but also engage in valuation *differently*. In such a case, "revaluation" would refer to *the form of the activity of valuing*, rather than replacement or reordering of values.[21] This seems to be Nietzsche's interest in the relation between health and music and his anticipation of a supra-European music, a synthesis of cultural and historical resources that *might* produce a "European of the future." Wagner can be regarded as a contemporary example of one who came closest (yet ultimately failed) to realizing a supranational community; he realized "*supra-German* sources and impulses," a combination Germanic and French sentiments and tastes, which nevertheless superseded and surpassed both. Siegfried is offered as an exemplar of "that *very free* man who may indeed be much too free, too hard, too cheerful, too healthy, too *anti-Catholic* for the taste of ancient and mellow cultured peoples" (§256).[22] Future philosophers, free-spirited "higher types" Nietzsche anticipates, will have to be more than knowers—they will have *to be* something new, *signify* (*zu bedeuten*) something new, represent (*darzustellen*) new values.[23] Nietzsche considers this creative project potentially to begin through the creation of "a new beauty and seduction" of the sort he finds in Bizet, whom he calls the musician of the "good European" (§254).

Nietzsche's preference for Bizet over Wagner is curious and turns on at least two points. First, Bizet is musically superior to Wagner in Nietzsche's later estimation just because by that time, Nietzsche considers Bizet a *musician* whereas he thinks Wagner is really an *actor* (see especially *CW*). The second major point of comparison can be made in juxtaposing Kundry and Carmen. In this respect, Nietzsche once more draws on his ideas about sexual agonistics and sexual reproduction as paradigmatic of creative fecundity. Carmen's consuming love of life exudes what Nietzsche later calls a "burnt sensibility" in language that recalls the end of his *BGE*, to be treated in the next chapter. Bizet's *Carmen* expresses "love translated back into nature": "love as *fatum*, as fatality, cynical, innocent, cruel—and precisely in this a piece of nature. That love which is war in its means, and at the bottom deadly hatred of the sexes!" (*CW* 2). Nietzsche associates this form of passion with "the south" and the "Mediterraneanization" of music he anticipates in section 255 and elaborates in *CW* 3.[24] Nietzsche goes on to contrast this form of passion, which he also associates with a form of elevating *pathos* needed for philosophy (*CW* 2), with the notion of love as selfless. While love as *fatality* is fecund, love as selfless is sterile, "chaste." Wagner's Kundry, we are told in section 47, is a flesh and blood personification of the *type* "das religiöse Wesen," who dies in her moment of redemption, which was accomplished by Parsifal whose powers stem from his chastity, which is achieved through renunciation, and compassion. What Nietzsche writes of Wagner's heroines generally is doubly true of her: "[. . .] Wagner's heroines never have children? *They can't.*—" (*CW* 9). Kundry fails to tempt Parsifal even when she lures him with mother's love—she neither gives birth nor succeeds in becoming a surrogate. She becomes free, free as a bird, in fact, only through the redemptive act of Parsifal's compassion, and only in release from human life.[25]

So, Nietzsche's task looking ahead will be to inquire about a possible sense of nobility that might be ignited and pursued by the alternative conceptions of love and redemption that he finds in Bizet rather than Wagner. Nevertheless, he finds Wagner's case—at once most promising *and* disastrous—to be quite instructive concerning the promises and pitfalls of this prospect and process.

CHAPTER 11

PART IX: "WHAT IS NOBLE?"

QUESTIONING

The concluding part of *BGE* has the curious distinction of having a question as its title, although this is not reflected in every English translation of the work. *Was ist Vornehm?* Nietzsche asks. It could well be that Nietzsche's question here is rhetorical so that little of great consequence is lost by omission of the punctuation—"*What is noble*, you ask? I, Nietzsche, will set you straight here at the end of the book." But if there is a real question in Nietzsche's mind about the nature, status, and possibilities of nobility, then there is quite a problem if this is literally lost in the translation of the title to the concluding part. One might miss the fact that there is a real inquiry here, that perhaps something is not yet known, still to be determined. Or, if it is Nietzsche's goal to *open up* questioning, to start rather than complete an inquiry, this would surely be jeopardized in omission of the question mark.

Readers of *BGE* often approach the book at least vaguely familiar with Nietzsche's apparent preference for noble values and forms of valuation over those slavish as outlined in *GM*, which was written after *BGE*. Conceptually, then, many read *BGE* looking backwards from what they regard as the main ideas of that text, but this is also problematic. It is easy to assume that the discussion of nobility in *GM* is immediately relevant if not identical to the *question* of nobility in *BGE*, but this is not at all clear. Moreover, the relation between Nietzsche's discussion of the prehistoric roots and invention of morality and his anticipation of the self-overcoming of Christianity—how it is necessary, what it entails, and what follows from it—is not at all clear and requires considered analysis. The expectation that the discussion of prehistoric nobility in *GM* reflects Nietzsche's ideas about future nobility might also predispose the reader to think that where Nietzsche raises the question of nobility in *BGE* he will provide an answer. Expectations are heightened by Nietzsche's own expressions of anticipation for great things to come throughout *BGE*. Nearly all of the preceding parts conclude with Nietzsche's shrill and sometimes histrionic expectations that another world is possible, one in which there is a reconsideration and reevaluation of what we currently extol as "good," that the axis of good and evil might be replaced or somehow superceded. So, we might arrive at Nietzsche's concluding question *Was ist Vornehm?* rightfully expecting to encounter some outline of a new nobility. Instead of looking forward to Nietzsche's next text (*GM*) for clues about the significance of his title question, one might look backward to *Z* and its peculiar focus on development, particularly in its account of self-overcoming and the perpetual process of *zugrunde gehen*, of going to ruin that characterizes a crucial part of the dynamic development of under-going and overcoming. Rather than solely giving us a new table of values at the end of *BGE*, Nietzsche unravels his own project and admires its demise. Where we might expect to find Nietzsche planting his flag *jenseits*—beyond—we instead find things falling apart. What follows from this largely anti-climactic conclusion is unclear, but we conclude our own text by exploring a few possibilities.

NIETZSCHE'S ANTICIPATIONS

Throughout *BGE*, Nietzsche builds expectations for what might be glimpsed on the horizon he sketches in the book—that *beyond*, that *future* indicated in the title and subtitle of the work. Nietzsche dramatically builds and heightens his readers' anticipations such that when they arrive at his concluding part, they might readily expect the completion of a sketch he has been drawing throughout. Examining the organizing structure of the book as a whole, we notice that nearly each part concludes with Nietzsche's vision of some possibility he imagines for the future and/or which he intends to realize in the course of the book. One of these is surely the perspective he anticipates near the end of part I "On the Prejudices of the Philosophers." In the penultimate section (§22), Nietzsche wonders whether it might be possible to reach similar conclusions about the world based on very different perspectives and modes of interpretation. He speculates this is indeed possible: a perspective that "picture[s] the unexceptional and unconditional aspects of all 'will to power' so vividly that almost every word, even the word 'tyranny' itself, would eventually seem unsuitable, or a weakening and attenuating metaphor" could still lead to a conclusion that the world is "necessary" and "calculable," not because nature is lawful but rather "because [laws] are absolutely *lacking*, and every power draws its ultimate consequences at every moment."

Further, from this new perspective, Nietzsche anticipates and describes in the final section of part I (§23) what he calls his "physio-psychology." Someone who achieves the perspective he scouts in earlier sections would "regard even the affects of hatred, envy, covetousness, and the lust to rule as conditions of life, as factors which, fundamentally and essentially, must be present in the general economy of life (and must, therefore, be further enhanced if life is to be further enhanced)."[1] This idea certainly can be nauseating, dangerous, and even painful, which is why he thinks his project is not advisable for many, if any, others to follow, so we might rightly expect there is a rather exclusive group anticipated and summoned here. Those admitted, those with the stomach for it, are invited to come aboard and "sail right *over* morality, [as] we crush, we destroy perhaps the remains of our own morality." We might be justified in expecting that at the end of the voyage a certain form of nobility would replace the battered morality Nietzsche envisions leaving behind.

By the end of part II "The Free Spirit," Nietzsche provides some further indication of the sort of people one might expect to encounter *beyond good and evil*: "a new species of philosophers" (§42). But we do not get much information about this type, only that they are expected to bear some resemblance to the "free spirited" community for which the author of *BGE* takes himself to be the spokesman; they will have a love of truth but will guard it jealously as *theirs*. And what we learn of the free spirits is rather frightening: this band considers the growth and development of humanity as relative to "the dangerousness of [its] situation," which "must first grow to the point of enormity, [its] power of invention and simulation ([its] 'spirit') had to develop under prolonged pressure and constraint into refinement and audacity, [its] life-will had to be enhanced into an unconditional power-will." As to how such enhancement might occur, Nietzsche writes, "hardness, forcefulness, slavery, danger in the alley and the heart, life in hiding, stoicism, the art of experiment and devilry of every kind, everything evil, terrible, tyrannical in man, everything in him that is kin to beasts of prey and serpents serves the enhancement of the species 'man' as much as its opposite does" (§44). We might rightly wonder *what* of this sort—"hardness, forcefulness, slavery, danger in the alley and the heart"—must occur in order to produce the new philosopher, and how he will stand in relation to others with whom he associates, particularly those who might suffer the ills of tyranny.

The picture becomes even more terrifying, and the tenor of Nietzsche's anticipation ever more shrill, at the end of part III, titled "What is religious" (which is *not* a question). There, Nietzsche returns to his vision of the future philosophers, described as having "the most comprehensive responsibility" because the development of humanity lies on their shoulders. And the process of development described at the end of part II is reiterated and amplified when Nietzsche continues: "this philosopher will make use of religions for his project of cultivation and education, just as he will make use of whatever political and economic states are at hand. The selective and cultivating influence, always destructive as well as creative and form-giving, which can be exerted with the help of religions, is always multiple and different according to the sort of human beings who are placed under its spell and protection" (§61). While religion might be useful for manipulating circumstances that would free one from public life, as the Brahmins did, Nietzsche also imagines that religion could "give[s] some of the ruled the instruction and opportunity to prepare themselves for future ruling and obeying" (§61). But, while it is clear that some form of ruling is central to Nietzsche's conception of this future type that bears a certain form of nobility, it is unclear whether Nietzsche envisions them as ruling states, groups of individuals, or primarily and exclusively, themselves. He continues, "those slowly ascending classes—in which, thanks to fortunate marital customs, the strength and joy of the will, the will to self-control

[*Selbstbeherrschung*] is ever growing—receive enough nudges and temptations from religion to walk the paths to higher spirituality, to test the feelings of great self-overcoming [*Selbstüberwindung*], of silence and solitude. Asceticism and Puritanism are almost indispensable means for educating and ennobling a race that wishes to become master over its origins among the rabble and that works its way up toward future rule" (§61). We shall certainly return to what might be entailed in this idea of *Selbstbeherrschung*, translated as "will to self-control" and *Selbstüberwindung*, translated as self-overcoming.

At least one of the goals is clear: what such ennobling process will entail is breaking the grip of the current vision of humanity—of all things human and earthly, which "inverts all love of the earthly and of dominion over the earth into hatred of the earth and the earthly—*that* is the task the church posed for itself and had to pose, until in its estimation 'becoming unworldly,' 'unsensual,' and 'higher men' were fused into a single feeling" (§62). We noted previously that Nietzsche thinks future philosophers might *either* take on the perspective of "an Epicurean god" and meet this scene with divine laughter, or be *enraged* and horrified, approaching "the work" (the form of humanity) wrought by Christianity with a "divine hammer," presumably to destroy or at the very least *rework* it. Part of what makes the creators of current humanity so inept, as Nietzsche assesses them, is that they are "not noble enough to see the abysmally different order of rank, chasm of rank, between man and man" (§62) they lack the ability to value and evaluate. Many of the epigrams we find in part IV emphasize precisely this lack of awareness, lack of sensibility for distance, ranking, and difference, and link them with the desire to make equal, make same.

And this is at the root of what Nietzsche repeatedly calls "herd morality," which although it is "sovereign" (§62) and presents itself as *exclusive*, is but one type among many possible, including "*higher*," "moralities" (§202). The process that led to the development of the human herd, Nietzsche tells us at the end of part V "Natural History of Morals," also yielded *democracy*. The kind of rule emphasized in part III that the future philosophers will be noble enough to acquire and execute masterfully is decidedly *not* democratic. And Nietzsche makes it clear that he opposes not only actual or possible instantiations of democratic political orders but also *democratic thinking more generally*, democratic values, which he thinks have actually *physiologically* weakened and sickened human beings, heightening what is *ignoble* in humanity. It would appear that future philosophers have as their task the cultivation of humanity (and not only themselves or even specific individuals) such that nobility is once again possible. Further detail about the route to this is sketched in part VI "We Scholars," where Nietzsche claims toward the end of the part that the task of philosophers is to be "the bad conscience of their time" (§212). They do this violently, brutally "by applying the knife vivisectionally to the chest of the very *virtues of their time*" (§212). And part VII, "Our Virtues," both assesses current virtues and charts those of the free spirits. One of the virtues of the free spirits is honesty, and Nietzsche provides testimony to what "is 'settled in him'" (§231), which includes ideas about an inherent tension in physiological as well as cultural reproduction.

An assessment of our inheritance as it relates to our vulnerabilities and frailties as well as our potencies and possibilities is advanced in the part VIII "On Peoples and Fatherlands.'" It is here that the urgency of the *question* of nobility, of what is now noble and what might be one day, gathers intensity and becomes clearer. In the preceding parts, what we have learned about how Nietzsche thinks about nobility can be summed up crudely as follows: What is definitive of nobility is not simply station in life but a way of *valuing* and *feeling*. Noble evaluative schemes make use of rank ordering on a scale of higher and lower, and they are accompanied by feelings of distance and difference that allow such distinctions to be recognized and meaningful. The feeling or *pathos of distance* indicated here draws on *aesthetic* sensibilities rather than more strictly *emotive* qualities in the production of this feeling. But, there is also an emotive charge relevant here. Despite Nietzsche's bombastic aggression and his disdain for the current condition of humanity, *love* plays an important role, as suggested at the end of the previous chapter. What we love, what we value and honor, matter very much to the kinds of lives we live. Crucial to Nietzsche's diagnosis of the condition of modern humanity is concern about our capacity to love, to truly prefer something, anything in particular. This can be summed up as a problem of taste. "Of Peoples and

Fatherlands" explores the variety of tastes that are part of European inheritance and are indicative of its capacities for revering and esteeming, the essential ingredients of a morality, of all moralities, which are means to what Nietzsche refers to in section 219 as "that high spirituality." How these capacities might become synthesized, coordinated, and fully utilized is a question Nietzsche does not answer and does not presume to be able to do so. It is perhaps the work of the future philosophers whose path is possibly prepared by the scouts that are the free spirits.

WHAT IS NOBLE?

We thus arrive at part IX *Was it vornehm?* and immediately, Nietzsche reiterates an idea we have encountered repeatedly in our review of the concluding sections of the preceding parts: "every enhancement of the type 'man' has so far been the work of an aristocratic society [. . .] a society that believes in the long ladder of an order of rank and differences in value between man and man, and that needs slavery in some sense or other" (§257). Nietzsche goes on to provide a micro version of a story we encounter in *GM* in which society's origin is located in an event during which a pack of "men of prey" seize the "weaker" and make them their subjects (§257). He sketches the basic difference between "master morality" and "slavish morality" (§260) and how these not simply characterize individuals or groups of individuals but can also be tendencies that inhabit the same "soul." He talks about the significance of "exploitation" and criticizes prohibitions against violence and revulsion to suffering as hostile to life. He repeatedly emphasizes the importance of an "instinct for rank" (§263), for the *feeling* of height (§265), and the significance of our heredity, which includes, perhaps most importantly, our ancestors' tastes as reflected in their life-ways (§264). Each of these ideas merits further investigation.

The first section emphasizing the role of aristocratic values and perspectives in achieving "enhancement of the type 'man'" explains this not in terms of physical superiority or the ability to enslave and brutalize. Instead, what Nietzsche draws to his readers' attention is how the aristocratic perspective achieves some distance, *pathos*. The significance of this was mentioned in the preceding chapter in light of Bizet's music, which had a similar effect for Nietzsche. He makes it clear in section 257, although it seems to be frequently overlooked, that he is not seeking to reinstate an aristocracy that would striate society, and he is not even claiming that it is absolutely *necessary*, although he thinks history shows that it has been "*until now*" (our emphasis) an effective means of producing a kind of *pathos of distance*. Although he does not explore it in great detail in this book (as he will in *GM*), Nietzsche thinks this social *pathos* is related to what he calls "that other, more mysterious pathos," which ignites a "craving for an ever new widening of distances within the soul itself, the development of ever higher, rarer, more remote, further-stretching, more comprehensive states" (§257). It is this, specifically, that propels the dynamic of self-overcoming, which takes on increasing significance in this chapter and is a crucial theme in Nietzsche's *Z*.

As Nietzsche relates an abbreviated version of the story of the origin of society in the enslavement of the weak by a stronger "barbarian caste," he qualifies the nature of their power in terms that are somewhat different from his later discussion in *GM*. Here, barbarian "predominance did not lie mainly in physical strength but in strength of the soul." And it is on account of such strength, Nietzsche claims, that "they were more *whole* human beings (which also means, at every level, 'more whole beasts')" (§257).[2] In the context of *BGE*, it is clear Nietzsche's reason for seeing these human beings as more bestial is that they are not motivated by certain *anti*-natural values that deform human beings (think of the human beings who are simply exaggerated individual body parts in *Z*). It is important to note here the difference between "anti-natural" and "unnatural." Nietzsche does not simply give a positive value to everything supposedly natural and denigrate the artificial. He also regards human culture-making (including practices of producing artifice) as part of nature. The kind of devaluation of human existence that morality, in particular Christian morality, advances, however, is *hostile to nature as such* and is therefore *anti-natural*. As long as nature is devalued, life itself, and particularly human life, needs otherworldly redemption or else one may conclude life is worthless. Thus, as we saw previously in *BGE* (§230), Nietzsche seeks to take a moral-free perspective on existence in order to disclose possibilities that are obscured by moral prejudices, which affect not only *how* things are seen but also *what* can be seen. And *what* Nietzsche sees, reflected in his "proposition" (§36), is that "life is *essentially* appropriation, injury, overpowering of what is alien and weaker; suppression, hardness, imposition of one's own forms, incorporation and at least, at its mildest, exploitation"; in short, "life simply *is* will to power," bearing that same basic spirit of the will, previously discussed in section 230. To categorically oppose this—to devalue, denigrate, and suppress it—is to *deny* life. This does not mean we must celebrate or even ignore violence. However, if we refrain from it and avoid it, we would do so on different grounds and under different conditions, as for example, in the expression of different constitutions as described in section 260.[3]

The anti-naturalism Nietzsche finds in moralities persists and takes its toll over time to the point that it begins to *corrupt* the instincts. That is the subject of section 258, where Nietzsche uses the English word "corruption" (see §233 for a specifically modern example pertaining to women).[4] In this section, Nietzsche emphasizes the connection between corruption and disorder, what he elsewhere calls "disgregation," which is related to the political imagery of the soul and Nietzsche's reflections on forms of political association and their attendant and underlying values: "Corruption as the expression of a threatening anarchy."[5] Two features of this discussion are particularly relevant: Nietzsche's reference to different kinds of organisms, which include individuals as well as political and cultural groups; and his observation that "a good and healthy aristocracy" does not regard itself merely as having a regulative function but as *expressive* of the "meaning and highest justification" for the organism in which they rule.

In section 260, we learn more about the meaning of the organism in relation to what takes itself as noble and other means of organization. Nietzsche sums up some of his conclusions on the basis of his initial work in creating and analyzing a "typology of morals" (§186). He sketches two basic types of moralities, emphasizing they are better thought of as moralizing tendencies (just as the Apollinian and Dionysian are artistic tendencies). These characterize not only individuals and groups, but can also be found *within* individuals, who can and often do bear these tendencies simultaneously. Masterly moralizing occurs when we find "exalted proud states conferring distinction and determining order of rank," and this way of according honor is "value-creating" in which "morality is self-glorification [*Selbstverherrlichung*]." The chief differences among these tendencies are *what* is valued and *how*, the condition and form of expression evident in each. Masterly moralizing expresses a "feeling of fullness" and "overflowing power," characterized by "happiness of high tension." It issues from a conscious desire to share and *bestow* wealth. It is not primarily motivated by pity, fear, or selflessness, as Nietzsche thinks Christian morality is. Masterly moralizing holds compassion in suspicion and it is entirely compatible with the notion of love as the basis for a healthy society, as suggested at the end of the last chapter and expanded below in this chapter.

It seems clear from this section that Nietzsche admires this masterful type, particularly its creative capacities expressed in bestowing honor, which Nietzsche describes as their "art" and "realm of invention" [*Erfinden*; cf. §12]. But, we are alerted to a significant difference between the type "masterly morality" and Nietzsche's anticipation of the prospects beyond good and evil, the *supra-moral* or extra-moral ("aussermoralische": §32). A rather different concern with the future is evident. The masterly type greatly esteems its ancestors: in honoring itself, it honors its origins and conditions for being. This sharply contrasts with Nietzsche's contemporaries who he finds increasingly have less respect for elders and the past and place greater hopes for and higher esteem of the future and the "progress" it promises. Clearly, Nietzsche does not embrace either of these views. As noted throughout the book and in the review at the beginning of this chapter, Nietzsche has a decidedly *future* orientation in his project. He aims to contribute positively to the creation of future possibilities, in part by naming some such possibilities and thereby creating or opening a course. But such a future might not be regarded as "progress," at least in moral terms (indeed, from the current moral perspective, it could seem rather decadent, "wicked" [§296]), and its *progressus* is tentative and tenuous at best, and certainly not necessary or inevitable as modern adherents to the faith in progress hold. So, what we find in Nietzsche is a different notion of the future, how it is produced, and what is entailed in its production. The latter, we have already seen, includes a particular relation to and appropriation of the past and the resources acquired therein. One of its past inheritances Nietzsche thinks it is vital to recapture and cultivate is *love as passion*, which he heralds as a "European specialty," and "of noble origin" (§260). This love as passion, discussed in the previous chapter, is one of humanity's atavistic resources that might be tapped in the production of the future beyond good and evil Nietzsche anticipates.

The next few sections of this part utilize the language of evolutionary biology and embryology in the context of discussing the history of the development of human culture, particularly the development of moralities. So, for example, Nietzsche thinks there are no pure types on account of "the intermarriage of masters and slaves," which resulted in an ambiguous mixture of masterly and slavish propensities. As to how one morality might master, in the sense of overpowering and dominating, the other, he goes on to describe the emergence of species and types (§262) as the products of struggles [*Kämpfe*] with "unfavorable conditions" and their relation to "breeding" or cultivation [*Züchtung*]. Species or types form and become durable through *endurance*, not protection and "superabundant nourishment": "the continual fight against ever constant *unfavorable* conditions is [. . .] the cause that fixes and hardens a type." Two things are particularly notable about this phenomenon. The first is that endurance conditions are necessary for the existence of any particular type. Type features are relative to endurance conditions that force the development of particular qualities and capacities. A second thing follows from this, namely that if all types are dependent upon endurance conditions for their perpetuation, and yet all types eventually seek to minimize or reduce risk (i.e., to actively diminish or ameliorate endurance conditions), then all types eventually undermine themselves. Nietzsche describes this phenomenon as *self-overcoming*, and he thinks morality itself has reached such a point. Nietzsche claims, now "the 'individual' [*Individuum*] appears, obliged to give himself laws and to develop his own arts and wiles for self-preservation, self-enhancement, self-redemption." But Nietzsche is not simply praising and admiring this development (as those who laud the appearance of the "sovereign individual" in *GM* II:2 are wont to do). The result of this precarious situation is that there are "all sorts of new what-fors and wherewithals; no shared formulas any longer; misunderstanding allied with disrespect; decay, corruption, and the highest desires gruesomely entangled" (§262).

Nobility of taste (*Vornehmheit des Geschmacks*) includes reverence and an instinct for rank (§263); it is related to egoism (§265), which includes "refinement and self-limitation in its relations with its equals." Nietzsche writes, "the noble soul gives as it takes" and has "an instinct of repayment"; "*it knows itself to be at a height*" and thus does not "look 'up.'" This recalls the *pathos* or feeling of distance identified previously as edifying, providing a perspective that allows one to see beyond what is more common (an idea that is not particularly new), and gives one a sense of ordering in relation to what is higher. In this respect, we might return to the curious idea expressed in the preceding chapter about *becoming what one is* and Nietzsche's claim in *EH* that in order to do this one should "not have the faintest idea what one is." We might see this in light of section 266, where Nietzsche cites Goethe to Rat Scholosser: "'Truly high respect one can have only for those who do not *seek* themselves.'" This means not looking up and above, to have an instinct of reverence but to know oneself to be at a height.[6]

Nietzsche emphasizes the point he made in elaborate detail in part VIII: Heredity, or "Herkunft," matters. In section 264, Nietzsche discusses this in the contexts of preferences of parents and ancestors, and the extent to which we bear their preferences and tastes. Although this has a ring of Lamarckism to it in speculating about the heritability of acquired characteristics, it seems Nietzsche at this point has something in mind that is more like the atavism he repeatedly advances, and which was discussed in the previous chapter. In this section, he links the idea of inheritance with eternal recurrence (see Chapter 5 on part III). Citing Horace,[7] he provides us with a further glimpse of how he thinks about eternal recurrence when he claims that "plebs" eternally returns; it resists education, even acculturation. Once again, we can make sense of this when we appreciate the strong connection Nietzsche thinks exists between tastes and ways of life, and how the values that organize our life activities also create an order of rank of the competing drives that constitute us. These are fully physiological and not merely psychological or specific to "states of soul." In part VIII Nietzsche has expressed the hope that it is not just the "plebs" that eternally returns, which is part of our fatality, but also our more noble and *ennobling* inheritance.

The question of "What is noble?" is explored negatively in the context of asking the question "What is common?" in section 268. We can take the term "common" in at least two senses: what is base ["Die Gemeinheit"] and in opposition to the noble, and what is shared (as in the sense of "gemeinsam").[8] We have seen Nietzsche wrestle with this problem specifically in the context of reflecting on the problems and possibilities of a European future in the preceding chapter. How does one create a community that preserves and even heightens its great resources rather than simply reducing it to the greatest degree of commonality? In this section, Nietzsche explores this question from the standpoint of language and inheritance, claiming that "Words are acoustical signs for concepts," which themselves have a basis in "recurring and associated sensations" (§268). The primary condition for becoming *a* people is having "long lived together under similar conditions (of climate, soil, danger, needs, and work)," which makes it possible for people to understand one another. On the basis of their commonalities, people are able to achieve further understanding even more rapidly through processes of association and abbreviation. Avoiding danger places increased demands on communication and reliability of a common sense in order to avoid fatal errors of miscommunication. Orders of rank within the soul are established on the basis of "which group of sensations is aroused, expresses itself, and issues commands in a soul most quickly," and these "ultimately determine[s] its table of goods." Moreover, "The values of a human being betray something of the *structure* of his soul and where it finds its conditions of life, its true need." So, in this section, we have some very interesting suggestions for effecting future development. If Europe "wants to become one" it will need to focus on shared experiences rather than military dominance, political unification, a *lingua franca*, currency, or mythical past—or, we might add, *simply* a constitutional process. Moreover, it matters what kinds of experiences we seek, since the sensations aroused therein effect the ordering of souls and the creation of values.

But this will be exceptionally difficult to accomplish, "the most powerful of all powers at whose disposal man has been so far" is "easy communicability of need." The similar and common have the greatest advantage and "propagate." The force needed to change this course is immense, and nearly *un*natural (but certainly not *anti*-natural), since there is an "all too natural *progressus in simile*" in the development of humankind. And thus we see in section 269 that it also matters very much what we love, since that directs what we seek and pursue as well as forego. Here again, Nietzsche returns to his concern about pity on the basis of a love of man, wanting to preserve and help even what ought to perish, and he sees this as one of the greatest temptations and frailties to which humankind is vulnerable while recognizing that it is at the same time quite potent. The incomparable suffering that can be produced on account of the love of man can also be ennobling insofar as it can separate (§270), create the distance of *pathos* that Nietzsche thinks facilitates philosophy and stimulates spiritual heightening. In this context, Nietzsche refers back to the idea of having "once been 'at home' in many distant, terrifying worlds" (§270; cf. §§41 and 44), and the extent of and desire for responsibility (§272; cf. §61) as indicative of nobility.

NIETZSCHE'S *ZWISCHENSPIELE*

Kaufmann is right to notice that there is a curious break in the narrative of Nietzsche's text at sections 274 and 275 (one might place it even earlier, thematically if not stylistically, perhaps at §§269 or 270). Kaufmann notices the especially personal tone of the more epigraphic sections, suggesting the shift is perhaps related to Nietzsche's anxiety about completing his task, as expressed in section 277. The sections are similar to those that comprise part IV, and like those and others we have noted throughout this book, they similarly function as Nietzsche's vehicle in his role as *Zwischenbegebnis*, a transitional moment, an occurrence between. Some are snippets of conversations with unidentified interlocutors, imagined dialogues that are incomplete. The more frequent use of the first person singular "I" suggests Nietzsche is ruminating on his possibilities and fate in the process of development he anticipates. These sections follow his consideration of how difficult the task is to accomplish (§268), the emotional toil it takes on the sensitive types involved (§269), the temptations that exist to avoid it (§270), the isolation and loneliness one can experience (§§271 and 2), and the precarious nature of the position insofar as it entails a great deal of waiting for the moment to arrive as it is not simply some project one can seize (§274). And he explores the difficulties of everyday life—relations, diets, daily practices—that occur once one begins to develop different tastes (e.g., §§282–4).

While these aphorisms recall some of the themes we have come to associate with the nobility of some possible future humanity, we no longer find the continuous and coherent narrative that has characterized the preceding parts and the first half of the concluding part. More familiar threads and manner of address reappear in the remaining dozen or so sections, though these are also punctuated with tempo and stylistic changes, which are again reminiscent of other epigrams we have seen in the book (e.g., parts IV and VII). The themes shift as well. No longer does Nietzsche talk about the *imposition* of order and rank or the necessity and significance of exploitation and suffering. Instead, we learn that nobility is self-reverence (§287), that philosophy seeks masks and itself *masks* other philosophies (§289), that philosophers are reluctant to share their insights not only out of jealousy but also in the interest of protecting others from the difficulties their views often bring (§290). Nietzsche strikes out against pity, the "cult of suffering," as the "newest kind of bad taste" (§293),[9] which as we learned from part III, leads us to want to preserve what ought to die.

And he heralds again *gay science* as the motivational force and ultimate goal of members of the community he anticipates (§293). Such gaiety involves both love of life previously discussed (§260) and an attendant and abiding ability to laugh. This is a theme that recurs in Z,[10] and recalls an important passage from part III of *BGE*. Nietzsche suggests an order of rank of philosophers according to their capacity to laugh, the highest of which would be "golden laughter." Compare this with the kind of laughter mentioned in section 62 in which we are presented with the dilemma of possible responses and reactions to the hideous image of what we have become: "Suppose we could contemplate the oddly painful and equally crude and subtle comedy of European Christianity with the mocking and aloof eyes of an Epicurean god, I think our amazement and laughter would never end." Alternatively, and perhaps more likely given our sorry condition, "Anyone, however, who approached this almost deliberate degeneration and atrophy of man represented by the Christian European (Pascal, for example), feeling the opposite kind of desire, not in an Epicurean spirit but rather with some divine hammer in his hand, would surely have to cry out in wrath, in pity, in horror [. . .]." The connection between laughter and love becomes clearer insofar as the section introducing the "genius of the heart" (§295) follows this one on laughter (§294), where instead of visions of exploitation and the imposition of form on a whole populace, we find Nietzsche writing about a lover who is also a tempter and pied-piper.

By way of conclusion to this book and our discussion of Nietzsche's work, we wish to focus on two features of the final part of the main text: the introduction of the curious figure of the "genius of the heart" and what precedes and follows it, insofar as the book appears to unravel toward the end. The genius of the heart is a figure not frequently explored in the scholarly literature and is one we strongly advise readers to explore in greater depth,[11] since we think it provides a deeper appreciation for Nietzsche's understanding of the relation between value-creation and love, a theme we have observed recurring throughout the text. And finally, we note that it might be somewhat appropriate that, in the end, Nietzsche's book comes undone, or "falls apart," as we think that it does. This serves two purposes. The first is to prevent us from becoming Nietzsche's followers, which he has clearly indicated would be a bad thing even though he tempts and lures many a reader throughout the text. In the end, Nietzsche decisively reclaims his truths as *his*. And secondly, Nietzsche has identified, as discussed above, a dynamic of self-overcoming that is characteristic of all development, and he proceeds ever-mindful of his own position within a larger course of social and historical development. He regards himself as *transitional*, as argued in the chapters on parts IV and VIII, and therefore as occupying a place between one form of life and another he anticipates as possible. He contributes what he can to bringing out the features of the current form of life that will eventually result in its demise, its features of self-overcoming, which include its commitment to truth and, for Nietzsche, the truth about the lack of necessity of the normativity of truth, about the mechanics of normativity as such and the relations between values and forms of life. Thus he finishes this part of his work no longer anticipating a form of future humanity, no longer offering physiological, cosmological, or philosophical propositions, as he has in previous chapters; he is not even engaging in the biting critical analysis of our current state of health and convictions. Instead, he portrays his own *Zugründegehen*, his fading, his passage beyond the point of ripeness, which, as we have already discussed, is crucial to *self-overcoming*. We offer some suggestions for what this portends in the final section of this book, but first we should meet the curious new character that Nietzsche introduces just prior to his "going under."

THE "GENIUS OF THE HEART"

The "genius of the heart" might remind us of how Nietzsche has described the future philosophers in section 42, near the end of part II where he writes about the *Versucher*, who both seeks and tempts. What does this figure do? He is a master of semblance, "silences all that is loud and self-satisfied, teaching it to listen," "smoothes rough souls and lets them taste a new desire" (§295). He teaches delicacy, gracefulness, and hope. Nietzsche claims, midsection, that he is talking about Dionysus and he takes on the mantle of his disciple, but the nature of this might be called into question. Rather than preaching teachings of what we might expect him to have learned from Dionysus, Nietzsche seems to be channeling and at times imitating his god. The goals he attributes to Dionysus might very well be ones we could regard as Nietzsche's in relation to his readers in *BGE*: "silencing all that is loud and self-satisfied," teaching them to listen to new voices that speak about different goals, giving them a taste of a new desire, offering a kind of self-reverence that is perhaps contrary to democratic tastes.

The appearance of Dionysus near the end of this book brings us back to the theme with which we began in section 1—namely, the value of truth, and the notion that our very commitment to truth, once it becomes genuine, leads us to question its value as intrinsically good. When associated with the real, the existent, and the empirically knowable, truth has a challenger in Dionysus, whose creative power lies in disintegrating the appearances associated with truth; recall that *behind* every mask on the Greek tragic stage is Dionysus. While he is the opposite of an actor who gives shape or form to a character, Dionysus nevertheless provides the life force, the animating power, of all action.[12]

The ultimate point of summoning Dionysus at the end of the book, a book that anticipates the self-overcoming of morality, is to bring forward the conclusion that morality itself is an artifice, a product of human invention and creativity, one perhaps spurred by a need that is symptomatic of a form of decadence or decline.[13] In his 1886 preface to a new edition of his first book, Nietzsche writes,

> Here, perhaps for the first time, a pessimism "beyond good and evil" is suggested. Here that "perversity of mind" gains speech and formulation against which Schopenhauer never wearied of hurling in advance his most irate curses and thunderbolts: a philosophy that dares to move, to demote, morality into the realm of appearance—and not merely among "appearances" or phenomena (in the sense assigned to these words by Idealistic philosophers), but among "deceptions," as semblance, delusion, error, interpretation, contrivance, art. (*BT* "Attempt at a Self-Criticism" 5)

Since "Christian teaching [. . .] relegates art, *every* art, to the realm of *lies*," it ultimately undermines itself, as Nietzsche aims to show in *GM*, which he writes after he revisits his earlier works.

For the artful nature of the task, consider the perspective drawn in section 291, which endeavors to glimpse the development of human morality, to see morality as an artistic product (forgery: *Fälschung*). It aims to catch sight of the soul (*vermöge deren überhaupt ein Genuss im Anblick der Seele möglich wird*), and it affords a view of the human as "a manifold, mendacious, artificial, and opaque animal."[14] This recalls the passage about the masterly as "more whole beasts" near the beginning of the part, section 257.[15] The later section continues, "from this point of view much more may belong in the concept of 'art' than is generally believed."[16] This is what Nietzsche has been trying to tap in his efforts at *erfinden*—invention—previously described as what might be utilized in the production of a new nobility (both type of persons and sense or value).

Summoning Dionysus near the book's conclusion also reinforces Nietzsche's interest in love insofar as Dionysus is neither alone nor with Euripides' mad women but rather with Ariadne, who was immortally transfigured in her love of Dionysus.[17] And Dionysus professes his love of humankind much as Nietzsche's Zarathustra does in the opening narrative scene in which Zarathustra descends from his mountain cave because he "loves man."[18] It is also in *Z* that Nietzsche presents a dynamic in which "things fall apart," go to ruin of necessity. The seeds of their destruction are somehow inherent in their very conditions of existence. After conjuring up an image that signals the self-overcoming of morality (i.e., that the truth about morality is that it is an artifice, which means that on its own terms it is a lie), Nietzsche acknowledges the same fate for his own thoughts.[19]

THINGS FALL APART

Things fall apart at the end of *BGE* for a variety of reasons. In the end, it is not the readers who are addressed but rather Nietzsche's own thoughts, his "*wicked* thoughts" (§296), which are described as already "on the verge of withering and losing [their] fragrance," birds who are so weary they can be caught by hand, who "cannot live and fly much longer" (§296). They are no fresh creations ready to take flight in the hearts and minds of Nietzsche's reader. This finale is surely not the one for which we've been prepared.

Taking on the mantle of Dionysus, it seems as though Nietzsche intentionally disrupts and disappoints our expectations for a new program for nobility. He lures and tempts (at least some, he hopes) into *wanting* as much, but he is not prepared to be its source, perhaps not even its inspiration. Along the way, he repeatedly undermines his capacity and authority to engage in the grander project. He repeatedly indicates that he discusses *his* propositions, *his* truths, and *his* prejudices. And he notes that what is noble is protective of its truths, thinks they are matters of personal entitlement on the basis of being earned at high costs, and that they are devalued and debased by being shared (§43). This does not follow from the idea that all truth is relative and individually subjective, rather Nietzsche thinks truth is something owned and felt rather than strictly known.

At the beginning of part V, "The natural history of morals," Nietzsche describes his task (the only activity he thinks is legitimate at the time) in terms of *preparing* "a *typology* of morals." Emphasis can be placed on the provisional and *preparatory* nature of this activity, which involves "collect[ing] material [. . .], conceptualiz[ing] and arrang[ing] a vast realm of subtle feelings of value and differences of value which are alive, grow, beget, and perish." Nietzsche's immediate goal is "perhaps [. . .] to present vividly some of the more frequent and recurring forms of such living crystallizations" (§186). He does this in a variety of ways, through collecting historical examples, providing illuminating citations, and even attempting to capture such crystallizations in epigraphic form on multiple occasions. He tries to reveal a progression and process of development from Platonism to Christianity to the modern ideals of democracy. He pinpoints a variety of cultural resources and tastes that are indicative of our current constitution and suggestive of future possibilities. To join Nietzsche might not take the form of seizing his conception of nobility or following a new program but rather practicing his form of inquiry, to join him in interrogating rather than propagating an answer to the question *What is noble?*

This ending is perhaps his way of creating that order of rank between spirit and star that he mentions in section 285, where he writes:

> The greatest events and thoughts—but the greatest thoughts are the greatest events—are comprehended last: the generations that are contemporaneous with them do not *experience* such events—they live right past them. What happens is a little like what happens in the realm of stars. The light of the remotest stars comes last to men; and until it has arrived man *denies* that there are—stars there. 'How many centuries does a spirit require to be comprehended?'—that is a standard, too; with that, too, one creates order of rank and etiquette that is still needed—for spirit and star.

With this conclusion, Nietzsche advances his own fading, hastens his own remoteness. It also affords Nietzsche some shelter, allows him to slip into obscurity and perhaps take some satisfaction in his incomprehensibility, as when he writes in section 289: "Every philosophy also *conceals* a philosophy; every opinion is also a hideout, every word also a mask." As Nietzsche has already noted, some deliberately seek masks (§§278, 270; recall also the language of the stage, actor, and mask in §§7, 25) and *want* to be misunderstood, perhaps to protect from what they see (e.g., §290: "Every profound thinker is more afraid of being understood than of being misunderstood").[20]

The final section of the book has none of the bombast of the concluding sections of previous books. It does not herald great and gruesome things to come, or anticipate the end of days. It is not addressed to the free spirits or even those who might aspire to be among them. Its audience is not those he derides or ridicules or even those he mocks or laughs away. Instead, it is addressed to his own thoughts, those who were the inspiration for the book and who, perhaps, have been betrayed by it, or at the very least have been let down by it. Nietzsche expresses concern that the vitality of his thoughts has been lost in translation to written word, that perhaps the very act of capturing and writing down his thoughts does them a disservice, makes them more likely to be *taken* as truths. What is "caught" or captured in this form is only what is already on its way toward passing away, what is "autumnal and yellow" (§296). The range of his palette of colors, his ability to create gradations and shades, is limited; he must work only with the hues of autumn and late day. We see only their fading and passing, and thus they cannot be alive for us. We can only scarcely guess, if at all, "how [they] looked in [their] morning, [those] sudden sparks and wonders of [Nietzsche's] solitude" (§296). All that is left to do then is—sing.

CHAPTER 12

"FROM HIGH MOUNTAINS": NIETZSCHE'S AFTERSONG

Nietzsche ends the book with a poem entitled "From High Mountains," and this was to become a feature of several of his late writings: for example, the second edition of *GS*, with its added fifth part, also ends with an appendix of songs, the songs of Prince Vogelfrei.[1] In the concluding aphorisms to each text, he questions the very value of words, of their ability to communicate his thoughts, and he seems to be speaking specifically of prose. Before translating his thoughts into words, he notes that they were once "so colorful" and "full of thorns and secret spices," which caused him to sneeze and laugh. But when he transforms such thoughts into words, they lose their fragrance or sensorial as well as musical dimension. In section 296 Nietzsche laments the fact that through prose his thoughts are destined to lose their novelty and he fears them becoming "truths": "they already look so immortal, so pathetically decent, so dull!" With the turn to poetry, then, Nietzsche might be attempting to overcome what he sees as the limits of prose which, as he proclaims, steal the color, prickliness, and fragrance of his thoughts.

Nietzsche has offered some important insights into the power of poetry in his earlier writings and they help to clarify his turn to it at the end of *BGE*. In *AOM* 135 he says that when a poet is not in love with reality then his music will also not be reality, and she will bear him only "hollow-eyed and fragile-limbed children." In *AOM* 114 he writes, however, that the poet does not deal with every reality but only a select one. The reality they concern themselves with is that of the dawning future and in which they are to ignore all the fantastic, superstitious, and faded subjects upon which the earlier poets had sought to prove their powers. More strongly, and highly resonant with the ambit of *BGE*, in *AOM* 99 he envisages the poet as a signpost to the future: "That poetic power available to men of today which is not used up in the depiction of life ought to be dedicated, not so much to the representation of the contemporary world or the to the reanimation and imaginative reconstruction of the past, but to signposting the future." Here he even speaks of poetry prefiguring the "ever increasing elevation of man." In *D* 551, entitled "Of future virtues," Nietzsche appeals to poets to realize their authentic or true vocation, which is to be, "*seers* who tells us something of the *possible*! . . . If only they would let us feel in advance something of the *virtues of the future!*"[2] It is this vocation of the poet that seems to inform the poem that ends *BGE* for it too heralds the future and future virtues.

The "Aftersong" that concludes *BGE* is a revised and expanded version of a poem Nietzsche had sent to Baron Heinrich von Stein in November 1884 imploring him to make the visit to the high mountains of Sils-Maria: "This is for you, my dear friend, to remember Sils Maria and in gratitude for your letter, *such* a letter" (cited in Kaufmann, p. 239). Nietzsche regarded von Stein as a possible acolyte whom he could recruit in his planned fraternity of free spirits or brotherhood of the gay science.[3] "Aftersong" translates literally the German "*Nach-gesang*," which is a literal translation of the Greek epode. An epode is a short lyric poem forming the final section of a three-part ode. The core theme of the poem is friendship and the search for the creation of new friends who can incarnate and fulfill the philosophy of the future. Nietzsche has a specific appreciation of the friend as someone who shares the struggle, the self-overcoming, of life but who is also someone we can honor as our enemy. As he puts it in *Z*: "In one's friend one should have one's best enemy. You should be closest to him in your heart when you strive against him . . . you shall be to him an arrow and a yearning for the Overhuman" (*Z* I: "On the Friend"). Nietzsche holds to this view because he thinks true friendship requires mutual sportive seduction into life's self-overcoming and not a relation of complacency.

The poem begins with the poet praising the noon of life as a time of celebration and summer festivity. The narrator of the poem is waiting for friends and inviting them to come as, "It is time. It's late!" All seems to be designed and ready for the friends to make their appearance and join the poet. However, when the friends do appear they do not find the man they have been seeking and they hesitate, amazed. The narrator's ancient friends show the "shock of love and fear" in the face of what they encounter: a hermit who has learned to dwell "where no one lives, in bleakest polar hell," and who has "unlearned mankind and god, prayer and curse," existing as if a ghost "that wanders over glaciers." He advises his old friends that they cannot live in the places where he resides and he advises them to depart for their own good and their own safety for among "distant fields of ice and rock" one must live as a "hunter" and only a few select kind will have the inclination for the hunt (as Nietzsche notes in §45, where the "great hunt" is to be found is where also the great danger begins). He has become a "wicked archer" and the ends of his bow kiss. Moreover, it is only the strongest in spirit that can bend the bow in the way he does: "No arrow strikes like that which my bow sends." But he also asks the friends to leave the gates of his residence open since "new friends may come along." We should let old friends go and not be memory-mongers. If we were once young, we are now becoming even younger (such is our appetite or desire for new life).

The author is forced to acknowledge that what was once hope and promise between him and his old friends has come to pass; the friends and of whom he once dreamed have aged and the old affinity has become lost: "One has to change to stay akin to me." Once again, in a repetition, the poet invokes the noon of life and waits for new friends, proclaiming once again that it is time and the time is late. Nietzsche's final stanza concludes that his song is now over and appeals to the "friend of noon"—we are invited not to ask after the identity of this particular friend[4]—for it is at noon "that one turned into two." With the coming of his friend Zarathustra the two celebrate a "feast of feasts," and the world now laughs, "rent are the drapes of fright," and the wedding of opposites, of light and darkness, is about to take place.

Here, at the very end of the poem, Nietzsche mimics the crucifixion of Christ: in both Matthew and Mark it is said that at noon on the day of Christ's death the sky grew dark like a coming together of light and darkness, and a few hours later Jesus cries out and dies; at this moment the curtain of the Temple is torn in half (Matthew 27.51; Mark 15.38). There could be a number of reasons why Nietzsche has chosen to reference Christ's crucifixion in the denouement to the poem.[5] Perhaps the most salient one is that the poem depicts a kind of death and resurrection and this captures the metamorphoses that characterize the book as a whole, including the free spirit's progress. As Burnham notes, there is depicted in the book a movement of change and self-overcoming that leads from new experiences, through synthesis and advancement, to new forms of life. There is also the case of the philosopher who, and as part and parcel of the enrichment of his mode of life, seeks to move away from himself only to return to himself; and, finally, there is the hope of a rebirth of nobility after the long wintry reign of Christianity.[6] In Nietzsche's poem it is not death that announces the tearing of the ancient curtain or veil but laughter.[7] The world now celebrates its liberation from the curse of Christendom and a new age and a new cheerfulness dawns.

There is without doubt an autobiographical aspect to the poem. By the middle of the 1880s Nietzsche's existence was becoming an increasingly solitary one with the friends from his youth and student days, including Paul Deussen, Franz Overbeck, and Erwin Rohde, feeling ever more estranged from him. We have mentioned the theme of friendship as being at the heart of the poem and of Nietzsche's concerns.[8] However, the poem connects with the rest of the book in several other ways. First, there are the references to noon or midday (*Mittag*), which foreground the problem of timeliness that is treated in the book: events can come too soon or too late. As Burnham notes, midday is an important image in Nietzsche, not so much a place in time but rather a join or "instantaneous transition" between the morning and the afternoon when shadows are shortest.[9] This imagery of the shortest shadow Nietzsche connects in *TI* with the "appearance" of Zarathustra and the meaning of his "event" in history.[10] The suggestion is that noon is a moment of opportunity when the chance of a fundamental change or transformation has to be taken or is lost. The shortest shadows of noon also signify what Nietzsche calls "the spirit of gravity," or one's inherited self-doubt, and noon is the time when one can jump over one's shadow.[11] There is also the imagery of the arrow and the tensed bow which echoes the book's preface. The basic idea is one of self-transformation in which one has gained in strength, including the strength "to hunt at a different level of philosophical prey," and this in turn encompasses hunting oneself in the form of a continual self-mastery and self-overcoming.[12]

The ultimate theme of the poem, then, is the need for perpetual change since growth is constancy: "*nur wer sich wandelt, bleibt mit mir verwandt*," that is, "Only those who change themselves remain akin to me."

STUDY QUESTIONS

These questions are approximately in the order of presentation of Nietzsche's text, and can be used to aid your understanding of and engagement with the book.

1. What does Nietzsche set out to question in the preface to the book and why?
2. Why is Nietzsche so concerned with raising the question of the *value* of truth?
3. How and for what ends does Nietzsche criticize the notion of the "will" and of "willing"?
4. Why is the concept of "will to power" not Nietzsche's substitute for Kant's "in-itself" or noumenon? How does it give us a new way of looking at the world?
5. Is Nietzsche a pessimistic thinker?
6. Can philosophy think without "prejudices"?
7. What is the "atomistic need" and why does Nietzsche criticize it so much?
8. What is the nature of Nietzsche's concern with "taste" in the book?
9. What is "perspectivism"?
10. Why is a will to unknowing not simply the opposite of a will to knowledge?
11. Why does Nietzsche oppose the idea of being a martyr for truth?
12. Why does Nietzsche take to task the Stoics in the way he does?
13. Examine the distinction Nietzsche forges between "free thinkers" and genuine "free spirits" or "free minds."
14. What alternative notion of the "soul" is Nietzsche putting forward in the book?
15. What does it mean to be an "attempter" or "experimenter"?
16. Why is the "intellectual conscience" so important for Nietzsche?
17. Examine Nietzsche's account of the saint and a saintly existence.

18. How does the eternal recurrence work as an ideal of super-human well-being?
19. Critically examine how Nietzsche construes the relation between philosophy and religion.
20. Do you agree with Nietzsche that Christianity is the most presumptuous and calamitous religion to date?
21. What is Nietzsche up to in part IV of the book on "epigraphs and interludes"?
22. Why does Nietzsche propose that we carry out a "natural history" of morality?
23. Why does Nietzsche think we should approach questions of morality in a spirit of modesty?
24. Critically examine Nietzsche's claim that European morality today is "herd-animal" morality.
25. Do we need philosophers to be legislators?
26. What is the nature of Nietzsche's concern with the scholar?
27. Why does the genuine philosopher live, according to Nietzsche, unwisely and impudently?
28. What is "great politics"?
29. Why does Nietzsche think that the question of what "our virtues" are is such a difficult one for us moderns to pose and answer?
30. Why must there be an "order of rank" among our values?
31. How do free spirits cultivate the virtue of "honesty" (*Redlichkeit*)?
32. What does it mean to translate the human being back into nature? What is the "eternal basic text" of "homo natura"?
33. Is Nietzsche a misogynist?
34. Why is Nietzsche concerned with "peoples" and "father-lands"? Why does he think that "becoming German" is a question of style?
35. Why is Wagner an important figure for Nietzsche to analyze in part VIII of the book?
36. Why does Nietzsche posit the need for a new nobility, and what would be "new" about it?
37. How does part IX of the text shed light on Nietzsche's "aristocratic radicalism"?
38. Examine the pertinence of Nietzsche's distinction between noble and slave moralities.

39. Why is Nietzsche so keen to stress that the "truths" of the book are primarily "his" truths?
40. What does it mean to philosophize "beyond good and evil"?

GUIDE TO FURTHER READING

INTRODUCTIONS

A large number of introductions to Nietzsche are now available. Of the established ones, the following can be recommended: Karl Jaspers, *Nietzsche: An Introduction to the Understanding of his Philosophical Activity*, trans. Charles F. Wallraff and Frederick J. Schmitz (Chicago: Regnery; Tucson, AZ: University of Arizona Press, 1965; repr. Baltimore, MD and London: Johns Hopkins University Press, 1997); and Walter Kaufmann, *Nietzsche: Philosopher, Psychologist, Anti-Christ*, 4th edn (Princeton, NJ and London: Princeton University Press, 1974). Two short introductions are J. P. Stern, *A Study of Nietzsche* (Cambridge and New York: Cambridge University Press, 1979), and Michael Tanner, *Nietzsche* (Oxford and New York: Oxford University Press, 1994). Of more recent works the following can be recommended: R. Kevin Hill, *Nietzsche: A Guide for the Perplexed* (London and New York: Continuum, 2007); Paul J. M. van Tongeren, *Reinterpreting Modern Culture: An Introduction to Friedrich Nietzsche's Philosophy* (West Lafayette, IN: Purdue University Press, 2000); and Rex Welshon, *The Philosophy of Nietzsche* (Durham, UK: Acumen, 2004). There are many important and helpful works on Nietzsche written in languages other than English. Serious students are strongly encouraged to explore this vast literature.

BIOGRAPHIES

Peter Bergmann's *Nietzsche: "The Last Antipolitical German"* (Bloomington, IN: Indiana University Press, 1987) offers an excellent biography focused on the "political" dimensions of Nietzsche's intellectual development. Other contributions include Lesley Chamberlain, *Nietzsche in Turin: An Intimate Biography* (New York: Picador, 1998); Ronald Hayman, *Nietzsche: A Critical Life* (London: Weidenfeld & Nicolson; New York: Oxford University Press, 1980); R. J. Hollingdale, *Nietzsche: The Man and his Philosophy*, 2nd edn (Cambridge and New York: Cambridge

University Press, 1999); Rüdiger Safranski, *Nietzsche: A Philosophical Biography*, trans. Shelley Frisch (New York: Norton; London: Granta, 2002); Robin Small *Nietzsche and Rée: A Star Friendship* (Oxford: Clarendon Press; New York: Oxford University Press, 2005). The most recent biography is Julian Young, *Friedrich Nietzsche. A Philosophical Biography* (Cambridge: Cambridge University Press, 2010).

EDITED COLLECTIONS

The following are recommended as helpful and important collections: Christa Davis Acampora and Ralph R. Acampora (eds), *A Nietzschean Bestiary: Becoming Animal Beyond Docile and Brutal* (Lanham, MD and Oxford: Rowman and Littlefield, 2004); Keith Ansell Pearson (ed.), *A Companion to Nietzsche* (Oxford and Malden, MA: Basil Blackwell, 2006); Daniel W. Conway with Peter S. Groff (eds), *Nietzsche: Critical Assessments*, 4 vols (London and New York: Routledge, 1998); Michael Allen Gillespie and Tracy B. Strong (eds), *Nietzsche's New Seas: Explorations in Philosophy, Aesthetics, and Politics* (Chicago and London: University of Chicago Press, 1988); Bernd Magnus and Kathleen M. Higgins (eds), *The Cambridge Companion to Nietzsche* (Cambridge and New York: Cambridge University Press, 1996); Jeffrey Metzger, (ed.), *Nietzsche, Nihilism, and the Philosophy of the Future* (London & New York, Continuum: 2009); John Richardson and Brian Leiter (eds), *Nietzsche* (Oxford and New York: Oxford University Press, 2001); Peter R. Sedgwick (ed.), *Nietzsche: A Critical Reader* (Oxford and Malden, MA: Basil Blackwell, 1995); Herman Siemens and Vasti Roodt, (eds), *Nietzsche, Power, and Politics* (Berlin and New York: Walter de Gruyter, 2008).

IMPORTANT MONOGRAPHS AND CRITICAL STUDIES

Of seminal monographs in the field of Nietzsche studies the following works in English merit attention: Gilles Deleuze, *Nietzsche and Philosophy*, trans. Hugh Tomlinson (London: Athlone Press; New York: Columbia University Press, 1983); Martin Heidegger, *Nietzsche* (San Francisco and London: Harper & Row, 1979–1987); Mazzino Montinari, *Reading Nietzsche*, trans. Greg Whitlock (Urbana-Champaign and Chicago: University of Illinois Press, 2003); Wolfgang Müller-Lauter, *Nietzsche: The Philosophy of Contradictions and the Contradictions of his Philosophy*, trans. David J. Parent (Urbana-Champaign and Chicago: University of Illinois Press, 1999); Alexander Nehamas, *Nietzsche: Life as Literature* (Cambridge, MA: Harvard University Press, 1985); Richard Schacht, *Nietzsche* (London and Boston: Routledge & Kegan Paul, 1983); Georg Simmel, *Schopenhauer and Nietzsche*, trans. Helmut Loiskandl, Deena Weinstein, and Michael Weinstein (Urbana-Champaign and Chicago: University of Illinois Press, 1991); Henry Staten, *Nietzsche's Voice* (Ithaca, NY and London: Cornell University Press, 1990).

TRUTH AND EPISTEMOLOGY

On this topic a seminal text is Maudemarie Clark, *Nietzsche on Truth and Philosophy* (Cambridge and New York: Cambridge University Press, 1990). Other important contributions include: Randall Havas, *Nietzsche's Genealogy: Nihilism and the Will to Knowledge* (Ithaca, NY and London: Cornell University Press, 1995); Peter Poellner, *Nietzsche and Metaphysics* (Oxford: Clarendon Press; New York: Oxford University Press, 1995); John Richardson, *Nietzsche's System* (New York and Oxford: Oxford University Press, 1996); Alan D. Schrift, *Nietzsche and the Question of Interpretation: Between Hermeneutics and Deconstruction* (London and New York: Routledge, 1990); and John T. Wilcox, *Truth and Value in Nietzsche: A Study of his Metaethics and Epistemology* (Ann Arbor, MI: University of Michigan Press, 1974).

NATURALISM

Two studies in particular merit the reader's attention on this topic: Christoph Cox, *Nietzsche, Naturalism, and Interpretation* (Berkeley, LA and London: University of California Press, 1999); and John Richardson, *Nietzsche's New Darwinism* (Oxford and New York: Oxford University Press, 2005).

ETHICS

On this topic some of the most important studies include: Peter Berkowitz, *Nietzsche: The Ethics of an Immoralist* (Cambridge,

MA, and London: Harvard University Press, 1995); Thomas H. Brobjer, *Nietzsche's Ethics of Character: A Study of Nietzsche's Ethics and its Place in the History of Moral Thinking* (Uppsala, Sweden: Uppsala University Department of History of Science and Ideas, 1995); Lester H. Hunt, *Nietzsche and the Origin of Virtue* (London and New York: Routledge, 1991); Brian Leiter, *Nietzsche on Morality* (London and New York: Routledge, 2002); Simon May, *Nietzsche's Ethics and his War on "Morality"* (Oxford: Clarendon Press; New York: Oxford University Press, 1999). See also the collection of essay edited by Richard Schacht, *Nietzsche's Postmoralism: Essays on Nietzsche's Prelude to Philosophy's Future* (Cambridge and New York: Cambridge University Press, 2001).

POLITICS

The most important and seminal studies on this topic are: Daniel W. Conway, *Nietzsche and the Political* (London and New York: Routledge, 1997); Bruce Detwiler, *Nietzsche and the Politics of Aristocratic Radicalism* (Chicago and London: University of Chicago Press, 1990); Don Dombowsky, *Nietzsche's Machiavellian Politics: The Outlaw Prince* (Basingstoke: Palgrave Macmillan, 2004); Lawrence J. Hatab, *A Nietzschean Defense of Democracy: An Experiment in Postmodern Politics* (Chicago and La Salle, IL: Open Court, 1995); David Owen, *Nietzsche, Politics and Modernity: A Critique of Liberal Reason* (London, Thousand Oaks, CA, and New Delhi: Sage, 1995); Tracy B. Strong, *Friedrich Nietzsche and the Politics of Transfiguration*, 3rd edn (Urbana-Champaign and Chicago: University of Illinois Press, 2000); Leslie Paul Thiele, *Friedrich Nietzsche and the Politics of the Soul: A Study of Heroic Individualism* (Princeton, NJ, and London: Princeton University Press, 1990); Mark Warren, *Nietzsche and Political Thought* (Cambridge, MA, and London: MIT Press, 1988). See also the edited collection of Paul Patton, *Nietzsche, Feminism and Political Theory* (London and New York: Routledge, 1993).

RELIGION

The following books and edited volumes on aspects of Nietzsche and religion are recommended: Giles Fraser, *Redeeming*

Nietzsche: On the Piety of Unbelief (London and New York: Routledge, 2002); Jacob Golomb (ed.), *Nietzsche and Jewish Culture* (London and New York: Routledge, 1997); John Lippitt and Jim Urpeth (eds), *Nietzsche and the Divine* (Manchester: Clinamen, 2000); Robert G. Morrison, *Nietzsche and Buddhism: A Study in Nihilism and Ironic Affinities* (Oxford and New York: Oxford University Press, 1997); James C. O'Flaherty, Timothy F. Sellner, and Robert M. Helm (eds), *Studies in Nietzsche and the Judaeo-Christian Tradition* (Chapel Hill, NC: University of North Carolina Press, 1985); Tyler T. Roberts, *Contesting Spirit: Nietzsche, Affirmation, Religion* (Princeton, NJ: Princeton University Press, 1998): Weaver Santaniello, *Nietzsche, God, and the Jews: His Critique of Judeo-Christianity in Relation to the Nazi Myth* (Albany, NY: State University of New York Press, 1994); Yirmiyahu Yovel, *Dark Riddle: Hegel, Nietzsche, and the Jews* (Oxford: Polity; University Park, PA: Pennsylvania State University Press, 1998).

ETERNAL RECURRENCE

On this complex and difficult thought in Nietzsche readers will profit from consulting the following texts: Lawrence J. Hatab, *Nietzsche's Life Sentence: Coming to Terms with Eternal Recurrence* (New York and London: Routledge, 2005); Martin Heidegger, *Nietzsche, Volume Two: The Eternal Recurrence of the Same*; Paul S. Loeb, *The Death of Nietzsche's Zarathustra* (Cambridge and New York: Cambridge University Press); Karl Löwith, *Nietzsche's Philosophy of the Eternal Recurrence of the Same*, trans. J. Harvey Lomax (Berkeley, LA and London: University of California Press, 1997); Joan Stambaugh, *Nietzsche's Thought of Eternal Return* (Baltimore, MD and London: Johns Hopkins University Press, 1972).

THE WILL TO POWER

Three important studies on the will to power in English are Jacob Golomb, *Nietzsche's Enticing Psychology of Power* (Ames, IA: Iowa State University Press; Jerusalem: Magnes Press, 1989); John Richardson's *Nietzsche's System* and the important essay by Wolfgang Müller Lauter, "Nietzsche's 'Doctrine' of the Will to Power,'" in Müller-Lauter, *Nietzsche: His Philosophy of Contradictions and the Contradictions of his Philosophy*, trans. David

J. Parent (Urbana-Champaign and Chicago: University of Illinois Press, 1999); and Linda L. Williams, *Nietzsche's Mirror: The World as Will to Power* (Lanham, MD, and Oxford: Rowman & Littlefield, 2000), pp. 122–61.

WOMEN

On this topic the most important and helpful books and edited volumes include: Peter J. Burgard (ed.), *Nietzsche and the Feminine* (Charlottesville, VA and London: University Press of Virginia, 1994); Carol Diethe, *Nietzsche's Women: Beyond the Whip* (Berlin and New York: Walter de Gruyter, 1996); Luce Irigaray, *Marine Lover of Friedrich Nietzsche*, trans. Gillian C. Gill (New York: Columbia University Press, 1991); Kelly Oliver, *Womanizing Nietzsche: Philosophy's Relation to the "Feminine"* (New York and London: Routledge, 1995), and with Marilyn Pearsall (eds), *Feminist Interpretations of Friedrich Nietzsche* (University Park, PA: Pennsylvania State University Press, 1998); and Caroline Picart, *Resentment and the "Feminine" in Nietzsche's Politico-Aesthetics* (University Park, PA: Pennsylvania State University Press, 1999).

PERSPECTIVISM

For a detailed examination of this topic in Nietzsche see Steven D. Hales and Rex Welshon, *Nietzsche's Perspectivism* (Urbana-Champaign and Chicago: University of Illinois Press, 2000); see also the relevant chapters in Nehamas, *Nietzsche: Life as Literature* (chapter 3) and Cox, *Nietzsche, Naturalism, and Interpretation* (chapter 3). Finally, for some novel insights see the recent essay by Ken Gemes, "Life's Perspectives," in Gemes and Richardson (eds), *The Oxford Handbook to Nietzsche* (Oxford: Oxford University Press, forthcoming).

PESSIMISM

There is a helpful chapter on Nietzsche's "Dionysian pessimism" in Joshua Dienstag's study, *Pessimism: Philosophy, Ethic, Spirit* (Princeton, NJ: Princeton University Press, 2006), pp. 161–201. Much helpful information, including context and background, can be found in Tobias Dahlkvist, *Nietzsche and the Philosophy of Pessimism* (Uppsala, Sweden: Universitet, 2007).

ON THE GENEALOGY OF MORALITY

There are now a significant number of books and edited volumes on this classic text by Nietzsche, which comes after *BGE* and was intended by Nietzsche to be a supplement and clarification of it. The following are recommended: Christa Davis Acampora (ed.), *Critical Essays on the Classics: Nietzsche's* On the Genealogy of Morals (Lanham, MD, and Oxford: Rowman and Littlefield, 2006); Daniel W. Conway, *Nietzsche's* On the Genealogy of Morals (London and New York: Continuum, 2008); Lawrence J. Hatab, *Nietzsche's* On the Genealogy of Morality: *An Introduction* (Cambridge and New York: Cambridge University Press, 2008); Christopher Janaway, *Beyond Selflessness: Reading Nietzsche's* Genealogy (Oxford: Oxford University Press, 2007); Dirk S. Johnson, *Nietzsche's New Darwinism* (Cambridge: Cambridge University Press, 2010); David Owen, *Nietzsche's* Genealogy of Morality (Stocksfield: Acumen, 2007); Aaron Ridley, *Nietzsche's Conscience: Six Character Studies from the "Genealogy"* (Ithaca, NY and London: Cornell University Press, 1998); Richard Schacht (ed.), *Nietzsche, Genealogy, Morality: Essays on Nietzsche's "Genealogy of Morals"* (Berkeley, LA and London: University of California Press, 1994).

THUS SPOKE ZARATHUSTRA

The following studies of *Zarathustra*, which has a complex relation to *BGE*, can be recommended: Robert Gooding-Williams, *Zarathustra's Dionysian Modernism* (Stanford, CA: Stanford University Press, 2001); Kathleen Marie Higgins, *Nietzsche's "Zarathustra"* (Philadelphia, PA: Temple University Press, 1987); Laurence Lampert, *Nietzsche's Teaching: An Interpretation of "Thus Spoke Zarathustra"* (New Haven, CT, and London: Yale University Press, 1986); Paul S. Loeb, *The Death of Nietzsche's Zarathustra*; Stanley Rosen, *The Mask of Enlightenment: Nietzsche's "Zarathustra"* (Cambridge and New York: Cambridge University Press, 1995).

BEYOND GOOD AND EVIL

To date there have been two major and helpful studies of *BGE*: Douglas Burnham, *Reading Nietzsche: An Analysis of "Beyond*

Good and Evil" (Stocksfield: Acumen, 2007); and Laurence Lampert, *Nietzsche's Task: An Interpretation of "Beyond Good and Evil"* (New Haven, CT, and London: Yale University Press, 2001). See also Laurence D. Cooper, *Eros in Plato, Rousseau, and Nietzsche* (University Park, PA: Penn State University Press, 2008). Paul van Tongeren's *Reinterpreting Modern Culture: An Introduction to Friedrich Nietzsche's Philosophy* (above) also focuses on *BGE*.

ESSAYS RELATING TO *BGE*

Despite the dearth of critical studies on *BGE* in English there are a number of important and helpful articles that can be recommended, including: Peter Berkowitz, "The Ethics of Knowing: *Beyond Good and Evil*," in Berkowitz, *Nietzsche: The Ethics of an Immoralist* (Cambridge, MA: Harvard University Press, 1995), pp. 228–61; Maudemarie Clark, "Nietzsche's Misogyny," in Kelly Oliver and Marilyn Pearsall (eds), *Feminist Interpretations of Friedrich Nietzsche* (University Park, PA: Pennsylvania State University Press, 1998), pp. 187–98; Robert Guay, "Our Virtues," *Philosophical Topics*, 34:1, pp. 71–87; Alexander Nehamas, "Who Are 'The Philosophers of the Future?': A Reading of *Beyond Good and Evil*," in Robert C. Solomon and Kathleen M. Higgins (eds), *Reading Nietzsche* (New York and Oxford: Oxford University Press, 1988), pp. 46–67; Gary Shapiro, "Peoples and Fatherlands: Nietzsche's Geophilosophy and the Direction of the Earth," *Journal of Nietzsche Studies* 2008, 35–6, pp. 9–28; Leo Strauss, "Note on the Plan of Nietzsche's *Beyond Good and Evil*," in *Studies in Platonic Political Philosophy* (Chicago: University of Chicago Press, 1983); Michael Tanner, "Friedrich Nietzsche, *Beyond Good and Evil*," in Godfrey Vesey (ed.), *Philosophers Ancient and Modern* (Cambridge and New York: Cambridge University Press, 1986), pp. 197–217; Gianni Vattimo, "Philosophy as Ontological Activity," in *Dialogue with Nietzsche*, trans. William McCuaig (New York: Columbia University Press, 2006), pp. 60–73.

NOTES

CHAPTER 1: NIETZSCHE'S LIFE AND WORKS IN CONTEXT

1 See Duncan Large, "Nietzsche's Use of Biblical Language," *Journal of Nietzsche Studies*, 22 (2001): pp. 88–115.
2 W. Wundt, "Philosophy in Germany," *Mind*, 2:8 (1877): pp. 493–518.
3 Nietzsche reports the meeting in a letter to his mother, emphasizing how greatly the journal is esteemed. Presumably, Robertson did not tell Nietzsche that the reference was not particularly positive! See pp. 509–10 of the 1877 issue cited above.
4 The following contributions are especially interesting: "Forgetfulness," "Pessimism: A History and A Criticism," "Study of Types of Character," "Mr. Sully on 'Physiological Aesthetics.'" The sections on "News" and "New Books" make references to many of the people Nietzsche offers as examples of various positions, especially in his later writings, and the "Books" section includes a summary and positive assessment of a book by Nietzsche's friend Paul Reé, whose work significantly influenced his *HH* and later *GM*.
5 Nietzsche rigorously pursued his science interests in 1873, when he read numerous works in astronomy, chemistry, physics, and physiology. See Thomas Brobjer, *Nietzsche's Philosophical Context* (Urbana-Champaign, IL: University of Illinois Press, 2008), and Gregory Moore, *Nietzsche, Biology, Metaphor* (Cambridge, MA: Cambridge University Press, 2002).
6 September 22, 1886, letter to Jacob Burckhardt, cited in Kaufmann's, "Translator's Introduction," to his translation of *BGE*, p. x.

CHAPTER 2: OVERVIEW OF THEMES

1 For further insight into this puzzle see Karsten Harries, "The Philosopher at Sea," in Michael Allen Gillespie and Tracy B. Strong (eds), *Nietzsche's New Seas: Explorations in Philosophy, Aesthetics, and Politics* (Chicago and London: University of Chicago Press, 1988), pp. 21–45.

CHAPTER 3: PART I: "ON THE PREJUDICES OF THE PHILOSOPHERS"

1 Helpful discussion of Nietzsche's views in the context of the history of aesthetics is found in Nicholas Martin, *Nietzsche and Schiller: Untimely Aesthetics* (Oxford: Oxford University Press, 1996). While Nietzsche is very interested in culture and how the arts are related to

forms of life, it is not clear whether he has much interest in theories of art and aesthetics per se. Nietzsche's *BT* briefly engages the aesthetic views of Aristotle and Schiller, but in his later writings, it is increasingly clear that he does not think aesthetic values and judgments are *separate and distinct* from rational and practical ones. In this respect, Nietzsche anticipates aspects of Dewey's thought, which includes the idea that there are aesthetic qualities in all experience and which form experiences *as* experience.

2 This theme is explored throughout the book, particularly in the context of what Nietzsche anticipates as the revaluation of appearances and the "will to appearance" in part VII.

3 Think of Aristotle's claim that poetry can be truer than history in its ability to capture what is true about human beings (even, precisely, in works that are not about actual living or past human beings). See Aristotle, *Poetics* IX.

4 Kant, of course, believed we could have other knowledge that was not dependent on experience, such as what might be called analytic truths, as for example, with the claim that all bachelors are unmarried men. All one needs to know are the meanings of the terms "bachelor" and "unmarried" to analytically conclude the truth of the claim, no further experience with any actual bachelors or men is necessary. Kant's *Critique of Pure Reason* aimed to show that what he called *synthetic a priori* judgments were also possible.

5 Nietzsche's relation to Schopenhauer is helpfully discussed in Christopher Janaway, *Beyond Selflessness: Reading Nietzsche's Genealogy* (Oxford: Oxford University Press, 2007).

6 In the subsequent work of part V of *The Gay Science* (added after publication of *BGE*), Nietzsche distinguishes kinds of pessimism, their origins and motivations, to show the differences between what he calls romantic pessimism (which he associates with Schopenhauer) and a pessimism of strength (which he associates with the ancient Greeks and his own retrieval of some of those ideas, including what he calls the "Dionysian"). Further discussion of Dionysus appears below and in Chapters 4 and 11.

7 There has been an explosion of interest in Nietzsche's knowledge of and engagement with science in recent years, much of which is not informed by early interpretations of Nietzsche's biologism and Heidegger's caution against it. See Martin Heidegger, *Nietzsche: Volume III: The Will to Power As Knowledge and As Metaphysics: Volume IV: Nihilism*, 2 Volumes in 1, translated and edited by David Farrell Krell (New York: Harper Collins, 1991), pp. 39–47. See also Gregory Moore, *Nietzsche, Biology, Metaphor* (Cambridge, MA: Cambridge University Press, 2002); John Richardson *Nietzsche's New Darwinism* (Oxford: Oxford University Press, 2004); and Dirk Johnson, *Nietzsche's Anti-Darwinism* (Cambridge: Cambridge University Press, 2010).

8 See elaboration of Nietzsche's views about drives in Richardson, *Nietzsche's New Darwinism* and John Richardson, *Nietzsche's System* (Oxford: Oxford University Press, 1996).

9 Useful discussion of Nietzsche's views of "soul," including comparison with Plato, can be found in Graham Parkes, *Composing the Soul: Reaches of Nietzsche's Psychology* (Chicago: University of Chicago Press, 1994).

10 Nietzsche's engagement with the ideas of Boscovich is explored in depth in Greg Whitlock, "Investigations in Time Atomism and Eternal Recurrence," *Journal of Nietzsche Studies*, 20 (2000): pp. 34–57. See also discussion of Nietzsche's interest in and critiques of materialism, particularly the views summarized and advanced by F. A. Lange, *Geschichte des Materialismus* [History of Materialism] 1866; Thomas Brobjer, *Nietzsche's Philosophical Context* (Urbana-Champaign: University of Illinois Press, 2008); George Stack, *Lange and Nietzsche* (New York and Berlin: Walter de Gruyter, 1983).

11 Cf. *TI*, "How the 'Real World' Became a Fiction"; on the influence of Spir, Teichmüller, and Lange on the ideas discussed in *BGE* I, see Nadeem Hussain, "Nietzsche's Positivism," *European Journal of Philosophy*, 12:3 (2004): pp. 326–68; and Maudemarie Clark and David Dudrick, "Nietzsche's Post-Positivism," *European Journal of Philosophy*, 12:3 (2004): pp. 369–85.

12 Cf. *GS* 374, and discussion by Werner Stegmaier, " 'Philosophischer Idealismus' und die 'Musik des Lebens.' Zu Nietzsches Umgang mit Paradoxien. Eine kontextuelle Interpretation des Aphorismus Nr. 372 der Fröhlichen Wissenschaft," *Nietzsche-Studien,* 33 (2004): pp. 90–129.

13 On the extent of Nietzsche's naturalism in *BGE*, see Maudemarie Clark and David Dudrick, "The Naturalisms of *Beyond Good and Evil*," in Keith Ansell Pearson (ed.), *A Companion to Nietzsche* (Oxford and Malden, MA: Blackwell Publishers, 2006), pp. 148–68.

14 Debate about whether Nietzsche is making assertions about freedom of the will or the phenomenology of willing in *BGE* I can be found in Clark and Dudrick, "Nietzsche on the Will: An Analysis of *BGE* 19" and Brian Leiter, "Nietzsche's Theory of the Will," both in Ken Gemes and Simon May (eds), *Nietzsche on Freedom and Autonomy* (Oxford: Oxford University Press, 2009).

15 Earlier, the Hellenistic philosophers and, later, Michel Foucault. See Foucault, *The History of Sexuality, Vol. 3: The Care of the Self*, translated by Robert Hurley (New York: Vintage Books, 1986).

16 See Kant's *The Critique of Judgment*. The centrality of taste for Nietzsche is still not well appreciated in English-language scholarship. This occurs both in his early conception of philosophy itself and the later preoccupation with its purification. An exception is Richardson, who devotes extensive discussion of the importance of the aesthetic in his *Nietzsche's New Darwinism* (see especially, pp. 257–8). As we shall see, Nietzsche also develops a very specific conception of the relation between the aesthetic and the sublime as a kind of taste for subtle knowledge, which is further related to the kind of intellectual conscience he anticipates for future

philosophers. One difference between the early and later Nietzsche on this point is that in Nietzsche's later writings the philosopher's taste has become, and needed to become in terms of his own project, more comprehensive and extensive (this informs how he understands "greatness"): the philosopher must have antennae for many types and forms of life and be able to see "value" in them; there is much on this in later parts of *BGE*, as we shall see, particularly in "Our Virtues," "On Peoples and Fatherlands," and "What is noble?".

17 See Nietzsche's early work, where he draws out the relation between *sophos* and *sapio* ("to taste") in his lectures on the Pre-Platonics (*KGW* II.4, pp. 217–18, in *The Pre-Platonic Philosophers*, translated by Greg Whitlock [Urbana-Champaign and Chicago: University of Illinois Press, 2001], p. 8).

18 Yet we can see similarities between Nietzsche's conception of the "soul" in terms of orders of rank and that of the Platonic Socrates in book VIII of *Republic* where the character Socrates describes constitutions of both cities and individual souls in terms of ruling parts weakening and giving way to lesser parts. The various constitutions (Aristocratic, Timocratic, Oligarchic, Democratic, and Tyrannical) are distinguished according to which drive rules. How drives rule is determined by the sort of drive it is and its capacity to know the good.

19 In this respect, Nietzsche's aesthetic views are more similar to those of Hume than those of Kant. See Hume's essay on "Of the Standard of Taste" (*David Hume, Selected Essays* [Oxford: Oxford University Press, 1998], pp. 133–54).

20 In this context, consider Nietzsche's views on the importance of the erotic as discussed by Robert Pippin, "Morality as Psychology; Psychology as Morality: Nietzsche, Eros, and Clumsy Lovers" in his *Idealism as Modernism: Hegelian Variations* (Cambridge: Cambridge University Press, 1997), and in the context of *amor fati* (loving fate) and eternal recurrence (discussed in later chapters) by Béatrice Han-Pile "Nietzsche and Amor Fati," *European Journal of Philosophy*, forthcoming, 2011.

21 See Gregory Moore's work tracing the variety of evolutionary theories emerging in Nietzsche's day and his knowledge of or access to such writings (*Nietzsche, Biology, Metaphor*, pp. 46–55), particularly on the work of Rolph (1884). Further helpful elaboration of the relation between the development and evolution of evolutionary theory itself, and thus the significance of Rolph's insights and, by extension, Nietzsche's use of them, see Stephen J. Gould, *The Structure of Evolutionary Theory* (Cambridge, MA: Harvard University Press, 2002). Gould does not notice these connections, although he does mention Nietzsche's anticipation of Gould's own concept of exaptation. See further discussion in Daniel Dennett, *Darwin's Dangerous Idea: Evolution and the Meanings of Life* (New York: Simon and Shuster, 1995). Interested readers might follow Gould's

suggestion (2002) that the future development of evolutionary theory also involves appreciation of its own development and historical roots to find further contributions or at least resonances to be found in Nietzsche's work for contemporary theorists of evolution, including evolutionary psychology, which was one of Nietzsche's primary interests.

22 Nietzsche's notebooks are fascinating to read and there are various collections available in English translation. Students should be cautious about conclusions based on this material as well as sources used to obtain it. There is considerable scholarly debate about using Nietzsche's notebooks as evidence of specific views he held that might not appear in his published writings. In general, Nietzsche scholars agree that published works have priority over unpublished notes. Furthermore, there is absolute agreement that a frequently cited source in English literature (including in this book), *The Will to Power*, translated by Walter Kaufmann and R. J. Hollingdale, is a compilation prepared by Nietzsche's sister and other editors, and it is *not* a book that Nietzsche drafted or even a reliable gathering of material from his notebooks. See further, p. viii.

23 See also *KSA* 11:36[22]: "Life should be defined as an enduring form of the *process of testing force*, where the different combatants grow unequally . . . Obeying and commanding are forms of martial art."

24 Nietzsche already seems to have this in mind in *GS* 109, where he describes his project as "de-deifying nature."

25 These ideas might be read as anticipating Heidegger's treatment of temporality and historicity in his *Being and Time* and relevant to his reading of the time of eternal recurrence in his *Nietzsche*, Vol. 2.

CHAPTER 4: PART II: "THE FREE SPIRIT"

1 These include: *Human-All-too-Human* (published in three parts), *Daybreak* or *Dawn*, and *The Gay Science*. See the back cover of the first edition of *GS*, which included only *GS* I–IV. For more discussion of the free spirit, see Amy Mullin, "Nietzsche's Free Spirit," *Journal of the History of Philosophy*, 38:3 (July 2000): pp. 383–405; Ruth Abbey, *Nietzsche's Middle Period* (Oxford: Oxford University Press, 2000); and Bernard Reginster, "What Is a Free Spirit? Nietzsche on Fanaticism," *Archiv für Geschichte der Philosophie*, 85:1 (2003): pp. 51–85.

2 See *D* 20 for Nietzsche's earlier, positive, discussion of "Freithäter und Freidenker."

3 Kathleen Marie Higgins discusses the history of the ass festivals and their relation to satyr plays in the context of the appearance of the ass in *Z* ("Nietzsche and the Mystery of the Ass" in *A Nietzschean Bestiary: Animality Beyond Docile and Brutal* (New York and Lanham, MD: Rowman & Littlefield Publishers, Inc., 2004), pp. 100–18). See also further discussion below.

4 Both philosophy and art are depicted as having "tragic" deaths (but also possible rebirths) in Nietzsche's very first book *The Birth of Tragedy*. Nietzsche also made extensive notes for, but never published, a work to be titled *Philosophy in the Tragic Age of the Greeks*, which considered the development of philosophy in tandem with the birth of tragedy.

5 For argument that part III of *Z* depicts the death of Zarathustra, a somewhat controversial claim given the character's appearance in part IV, see Paul S. Loeb, *The Death of Nietzsche's Zarathustra* (Cambridge: Cambridge University Press, 2010).

6 Cited in Jennifer Michael Hecht, *Doubt: A History* (New York: Harper Collins, 2003), p. 294.

7 Nietzsche finished *BGE* in early summer 1885. During the period when he was writing the text he spent time in Venice, a home of Bruno, and during 1885, a group of notable figures formed an international committee to erect a monument to Bruno on the site of his execution in Rome. (The committee included Victor Hugo [cf. *TI* "Skirmishes": 1], Herbert Spencer, Ernest Renan [cf. *TI* "Skirmishes": 2], Ernst Haeckel, Henrik Ibsen, and Ferdinand Gregorovius.) The statue was eventually erected in 1889.

8 For helpful discussion of some relevant parts of *BT* see Douglas Burnham and Martin Jesinghausen, *Nietzsche's* The Birth of Tragedy: *A Reader's Guide* (London: Continuum, 2010), pp. 97–102.

9 *KSA* 1, p. 789; translation is ours. Compare this with *HH* 158: "The most fortunate thing that can happen in the evolution of an art is that several geniuses appear together and keep one another in bounds; in the course of this struggle the weaker and tenderer natures too will usually be granted light and air." Cf. *KSA* 8:5[146] in a section titled "Critique of Development": "Der glücklichste Fall in der Entwicklung, wenn sich mehrere Genie's gegenseitig in Schranken halten."

10 These ideas are also reflected in Nietzsche's views about complementary characters or spirits (§28), as for example, that between Plato and Aristophanes in which the former allegedly sought relief through the latter by sleeping with a copy of Aristophanes' works under his pillow: "How could even Plato have endured life— a Greek life he repudiated—without an Aristophanes?"

11 Epicurus is discussed by Diogenes Laertius (third century AD), a likely source for Nietzsche, and his views are propounded and expanded by the later philosopher Lucretius (94–49 BCE).

12 The Stoics also denounced pity, and Martha Nussbaum has used that particular point as an entrée to considering the intersection between Nietzsche's views and those of the Stoics: "Pity and Mercy: Nietzsche's Stoicism," in Richard Schacht (ed.), *Nietzsche, Genealogy, Morality* (Berkeley, CA: University of California Press, 1994), pp. 139–67, p. 146. On this view, external goods are in the control of fortune, only intrinsic goods are within one's control and reach. Major emotions are supposed to be tied to the former. Nussbaum

considers six arguments Nietzsche advances against pity, comparing them with Stoic views, and then uses this as a basis for a more elaborate discussion of Nietzsche's account of punishment and mercy in *GM*. This is supposed to show that Nietzsche sides clearly with Senecca against Aristotle in "his stand against cruelty and in favor of self-command" (149). Nietzsche is famously critical of pitying; see, for example, the discussion "On the Pitying" in *Z* and note that Zarathustra's "last temptation" was pity for the last man. Nussbaum directs her readers to Nietzsche's earlier *D* 251, where Nietzsche ties pity, especially in the Stoic tradition, to a desire to dominate (Nussbaum, p. 151). According to Nussbaum, Zarathustra's emphasis on self-directed activity makes him resemble the Stoic. Whether or not one is convinced by Nussbaum that Nietzsche's arguments against pity are ultimately tied to a positive reception of Stoicism, one can appreciate her subtle discussion of Nietzsche's repudiation of cruelty.

13 On Nietzsche's repeated use of the figure of the satyr (including and beyond its association with Dionysus), see Lawrence J. Hatab, "Satyr: Human-Animality in Nietzsche," in Christa Davis Acampora and Ralph R. Acampora (eds), *A Nietzschean Bestiary: Animality Beyond Docile and Brutal*, pp. 211–19. Also see discussion of hybrids in the chapter on *BGE* VIII.

14 It is notable that Nietzsche uses the term "der Liebhaber der Erkenntniss" (translated here "lover of knowledge") rather than "lover of wisdom." This could be to distinguish his new philosopher, distinctive because of his *seeking* (as *Versucher*), from the traditional view of the philosopher as in pursuit of something that is somehow distinct from other kinds of knowledge-seeking (and perhaps regarded as exempt from certain standards of evidence and argument). In the preceding section 25, which discusses philosophers in the context of tragedy and farce, Nietzsche uses the German term *Philosophen*.

15 See also Graham Parkes, *Composing the Soul: Reaches of Nietzsche's Psychology* (Chicago: University of Chicago Press, 1994).

16 For example, *HH* 39, *GS* 117, and *TI* "Four Great Errors" 3.

17 Well known, critical discussions of these types can be found in Bernard Williams, *Shame and Necessity* (Berkeley, CA: University of California Press, 1993) and Alasdair MacIntyre, *After Virtue* (Notre Dame: University of Notre Dame Press, 1981).

18 A double negative; Nietzsche uses versions of *Abhängigkeit* in *GM* III:7, *GM* III:8, and *GM* III:27. Cf. *BGE* 6, 20, 29, 39, 41, 44, 61, 199, 201, 203, 204, 206, 208, 242, 260, and 261.

19 *Selbständigkeit* is used in *BGE* 239, and derivatives in sections 62 and 232. Nietzsche does not use the term at all in *GM*.

20 For an interesting contemporary take on this idea, see Wendy Brown's chapter on "Wounded Attachments" in her *States of Injury: Power and Freedom in Late Modernity* (Princeton, NJ: Princeton

University Press, 1995), which explores *ressentiment* as a particularly destructive form of not "letting go."

21 Nietzsche identifies another instance of "pushing" his ideas "to the limits" in section 56, in which he describes thinking through pessimism to its end and liberating it from its "half Christian" evaluative limitations. Nietzsche imagines such thought might lead to an ultimate affirmation: "the most high-spirited, most alive, and most world-affirming human being" ever [Kaufmann's translation modified]. This kind of affirmation is anticipated as something Nietzsche longs to achieve at the beginning of book IV of *GS* (§§276 and 267) in which he famously makes reference to *amor fati* and anticipates his negations as taking the form of "looking away," a notion reinforced in his metaphor of "sailing right over morality" (*BGE* 23). Section 56 is discussed at greater length in the next chapter.

22 One might still wish for even greater elaboration of these ideas given their scope and consequence. Nietzsche tells us in section 28 that free-spirited thought is "presto," and this arguably takes that to an extreme. There's no doubt that Nietzsche has not given us a conclusive proof of his "proposition," but it is not clear he has offered it to convince his reader—philosophers of the future are rather guarded about and protective of their "truths," reserving them for themselves. The important thing to note here, again, is that Nietzsche is scoping out a new vista, a new perspective, and reporting out from it.

23 "Die Welt von innen gesehen, die Welt auf ihren 'intelligiblen Charakter' hin bestimmt und bezeichnet—sie wäre eben 'Wille zur Macht' und nichts ausserdem."

24 For an elaborate account of how Nietzsche's free spirit is neither simply animated by a spirit of truthfulness (and thus free insofar as he is liberated from prejudices) nor the model of autonomy (because such "good government" cannot be specified in advance), see Reginster, "What Is a Free Spirit? Nietzsche on Fanaticism," 2003. Reginster's discussion of the differences between Nietzsche's and Kant's conception of autonomy is particularly useful. See also in Nietzsche, *D* 339, *GS* 335, *A* 11.

CHAPTER 5: PART III: "WHAT IS RELIGIOUS"

1 See, for example, *HH* chapter 3, "The Religious Life" and *D* book I, especially sections 57–96. It is in *GS* 125 that Nietzsche has a madman famously declare "God is dead and we have killed him."

2 See Laurence Lampert, *Nietzsche's Task: An Interpretation of "Beyond Good and Evil"* (New Haven, CT: Yale University Press, 2001), p. 102.

3 Nietzsche mentions eight figures in all, divided into four pairs: Epicurus and Montaigne, Goethe and Spinoza, Plato and Rousseau, Pascal and Schopenhauer.

4 In *D* 64 Nietzsche had noted that Christianity "possesses the hunter's instinct for all those who can by one means or another be brought to despair" and that Pascal "attempted the experiment of seeing whether, with the aid of the most incisive knowledge, everyone could not be brought to despair." And he concludes wittily: "the experiment miscarried, to his twofold despair." In *D* 86 Nietzsche further notes how Pascal sought to interpret physiological phenomena, such as the stomach, the beating of the heart, the nerves, the bile, and the semen, as moral and religious phenomenon, asking whether salvation or damnation was to be discovered in them, and how this led him to twist and torment his system of thought and himself so as to be in the right. See also *D* 91.

5 Lampert, *Nietzsche's Task*, p. 103.

6 Walter Kaufmann, *Nietzsche. Philosopher, Psychologist, and Antichrist*, 4th edn (Princeton, NJ: Princeton University Press, 1974), p. 111.

7 See Lampert, *Nietzsche's Task*, p. 112.

8 The concern with secularization can be traced back to Nietzsche's early writings, such as *The Birth of Tragedy* (1872) and the untimely meditations, notably *Schopenhauer as Educator* (1874). See also *KSA* 7:19[7]; 7:19[29].

9 Douglas Burnham, *Reading Nietzsche: An Analysis of "Beyond Good and Evil"* (Stocksfield: Acumen Press, 2007), p. 81.

10 One of Nietzsche's earliest sketches of the thought of eternal recurrence provides an "ethics" along these lines. Nietzsche asks, "if everything is necessary or preordained how can I exert an influence on my actions? For example, do not food, location, air, and company condition and transform me?" Nietzsche then points out that our opinions do so even more since they determine our choice of these things. He then concludes the sketch: "If you incorporate the thought of thoughts within yourself, it will transform you. The question in everything that you want to do: 'is it the case that I want to do it countless times?' is the *greatest* weight," *KSA* 9: 11[143]; translation available in Keith Ansell Pearson and Duncan Large (eds), *The Nietzsche Reader* (Malden, MA: Blackwell, 2006), p. 239.

11 In *EH* (BT 3), Nietzsche says that the doctrine of eternal recurrence—"of the unconditional and infinitely repeated circulation of all things"—could have already been taught by Heraclitus and that the Stoics shows traces of it. In fact there are a number of modern sources for the thought and Nietzsche had encountered most of them in his reading, including Hume, Giacomo Leopardi, and Schopenhauer. Perhaps the most intriguing modern source is August Blanqui's text of 1872 (written while he was in prison), *L'Éternité par les Astres* ("Eternity by the Stars"), which anticipates Nietzsche's articulation of the doctrine to an uncanny degree, even containing the image of the "hourglass" of existence: "What I am writing at this moment, in a dungeon of the Fort du Taureau, I have written it and I shall write it again forever, on a table, with a feather, under

clothes and in entirely similar circumstances. And so it is for every one of us. All of these earths stumble, one after the other, into the rejuvenating flames, so as to be born again and to stumble again, in the monotonous flow of an hourglass eternally turning itself over and emptying itself" (Paris: Les Impressions Nouvelles, 2002), p. 107. Nietzsche mentions Blanqui's text in a note of 1883 but it is not known for sure that he read it (*KSA* 10:[73]).

12 Schopenhauer famously writes that at the end of his life no sincere human being in sound possession of his faculties, "will ever wish to go through it again. Rather than this, he will much prefer to choose complete non-existence." See *The World as Will and Representation*, Volume 1, translated by E. F. J. Payne (New York: Dover, 1966), p. 324.

13 See *EH* "Why I am a Destiny" 3, "Zarathustra was the first to see in the struggle of good and evil the true driving-wheel in the machinery of things—the translation of morality into the metaphysical . . . is *his* doing . . . Zarathustra *created* the disastrous error that is morality: thus he must also be the first to *acknowledge* the mistake . . . The self-overcoming of morality out of truthfulness, the self-overcoming of the moralist into his opposite—*me*—this is what the name of Zarathustra means in my mouth."

14 Here we follow the argument of Loeb, *The Death of Nietzsche's Zarathustra* (Cambridge: Cambridge University Press, 2010), p. 190, rather than Lampert, *Nietzsche's Task*, pp. 120–1, or Burnham, *Reading Nietzsche*, pp. 87–9.

15 Again, we are more impressed by Loeb on this point, *The Death of Nietzsche's Zarathustra*, pp. 190–1, than either Lampert, *Nietzsche's Task*, pp. 119–20 or Burnham, *Reading Nietzsche*, pp. 84–6.

16 Lampert answers in the affirmative to this question in his exegesis of *BGE* 56.

17 The word religion has a twofold root: *relegere*, meaning to take into account or to pick up, and *religare*, meaning to connect or to fasten. See Ulrich Haase, *Starting with Nietzsche* (London: Continuum, 2008), p. 160.

18 Thanks to Paul S. Loeb for drawing our attention to this discourse in Z.

19 See H. W. Siemens, "Nietzsche's Critique of Democracy," *Journal of Nietzsche Studies*, 38 (2009): pp. 20–38, pp. 30–2.

CHAPTER 6: PART IV: "EPIGRAMS AND INTERLUDES"

1 In part IX, Nietzsche ambivalently embraces (or anticipates a time when it will be possible to embrace) divine laughter. See section 294.

2 Part I of *Thus Spoke Zarathustra* was completed in February 1883, but the fourth and final part was not completed until 1885. The four parts of the book were originally published separately.

3 See *KSA* 10:3[1].1–445.

4 These ideas recall the discussion of independence (*Unabhängenkeit*) in sections 29 and 41, and in section 260 in the context of considering humanity's "noble" and "slavish" inheritance, discussed in Chapter 11 of this book.

5 In his retrospective preface of 1886, Nietzsche describes what motivates his writing *The Gay Science* in terms of overflowing with gratitude (*GS* P2:1), and he goes on to identify a concern of the psychologist as "the relation of health and philosophy," which is capable of distinguishing whether "deprivations" are doing the philosophizing or whether "riches and strengths" are at work. (See also *GS* 76, 100, 107, 171, 295, 338, 343, 351, 363, 366, and 370.) Compare this with the contrast Nietzsche appears to be drawing between an evolutionary theory of conservation and one of discharging strength (*BGE* 13), and the danger of the free spirit in terms of its "hospitality" (*BGE* 41).

6 And these can be compared with claims about love elsewhere. Consider how unconditionally loving or hating are indicative of immaturity (§31; cf. §46), how the "love [of] man *for God's sake*"(§60) is described as both noble but going "astray" (§60), how the "love of *one* is a barbarism for it is exercised at the expense of all others" (§67); the connection between love, gratitude, and overflowing (§79); how "tethering the heart" is connected with being a "free spirit" (§87); how love and hatred distinguish the heavy spirited from the light (§90); the "impotence of the love of men" in Christianity (§104); the connection between sexual love and shame (§114); the importance of "woman's love in sexual relations and women's existence"(?!) (§§115, 139); the bodily character of "true" love (§142); how "love" is "beyond good and evil" (§153); the connection between love and jealousy (§160); the transfiguring perspective of love (§§163, 102).

7 What distinguishes something *as* an aphorism from other sections that have more narrative or discursive formats (or those that are poems, songs, or dithyrambs) is difficult to discern with precision. Jill Marsden describes them as "modular assertions which function independently in the work [. . .] The context of the aphorism is no broader than its terms," "Nietzsche and the Art of the Aphorisms," in Keith Ansell Pearson (ed.), *A Companion to Nietzsche* (Oxford and Malden, MA: Blackwell, 2006), p. 27.

8 One matter has now largely been resolved, namely *which* epigraph he is referring to. Previously, scholars engaged in a good deal of interpretative contortionism to explain how the epigraph from *Zarathustra* could be the object of the exegetical work in *GM* III, and this had puzzling suggestions for what it might mean to read and interpret Nietzsche. However, there is now general agreement that what appears as the first numbered section of that essay is the object of the exegesis, and several solid accounts show how Nietzsche sets about his task and how we might make use of that example. Agreement was reached more or less simultaneously using

two different methods. Clark's and Wilcox's empirical analysis of the archive materials showed the *Zarathustra* epigraph was added after the essay was written and thus could not be the primary subject of the exegesis therein. On hermeneutical grounds, Janaway shows how the essay comments on section 1 specifically, and Babich argues how the *Zarathustra* epigraph *reflects* this. Hatab elaborates the significance of interpreting the text as a whole with this understanding of the structure of the third essay. See Christopher Janaway, *Beyond Selflessness: Reading Nietzsche's Genealogy* (Oxford: Oxford University Press, 2007); Babette Babich, "The Genealogy of Moral and Right Reading: On the Nietzschean Aphorism and the Art of Polemic" in Christa Davis Acampora (ed.), *Critical Essays on Nietzsche's* On the Genealogy of Morals (New York and Lanham, MD: Rowman & Littlefield Publishers, Inc., 2006), pp. 177–90; and Lawrence J. Hatab, *Nietzsche's* On the Genealogy of Morality: *An Introduction* (Cambridge: Cambridge University Press, 2008).

9 Consider that the aphoristic style and Nietzsche's own ways of using it disrupt certain narrative and grammatical structures that presuppose certain metaphysical ideas about subjectivity (as for example, subjective unity and authority, agency, etc.; see *GS* 249 (polyphony), *GS* 256; cf. Marsden, "Nietzsche and the Art of the Aphorisms," p. 28).

10 Marsden, "Nietzsche and the Art of the Aphorisms," p. 27.

11 On the ontological significance of music (and how it allows the disclosure of being that cannot be simply expressed in language), see Christoph Cox, "Nietzsche, Dionysus, and the Ontology of Music," in Keith Ansell Pearson (ed.), *A Companion to Nietzsche* (Oxford and Malden, MA: Blackwell, 2006), pp. 495–513.

12 On Nietzsche's views about decadence as they reflect his interest in music (and de-cadence) see Bruce Ellis Benson, *Pious Nietzsche: Decadence and Dionysian Faith* (Bloomington, IN: Indiana University Press, 2008).

13 Wagner's letter to Mathilde Wesendonck, October 29, 1859, cited in Christopher Morris, *Reading Opera between the Lines: Orchestral Interludes and Cultural Meaning from Wagner to Berg* (Cambridge: Cambridge University Press, 2002), p. 9, n. 15.

14 Wagner's letter to Ferdinand Heine, August 1843, cited in Morris, p. 7, n. 14.

15 See Graham Parkes, "Introduction," *Thus Spoke Zarathustra*, translated by Graham Parkes (Oxford: Oxford University Press, 2005). Parkes aims to explicitly bring out the musicality of Nietzsche's book in his translation.

16 In the preface to *EH* Nietzsche writes, "Nobody is free to have ears for Zarathustra."

17 In *EH*, Nietzsche claims eternal recurrence is the "highest formula of affirmation that is at all attainable." But recall, this is not a blind cheerfulness or simple celebration of life; rather, Nietzsche regards

it as the outcome of pessimism taken to its limits "beyond good and evil," which means liberated from the "spell and delusion of morality" (*BGE* 56).

18 Himself "looking back," Nietzsche links his insight with a specific time and place, he locates it in a specific moment that seems to change his life forever. More on this appears below.

19 The change is presumably from Wagner's conception to something "lighter" and more vibrant, which he later associates with Bizet: "the phoenix of music flew past us with lighter and more brilliant features than it had ever displayed before" (*EH Z*: 1). On Bizet and what is meant by "lighter" and the form of love it conveys, see Chapter 10 in this book.

20 Likely similarly reconstructed or fabricated after the fact, much as Nietzsche's own recollection was.

21 Later mentioned in terms of palingenesis. Klaus Kropfinger, *Wagner and Beethoven: Richard Wagner's Reception of Beethoven*, translated by Peter Palmer (New York and Cambridge: Cambridge University Press, 1991), especially pp. 23–6.

22 *KSA* 10:3[1].293: "Die Liebe zum Leben ist beinahe der Gegensatz der Liebe zum Lang-Leben. Alle Liebe denkt an den Augenblick und die Ewigkeit—aber nie an 'die Länge.'"

23 Tracing out these curious connections, and mindful of the necessarily tentative and speculative nature of the suggestion, we might see *BGE* as *prelude* to *Z*, or at least more like a "prequel" than a sequel insofar as the philosophical views it anticipates are enacted by Nietzsche in the book that precedes it. This claim, of course, requires significantly more support and elaboration to sustain. For the idea of "prequel" in relation to Nietzsche's writing, see Paul S. Loeb's account of how book IV of *Z* is a like of "prequel" insofar as it relates events that are "internally analeptic" in *The Death of Nietzsche's Zarathustra* (Cambridge: Cambridge University Press, 2010), pp. 90–4. Loeb argues that part IV is like a prequel insofar as the events it portrays are like extended "flashbacks" of portions contemporaneous with the preceding events related. For Loeb, Nietzsche utilizes this narrative structure to illustrate his thought of eternal recurrence in which case Zarathustra's life recurs eternally. (Thus, eternal recurrence is *not* principally given as Zarathustra's idea or one that he especially effectively embraces.)

CHAPTER 7: PART V: "NATURAL HISTORY OF MORALITY"

1 See Walter Kaufmann, "How Nietzsche Revolutionized Ethics," in Kaufmann, *From Shakespeare to Existentialism* (Princeton, NJ: Princeton University Press, 1959), pp. 207–19.

2 On the "dangerous" distinction between "theoretical" and "practical" see *KSA* 13:14 [107]; *WP* 458.

3 W. E. H. Lecky, *History of European Morals in two volumes*, volume 1 (London: Longmans, Green & Co., 1920). Lecky's conception of

"natural history" has a number of aspects: (a) it must inquire into the sources of morals (e.g., not only explaining what constitutes a duty but how we obtain the notion); (b) it seeks to trace the action of external circumstances upon morals and ascertain what have been the main moral types in different ages and "by what causes they have been modified, impaired, or destroyed" (p. 160); (c) it has a suspicion about positing immaterial substances, such as a moral "faculty," and recognizes that the term "faculty" is simply an expression of classification.

4 For further insight see Thomas H. Brobjer, *Nietzsche and the "English"* (New York: Humanity Books, 2008), pp. 40–1.

5 For insight into Guyau see K. Ansell Pearson, "Free Thinkers and Free Spirits: Nietzsche and Guyau on the Future of Morality," in J. Metzger (ed.) *Nietzsche, Nihilism and the Philosophy of the Future* (London: Continuum, 2009), pp. 102–24; for insight into Rée see Janaway, *Beyond Selflessness: Reading Nietzsche's Genealogy* (Oxford: Oxford University Press, 2007); for insight into Rolph see Moore, *Nietzsche, Biology, Metaphor* (Cambridge, MA: Cambridge University Press, 2002).

6 For insight into how this "science" was envisaged in Nietzsche's time see Guyau's *A Sketch of Morality without Obligation or Sanction*, translated by Gertrude Kapteyn (London: Watts and Co., 1898). Guyau's text is one of the most sophisticated renditions of moral naturalism of its time.

7 See Arthur Schopenhauer, *On the Basis of Morality* (Oxford and Providence: Berghahn Books, 1995), p. 149. Schopenhauer speaks, as Nietzsche quotes him in *BGE* 186, of "the *real* basis of ethics" (*das eigentliche Fundament der Ethik*). For the most part Nietzsche prefers the word "Moral," though in many of his notes on "morality" from the period of *BGE* he too will employ the word "Ethik."

8 The Swiss historian Jacob Burckhardt, whose lectures on world history at Basel Nietzsche attended, may have exerted an influence on Nietzsche's conception of a "natural history of morality." For example, Burckhardt speaks of studying phenomena that are "*recurrent, constant* and *typical*" (p. 74). In addition, Burckhardt accords importance to the actions of "exceptional individuals"—the great individual for him is an "exception" and not an "example"—and has a notion of the "herd." See J. Burckhardt, *Force and Freedom*, James Hastings Nichols (ed.) (New York: Meridian Books, 1955).

9 For Wittgenstein philosophical problems "arise when language *goes on holiday*" and one of his main aims was to "bring words back from their metaphysical to their everyday use," *Philosophical Investigations*, translated by G. E. M. Anscombe (Oxford: Blackwell, 1967), sections 38 and 116. For insight into the intellectual affinities between Nietzsche and Wittgenstein see Erich Heller, *The Importance of Nietzsche: Ten Essays* (Chicago: University of Chicago Press, 1988), pp. 141–58. Nietzsche's approach to "morality" has been instructively compared to Wittgenstein by Raymond Geuss

in his essay, "Nietzsche and Morality" in Geuss (ed.) *Morality, Culture, and History* (Cambridge: Cambridge University Press, 1999), pp. 167–97.

10 See Immanuel Kant, *Groundwork of the Metaphysics of Morals*, translated by H. J. Paton (New York: Harper & Row, 1956), pp. 69–71.

11 See *D* 187, *GS* 335, and *A* 12.

12 Nietzsche has been deploying the word "herd" since as early as his untimely meditation on Schopenhauer. See *SE* 1.

13 Henri Bergson, *The Two Sources of Morality and Religion*, translated by R. Ashley Audra and Cloudesley Brereton (Notre Dame: University of Notre Dame Press, 1977), p. 26.

14 For further insight into Nietzsche's estimation of Napoleon, see Paul F. Glenn, "Nietzsche's Napoleon: The Higher Man as Political Actor," *Review of Politics*, 63:1 (2001): pp. 129–58, and Don Dombowsky, "Nietzsche as Bonapartist," in Herman Siemens and Vasti Roodt (eds), *Nietzsche, Power, and Politics* (Berlin and New York: Walter de Gruyter, 2008), pp. 347–71.

15 This aphorism is the first in Nietzsche's corpus to feature the contrast between the "morality of custom" and the "sovereignty of the individual" (*Selbstherrlichkeit des Einzelnen*). See also *GM* II:2.

16 Compare *D* 202, *Z* I "On the Pale Criminal," and *GM* II:10 on the "self-sublimation" of justice into mercy.

17 The nature of *Mitleid*, typically translated as "pity," is subjected to critical analysis by Nietzsche in several of his texts. See, for example, *D* 132–8 and *GM* preface. For further insight see David E. Cartwright, "Kant, Schopenhauer, and Nietzsche on the Morality of Pity," *Journal of the History of Ideas*, XLV: 1 (1984): pp. 83–98, and by the same author, "Schopenhauer's Compassion and Nietzsche's Pity," *Schopenhauer Jahrbuch*, 69 (1988): pp. 557–65. See also Gudrun von Tevenar, "Nietzsche's Objections to Pity and Compassion," in von Tevenar (ed.), *Nietzsche and Ethics* (Bern: Peter Lang, 2007), pp. 263–81.

18 For further insight see John Richardson, *Nietzsche's New Darwinism* (Oxford: Oxford University Press, 2004), pp. 190–200.

19 It is this kind of insight that informs Nietzsche's concern about socialism: "To have and to want to have more—*growth*, in one word—that is life itself. In the doctrine of socialism there is hidden, rather badly, a 'will to negate life;' the human beings or races that think up such a doctrine must be bungled" (*KSA* 11:37[11]; *WP* 125). This does not prevent Nietzsche from appreciating the possible therapeutic value of socialism: he holds that it delays "peace on earth" and works against the "total mollification of the democratic herd animal" (ibid.). See also Burckhardt, *Force and Freedom*, pp. 318–19: " . . . permanence means paralysis and death. Only in movement, with all its pain, is life."

20 This new virtue plays an important role in Nietzsche's thinking of the 1880s, including *BGE*, and will be examined in the chapter on "Our Virtues."

21 Schopenhauer, *On the Basis of Morality*, p. 212.
22 *WP* 269 gives a severely truncated version of this note.
23 This note, given as a few lines in *WP* 287, runs to ten pages in the *KSA*.
24 This negative valuation of happiness is something Nietzsche shares with Burckhardt. See *Force and Freedom*, pp. 295–6, p. 318.

CHAPTER 8: PART VI: "WE SCHOLARS"

1 Lampert, *Nietzsche's Task: An Interpretation of "Beyond Good and Evil"* (New Haven, CT: Yale University Press, 2001), p. 180.
2 Nietzsche is writing his texts in Germany at a time when the "back to Kant" movement is well underway and neo-Kantianism, often associated with the reduction of philosophy to the theory of knowledge, is a dominant force in German universities. However, as one commentator has noted, the view that it had reduced philosophy to the theory of knowledge is unfair and was rejected by a number of neo-Kantians themselves. Herbert Schnädelbach, *Philosophy in Germany 1831–1933*, translated by Eric Matthews (Cambridge: Cambridge University Press, 1984), p. 106. Their achievements included: developing philological research that helped establish Kant's monumental role in the history of modern European philosophy, establishing important trajectories in epistemology and the philosophy of science, and developing Kantian thought in diverse areas such as the theory of value, ethics, and social and political philosophy.
3 Suzanne Guerlac, *Thinking in Time: An Introduction to Henri Bergson* (Ithaca, NY and London: Cornell University Press, 2006), p. 21.
4 Gary Gutting, *French Philosophy in the Twentieth Century* (Cambridge: Cambridge University Press, 2001), p. 8.
5 Recent studies have encouraged us to appreciate Comte as a much more subtle and delicate thinker than is widely supposed. In his *Comte after Positivism* (Cambridge: Cambridge University Press, 1995), for example, Robert Scharff seeks to show that Comte, while holding scientific philosophy to be the final stage of intellectual development, did not simply reject theology and metaphysics; rather, he has a historic-critical appreciation of the situation in which philosophy's past is relevant to its future practice and this involves a *critical appropriation* of the theologico-metaphysical legacy (Scharff, p. 5). This is arguably the strategy Nietzsche adopts in his free spirit trilogy.
6 This is a criticism Karl Jaspers levels at Nietzsche and argues that to imitate pre-Socratic thinking today amounts to a ludicrous and despicable exercise. See Jaspers, *Anaximander, Heraclitus, Parmenides, Plotinus, Lao-Tzu, Nagarjuna*, translated by Ralph Manheim (New York and London: Harcourt Brace Jovanovich, 1966), p. 31.
7 Lampert, *Nietzsche's Task*, p. 184.

8 See also *HH* P:4 on the relation between "great health" and living experimentally: "the excess that gives to the free spirit the dangerous privilege of living *for experiments* and of being allowed to offer itself to adventure: the master privilege of the free spirit!"

9 As noted by Burnham, *Reading Nietzsche: An Analysis of "Beyond Good and Evil"* (Stocksfield: Acumen Press, 2007), p. 139. See also Lampert, *Nietzsche's Task*, p. 185: "To play *the* wicked game is to make oneself an actor in the highest of all games, a knowing actor who has been forced to believe that he has a right to a judgment about the worth of life."

10 *Biederkeit* means integrity, honesty, sincerity, uprightness, so that a *Biedermann* is a man of honor, a man of his word; less charitably the word also denotes middle-class respectability. When Nietzsche puts probity or honesty to work in his later work, from *Daybreak* onward, the word he invariably uses is *Redlichkeit*, which has the same set of meanings, and he also makes use of *Rechtschaffenheit* (e.g., *A* 12). In *D* 465 this is said to be "our youngest virtue;" it is examined in the next chapter. In the early writings probity or integrity is seen by Nietzsche to be almost wholly tied to convention in which one typically tells the truth only in simple things, and where probity is distrustful of the innovator, the desire is to employ probity in order to conserve the old wisdom and established truths. See also *GS* 366.

11 On the need to regulate one's pro and con, the necessary injustice in life's perspectivism and need for a comprehensive point of view, see *HH* P:6: "You must learn to grasp the *necessary* injustice in every For and Against, injustice as inseparable from life, life itself as *conditioned* by perspective and its injustice. Above all, you must see with your own eyes where injustice is always the greatest: namely, where life has developed in the smallest, narrowest, and neediest, most preliminary ways and yet still cannot avoid taking *itself* as the purpose and measure of things . . . you must see with your own eyes the problem of establishing *rank orderings* and how power and right and comprehensiveness of perspective grow up into the heights together."

12 See *KSA* 12:2[127]: "Skepsis an der Moral ist das Entscheidende." A note from 1885 also speaks of the need to cultivate an "absolute skepticism toward all inherited concepts" (*KSA* 11:34[195]; *WP* 409).

13 On art for art's sake see also *BGE* 254 and *TI* "Skirmishes of an Untimely Man" 24.

14 See also *GS* 283: "I welcome all signs that a more virile, warlike age is about to begin, which will restore honor and courage above all. For this age shall prepare the way for one yet higher, and it shall gather the strength that this higher age will require some day— the age that will carry heroism into the search for knowledge and that will *wage wars* for the sake of ideas (*Gedanken*) and their consequences." See also, from the 1887 edition, *GS* 362.

15 For insight into the role played by classical philology in the German university system in the eighteenth and nineteenth centuries see,

Nicholas Boyle, *German Literature. A Very Short Introduction* (Oxford: Oxford University Press, 2008), pp. 8–11.

16 Nietzsche employs this notion of "the passion of knowledge" to significant effect in book V of *D*. See especially *D* 429 entitled "The new passion."

17 The need for cleanliness runs like a refrain throughout Nietzsche's writings, starting with the unfashionable observations. Nietzsche argues that the sense for '"cleanliness" (*Reinlichkeit*) should be kindled in a child to the point of passion, attending all its talents "like an aureole of purity" that bears happiness within it and spreading happiness around it (*AOM* 288). In *GS* 335 Nietzsche advises us as follows: "Let us therefore *limit* ourselves to the purification of our opinions and valuations and to the *creation our own new tables of what is good* . . . " See also *EH* P:3, "Every achievement, every step forward in knowledge is the *consequence* of courage, of toughness toward oneself, of cleanliness (*Sauberkeit*) towards oneself," and *EH* "Why I am so Wise" 8: "I have an instinct for cleanliness that is utterly uncanny in its sensitivity . . ."

18 The note for this section of *BGE* can also be profitably read. See *KSA* 11:38[13]; *WP* 972.

19 See A. Schopenhauer, *The World as Will and Representation*, translated by E. F. J. Payne (New York: Dover, 1966), chapter XXXI.

20 Translated into English as *Force and Freedom*.

21 J. Burckhardt, *Force and Freedom*, James Hastings Nichols (ed.) (New York: Meridian Books, 1955), p. 269. Burckhardt maintains that it is with the "great philosophers" that we enter the domain of greatness properly speaking, a domain of uniqueness and irreplaceability, where more than ordinary powers are at work and the world as a whole is addressed (p. 276).

22 See Nietzsche's letter to Franz Overbeck, July 30, 1881.

23 With regards to philosophers Nietzsche says, "they must no longer merely let themselves be given concepts, no longer just purify and clarify them, but first of all must *make* them, *create* them, present them and persuade in their favor. Up to now, one on the whole trusted in one's concepts as a miraculous *dowry* (*Mitgift*) from some miracle world: but in the end they were the legacies left us by our most distant, stupidest and yet cleverest forebears" (*KSA* 11:34[195]).

24 Lampert, *Nietzsche's Task*, p. 206.

25 Bergson, *The Two Sources of Morality and Religion*, translated by R. Ashley Audra and Cloudesley Brereton (Notre Dame: University of Notre Dame Press, 1977), pp. 281–3; G. Vattimo, *Nihilism and Emancipation: Ethics, Politics, and Law*, translated by William McCuaig (New York: Columbia University Press, 2004), pp. 116–17.

26 In a note from 1885–1886 Nietzsche writes of the use of the modern democratic movement by a superior force that will "perfect" it through a "sublime (*sublimen*) elaboration of slavery;" the

"higher species of masterful and imperial spirits" need this slavery "for new, previously impossible prospects, for *its* prospects . . . For *its* tasks . . . " (*KSA* 12:2[13]).

27 Peter Bergmann, *Nietzsche, the "Last Anti-Political German"* (Bloomington, IN: Indiana University Press, 1987), p. 162.

28 This theme is continued in the next appearance of the term in Nietzsche's published writings, *D* 189.

29 Ibid.

30 That is, Germany is becoming "shallow."

31 One commentator has even suggested that *Geisterkrieg* is a reference to what has come to an end, the old notion of politics and which "has dissolved" (*aufgegangen*) into a war of specters or ghosts, possibly lost causes. It might be relevant to note that in the denouement to this passage Nietzsche writes: "there will now be wars the like of which have never been seen before on earth" and, "only since I came on the scene has there been *great politics* on earth." See Paul van Tongeren, "Nietzsche as Über-Politischer Denker," in Herman Siemens and Vasti Roodt (eds), *Nietzsche, Power, and Politics*, pp. 69–85; Hugo Drochon has proposed "Mind War" as the most accurate translation of *Geisterkrieg* and which is best construed not in terms of a war between peoples or classes but between "ascending" and "descending" forms of life. See Drochon, "The time is coming when we will relearn politics," *Journal of Nietzsche Studies*, 39 (Spring 2010): pp. 66–86, and Nietzsche, *KSA* 13:25[1].

32 "If we could dispense with wars, so much the better. I can imagine more profitable uses for the twelve billion now paid annually for the armed peace we have in Europe; there are other means of winning respect for physiology than field hospitals." Cited in Walter Kaufmann (ed.), *On the Genealogy of Morals and Ecce Homo* (New York: Random House, 1968), p. 344. In 1878 Nietzsche recognizes that one problem facing modern Europe is that of war (*HH* 477). He is not sure that culture can exist without passions, vices, and acts of malice, so we need to recognize this and find new means of releasing such instincts and energies. If such instincts are not gratified they will find release in new persecutions and relapses into barbarism. In *WS* 284 entitled "The means to real peace" Nietzsche seems to appeal to something akin to a superhuman act or deed that would bring about world peace: "The tree of the glory of war can be destroyed only at a single stroke by a lightning-bolt: lightning, as we know well, comes out of a cloud and from on high."

33 See Drochon, "The time is coming when we will relearn politics," 2010; and Karl Jaspers, *Nietzsche: An Introduction to his Philosophical Activity*, translated by Charles F. Wallraff and Frederick J. Schmitz (Chicago: Regnery; Tucson, AZ: University of Arizona Press, 1965; repr. Baltimore, MD and London: Johns Hopkins University Press, 1997), chapter 4.

CHAPTER 9: PART VII: "OUR VIRTUES"

1 Kant places the stress on the incomprehensible nature of the moral law for us, and this is something that irritates Nietzsche. See, for example, *D* 142: "Let us ask ourselves whether anyone who feels happy in believing in the *incomprehensibility* of moral things can be sincerely interested in acquiring knowledge of them!"

2 See Lampert, *Nietzsche's Task: An Interpretation of "Beyond Good and Evil"* (New Haven, CT: Yale University Press, 2001), pp. 211–12; Burnham, *Reading Nietzsche: An Analysis of "Beyond Good and Evil"* (Stocksfield: Acumen Press, 2007), p. 157.

3 See Robert Guay, "Order of Rank," in Ken Gemes and John Richardson (eds), *The Oxford Handbook to Nietzsche* (Oxford: Oxford University Press, 2011, forthcoming).

4 Ibid.

5 Ibid.

6 Ibid.

7 In the *Critique of Judgment* (1790), Kant says that in order to judge in matters of taste we must not be in the least biased in favor of the thing's existence but must be wholly indifferent about it. This means we need to distinguish between the merely "agreeable" in sensation and the "beautiful," which ultimately concerns not sensation but reflection. Indeed, Kant says that the judgment of the beautiful is, when properly understood, a judgment peculiar to the human animal. All kinds of animals find objects agreeable, but only the human being has the capacity for the judgment of the beautiful.

8 In his early writings Nietzsche sees the value and validity of Kant's account of aesthetic experience in terms of disinterested contemplation. See *KSA* 7:[17] and 29[20]. See also *GM* III:6 for another take on the issue.

9 Schopenhauer, *On the Basis of Morality* (Oxford and Providence: Berghahn Books, 1995), p. 140

10 Nietzsche subjects *Mitleid* to critical treatment in a series of aphorisms in *D* (132–42). On Schopenhauer and integrity consider this note from 1880 in which Nietzsche writes: "I find Schopenhauer somewhat superficial in psychological matters, he neither enjoyed himself much nor suffered much; a thinker should beware of becoming *harsh*: where would he get his material from then. His passion for knowledge was *not great* enough for him to suffer on its behalf: he barricaded himself in. His pride, too, was greater than his thirst for knowledge . . . " (*KSA* 9:6[381]).

11 On the future of laughter compare *GS* 1.

12 See also *GS* 337: "When I contemplate the present age with the eyes of some remote age, I can find nothing more remarkable in present-day humanity than its distinctive virtue and disease which goes by the name of 'the historical sense.'" Nietzsche's ambivalence toward the historical sense is once again evident here (it is said to be a virtue and a disease), but he also wonders whether in time it

might become a marvelous growth with a marvelous scent that might make the earth more agreeable to live on.

13 See *HL* 10 on the need to organize the chaos within us.

14 See also *D* 169.

15 Compare the analysis Nietzsche carries out in *HH* 221.

16 See Alan White, "The Youngest Virtue," in Richard Schacht (ed.), *Nietzsche's Postmoralism* (Cambridge: Cambridge University Press, 2001), pp. 63–78. Nietzsche writes extensively on "integrity" in his notebooks with several sketches for planned books bearing the title "Die Leidenschaft der Redlichkeit" (see *KSA* 9, p. 316). In *KSA* 9: 6[130] he writes: "the will to power, to the infallibility of our person, resides in our greatest justice and integrity: skepticism just applies to all authority, we do not want to be duped, not even by *our drives!*" And in *KSA* 9:7[53] he writes: "I am not in a position to acknowledge anything great which is not connected to *integrity towards oneself*; playacting towards oneself fills me with horror . . . " Finally, in *KSA* 9:7[262] he notes a comparison with Pascal: "don't we, like him, have our strength in beating ourselves into submission? He in aid of God, and we in aid of integrity?" These notes date from 1880. According to one commentator there is less emphasis on intellectual honesty in Nietzsche's later works, such as *BGE*, than his middle period works. See Holger Zaborowski, "From Modesty to Dynamite, from Socrates to Dionysus: Friedrich Nietzsche on Intellectual Honesty," *American Catholic Philosophical Quarterly*, 84:2 (2010): pp. 337–56. For important deployments of "intellectual integrity" in the late Nietzsche see, for example, *A* 12 and *A* 50.

17 Later in this section Nietzsche speaks of becoming "hardened in the discipline of science." In *GS* 293 he also describes "science" as severe and says that those who become accustomed to it dwell in a virile or masculine air. It is perhaps interesting to reflect on the fact that in *BGE* 230 Nietzsche refers to the counter-tendency of the will to knowledge which seeks the depths as "sublime" (though he used the word "sublime" here, not the typical word in German for the sublime which is "Erhabene"). It is typical in the modern literature on the sublime to associate it with the masculine and the cruel, as we find, for example, in Kant's pre-critical treatment of it in *Observations of the Feeling of the Beautiful and Sublime* (1763): "The fair sex has just as much understanding as the male, but it is a *beautiful understanding*, whereas ours should be a *deep understanding*, an expression that signifies identity with the sublime" (Kant 1960, p. 78).

18 Sarah Kofman, *Nietzsche and Metaphor*, translated by Duncan Large (London: Athlone, 1993), p. 92. Our reading of *BGE* 230 has been greatly aided by Kofman's insights.

19 Lampert, *Nietzsche's Task*, p. 233.

20 See Julian Young, *Nietzsche: A Philosophical Biography* (Cambridge: Cambridge University Press, 2010), p. 287 and chapter 20 on "Nietzsche's Circle of Women," pp. 387–406. See also the study by

Carol Diethe, *Nietzsche's Women: Beyond the Whip* (Berlin and New York: Walter de Gruyter, 1996).

21 Ibid., p. 287.

22 Maudemarie Clark, "Nietzsche's Misogyny," in Kelly Oliver and Marilyn Pearsall (eds), *Feminist Interpretations of Friedrich Nietzsche* (Pennsylvania, PA: The Pennsylvania State University Press, 1998), pp. 187–98, p. 189.

23 Ibid., p. 192.

24 Nietzsche borrows the phrase "eternal feminine" from the words of the "Chorus Mysticus" that appear in the conclusion of part II of Goethe's *Faust*: "The eternal feminine/Draws us on." For further insight into Nietzsche on the "eternal feminine" see Sarah Kofman, "The Psychologist of the Eternal Feminine (Why I write such good books, 5)," *Yale French Studies*, 87 (1995): pp. 173–89.

CHAPTER 10: PART VIII: "ON PEOPLES AND FATHERLANDS"

1 It should be remembered that Zarathustra struggles with a feeling of homelessness and the temptations of hospitality.

2 *CW* 9; Nietzsche's discussions of various types and exemplary figures (such as Plato, Paul, and Wagner) are often organized around what appears to be most needed in their life's work, what he calls the "secret wishes of the heart" earlier in *BGE* 5. For example, this is at the core of his problem with Wagner (see *CW* 9), and raised elsewhere in his writings, for example, *HH* 486 and, famously, *GS* 290, where Nietzsche writes that "one thing is needful—to give style to one's character." The phrase, "one thing is needful" is a citation of Luke 10.42, and is a theme found in the popular Lutheran hymn, Schröder's "Eins ist noth, ach Herr dies eine." Bach also composed a work titled "Eins ist Noth! ach Herr, diess Eine." Drafts of the famous passage from *GS* are part of the "Tautenburger Aufzeichnungen für Lou von Salomé," during which time Nietzsche sets to music Salomé's "Prayer to Life" ("Gebet an das Leben") (see *KSA* 10:1[109].1, p. 38).

3 Some comparison with the tradition of aesthetics on the question of whether taste can be taught, is native, or acquired through certain experiences might be illuminating. Yet, knowledge, perception, and insight are important. See Keith Ansell Pearson on Nietzsche's conception of the sublime and the project of future humanity, where he argues that Nietzsche applies the sublime to perception and insight (cf. chapter 7 with " 'Holding on to the Sublime': Nietzsche on Philosophy's Perception and the Search for Greatness," *Nietzsche, Power and Politics: Rethinking Nietzsche's Legacy for Political Thought* [Berlin: Walter de Gruyter, 2008], pp. 767–800).

4 Tracy Strong recently explored the relevance of the cultural project of *BT* for the cultural-political one of *BGE*. Most central is the transformative project that turns on the possibility of *love*, which would include but not be limited to "taste" as we have indicated.

Strong also discusses the relation between love and freedom insofar as love pulls us out of ourselves: "'What have you . . . truly loved? What has pulled out your soul, mastered it, and at the same time made it joyful?' (*SE* 6?) Love pulls us away from ourselves and dissolves the self into what Nietzsche here calls 'freedom.' Love and freedom are linked." (Tracy Strong, "Nietzsche and the Political: Tyranny, Tragedy, Cultural Revolution, and Democracy," *Journal of Nietzsche Studies* 35/36 [2008]: p. 54.) See the discussion of love at the end of this chapter.

5 Oddly Kaufmann translates this as "*entr'acte*" and without acknowledging a similar word is used in the title of part IV.

6 For discussions of Nietzsche's first effort to pinpoint this as Wagner's problem see Julian Young's "Richard Wagner and the Birth of *The Birth of Tragedy*," *International Journal of Philosophical Studies*, 16:2 (2008): pp. 217–45; and Gary Shapiro, "Nietzsche's Unmodern Thinking: Globalization, the End of History, and 'Great Events,'" *American Catholic Philosophical Quarterly*, 84:2 (2010): pp. 205–30. Shapiro's article focuses on Nietzsche's *UM*, *Z*, and *BGE* (particularly part VIII), and how his conceptions of the "great event" and the problem of the future develop, especially in light of his concern to overcome Hegel's conception of world historical development.

7 On the will to appearance, see Robert Rethy, "*Schein* in Nietzsche's Philosophy" in Keith Ansell Pearson (ed.), *Nietzsche and Modern German Thought* (London and New York: Routledge, 1991), pp. 59–87. See also Acampora, "Naturalism and Nietzsche's Moral Psychology," in Keith Ansell Pearson (ed.), *A Companion to Nietzsche* (Oxford and Malden, MA: Blackwell, 2006), pp. 314–33.

8 Translated by Greg Whitlock in Mazzino Montinari, *Reading Nietzsche* (Urbana-Champaign: University of Illinois Press, 2003). The passage cited is part of a replacement text he submitted for *EH* "Wise" 3, when he returned the first and second signatures to the publisher on December 18, 1888. It does not appear in the Kaufmann translation. This passage is somewhat at odds with *BGE* 264, which underscores that it is "absolutely impossible" not to embody the "qualities and preferences" of one's parents. These passages can be reconciled if one grants that Nietzsche holds that one is not *merely* what one inherits most immediately and that in higher types the ancient inheritances are enhanced and more pronounced.

9 Translated by Greg Whitlock. "Aber auch als Pole bin ich ein ungeheurer Atavismus. Man würde Jahrhunderte zurückzugehn haben, um diese vornehmste Rasse, die es auf Erden gab, in dem Masse instinktrein zu finden, wie ich sie darstelle" (*KSA* 6, p. 268). On "atavism" in *BGE*, see also §§ 149, 241, and 261.

10 Cf. *EH* "Books" 4: "multiplicity of inward states is exceptionally large in my case, I have many stylistic possibilities—the most multifarious art of style that has ever been at the disposal of one man."

11 Compare the Preface where Nietzsche writes, "It seems that all great things first have to bestride the earth in monstrous and frightening masks in order to inscribe themselves in the hearts of humanity with eternal demands [. . .]."

12 Gary Shapiro argues that Nietzsche *emphasizes* rather than diminishes the significance of place and geography, and that he reorients the dominant forms of determining significance temporally and historically toward the geological and territorial. See his "Beyond Peoples and Fatherlands: Nietzsche's Geophilosophy and the Direction of the Earth," *Journal of Nietzsche Studies,* 35:36 (2008): pp. 9–27.

13 See also Strong, "Nietzsche and the Political."

14 Nietzsche's next book, *On the Genealogy of Morality*, extensively develops the theme of the significance and meanings as well as methods of detection of origins, ancestry, and descent. Compare discussion of "What is German" with *BGE* 208 and 209; also compare with the theme in part III of differences between "northern" and "southern" capacities for religiosity.

15 See the example of Kotzebue (cf. *AOM* 170) and *FEI* 5, which mentions his murder and has language reminiscent of this section when Nietzsche claims, "all culture begins with obedience," but it sharply diverges from the ultimate message of part VIII of *BGE*, when Nietzsche claims something much like the first "old patriot" who thinks that "great leaders are necessary," and, like the second patriot when he claims that "in the midst of victory ['on the field of battle'] with his thought turned to his liberated fatherland, he made the vow that he would remain German. German!" (*KSA* 1, p. 749).

16 This is surely relevant to Nietzsche's idea that moralities are "sign languages" of the affects (*BGE* 187), discussed above.

17 Compare *Z*:I "On Reading and Writing" as well as *GM* P:7.

18 The direction of *hearing* and *listening* is an important theme that recurs in Nietzsche's works. Wagner's essay on Beethoven, written in 1860, significantly influenced Nietzsche. Wagner detected a crucial innovation in Beethoven's use and development of melody as something sustained throughout the composition, and Wagner sought to achieve this in the opera, including during times the audience would be expecting a "break," the *Zwischenspiele* and *Zwischenakte*. (See Klaus Kropfinger, *Wagner and Beethoven: Richard Wagner's Reception of Beethoven* [New York and Cambridge: Cambridge University Press, 1991].) In *CW*, however, Nietzsche comments that Bizet made him a better listener (*CW* 1), and he criticizes Wagner's "unending melody" as inhibiting development in his work (*CW* 1). See our discussion in Chapter 6.

19 See Janet Lungstrum's "Nietzsche writing woman/woman writing Nietzsche: The Sexual Dialectic of Palingenesis" in Peter J. Burgard, *Nietzsche and the Feminine*. Charlottesville: University of Virginia Press, 1994, and Caroline Joan Picart, *Resentment and the "Feminine"*

in Nietzsche's Politico-Aesthetics (State College: Penn State University Press, 1999).

20 On "spiritual perception" see Chapter 8 in this book, and Keith Ansell Pearson, " 'Holding on to the Sublime,' 2008, pp. 768–9: "For Nietzsche, philosophy is 'spiritual perception' (or vision) (*BGE* 252) [. . . which entails] a sublime exercise and operation in that it entails elevating individuals to greatness and nobility and creating a people, or a humanity, equal to this concept."

21 On this sense of revaluation, see Aaron Ridley, "Nietzsche and the Re-evaluation of Values," in Christa Davis Acampora (ed.), *Critical Essays on Nietzsche's* On the Genealogy of Morals (Lanham, MD and New York: Rowman & Littlefield Publishers, Inc., 2006), pp. 77–92.

22 Further reading on the distinction between *Menge* and *Masse* in Nietzsche, and as it is discussed in contemporary political theory, can be found in Shapiro, "Beyond Peoples and Fatherlands: Nietzsche's Geophilosophy and the Direction of the Earth," 2008.

23 Consider how this is related to rebaptizing and renaming in sections 42, 210, and 227.

24 Interestingly, Nietzsche is more specific in *CW* about what he intends by the geographic locator of "south" in *BGE* 255: it is "African"; thus, what Nietzsche anticipates in "the good European" is *"supra*-European" insofar as it intensifies and maximizes diversity and hybridity rather than simplifies and eradicates what would be regarded as "foreign" by his contemporaries.

25 Readers might explore whether and how the rhymes exhibit the qualities of language and tempo discussed earlier in the part, and their relation to the rhymes in section 237 (on women).

CHAPTER 11: PART IX: "WHAT IS NOBLE?"

1 It is worth pursuing how this conclusion stands in relation to Nietzsche's prior discussion of what he here calls "the reciprocal dependence of the 'good' and 'wicked' drives" (cf. §2), an idea that meets with "unconscious resistance in the heart of the investigator" (cf. §5).

2 But recall *GM* I:6, mentioned in the previous chapter, which appears to valorize the *depth of soul* that the priestly revolt in morality accomplishes.

3 Possibly also suggested in section 293.

4 This section should be read alongside "The little women's sayings" of section 261 and those that appear to denigrate women.

5 Cf. *GS* 23, 149, and 358. For a discussion of how Nietzsche regards "corruption" as a potentially transitional state, see Renate Reschke, " 'Korruption': Ein kulturkritischer Begriff Friedrich Nietzsches zwischen Geschichtsphilosophie und Ästethik," *Nietzsche-Studien* 26 (1992), pp. 137–62.

6 Compare also with section 287: "It is not the works, it is the *faith* that is decisive here, that determines the order of rank—to take up again an ancient religious formula in a new and more profound sense: some fundamental certainty that a noble should have about itself, something that cannot be sought, nor found, nor perhaps lost. *The noble soul has reverence for itself.*"

7 Horace *Epistles* I:10, 24: "*usque recurret*"; cf. *BGE* 56.

8 Nietzsche draws attention to this dual sense in section 284, where he writes, "All community makes men—somehow, somewhere, sometime 'common'." (Jede Gemeinschaft macht, irgendwie, irgendwo, irgendwann — "gemein".)

9 The referent here for the new taste as a cult of suffering is presumably evident in Wagner's celebration of compassion as *Mitleid* in *Parsifal*, discussed in the preceding chapter, as well in various liberal social projects and researches in which pity for the suffering of humankind might be evident as motivating force. Nietzsche's praise of laughter must partially be an overcoming of Wagner's *Parsifal* in which Kundry is condemned to only laugh, and she sees this as a curse.

10 The most extensive discussion of the theme of laughter and comedy in *Thus Spoke Zarathustra* is Kathleen Marie Higgins' *Nietzsche's Zarathustra* (Philadelphia, PA: Temple University Press, 1987). See also her *Comic Relief: Nietzsche's "Gay Science"* (Oxford: Oxford University Press, 2000).

11 This "genius" is Dionysus, who of course *has* received extensive discussion in the scholarly literature, but rarely *as* "genius of the heart." As a notable exception, see Günter Figal, "Nietzsches Dionysos," *Nietzsche-Studien*, 37 (2008): pp. 51–61. Nietzsche cites this part of his text at the end of his final general section under the heading "Why I write such good books" in *Ecce Homo* (*EH* "Books" 6).

12 Space does not permit us to elaborate the development of Nietzsche's conception of what is Dionysian and its role in his philosophy. We are inclined to think the difference between the earlier and later versions is exaggerated, however, see Adrian Del Caro, "Nietzsche's Self-transformation and the Transformation of the Dionysian," in Salim Kemal (ed.), *Nietzsche, Philosophy, and the Arts* (Cambridge: Cambridge University Press, 1998), pp. 70–91.

13 One should be specific about the target here. Morality as such is regarded by Nietzsche as an invention because moral values are not *found* in the world, "there are no moral facts." Morality as such is not necessarily anti-natural, as evident in Nietzsche's comparison of masterly and slavish moralities. So, within the genre of the artifice of morality, so to speak, there are various styles and forms of expression, some of which are decadent, others of which evince a form of growth and enhancement of the type human. It is clear that Nietzsche thinks the anti-naturalism of Christian morality, which Nietzsche thinks has its roots in Platonism, is decadent.

14 "Der Mensch, ein vielfaches, verlogenes, künstliches und undurch-
sichtiges Thier [. . .]" (*BGE* 291). Dionysus also describes human
beings as animals and ascribes three characteristics to them: " 'man
is to my mind an agreeable, courageous, inventive animal that has
no equal on earth [. . .] I often reflect how I might yet advance him
and make him stronger, more evil, and more profound than he is.' "
[" 'der Mensch ist mir einangenehmes tapferes erfinderisches Thier,
das auf Erden nicht seines Gleichen hat, [. . .] ich denke oft darüber
nach, wie ich ihn noch vorwärts bringe und ihn stärker, böser und
tiefer mache, als er ist.' "] In section 284, Nietzsche suggests the
future noble might have four virtues: "courage, insight, sympathy,
and solitude" [des Muthes, der Einsicht, des Mitgefühls, der
Einsamkeit].

15 For extensive discussion of Nietzsche's views of the human as
cultural animal, see Vanessa Lemm, *Nietzsche's Animal Philosophy:
Culture, Politics, and the Animality of the Human Being* (New York:
Fordham University Press, 2009).

16 "Unter diesem Gesichtspunkte gehört vielleicht viel Mehr in den
Begriff 'Kunst' hinein, als man gemeinhin glaubt" (*BGE* 291).

17 This evokes the sexual agonistics discussed above at the same time
that it conjures images of creativity and fecundity. Note the contrast
between the conception of love as "merely a more refined form
of parasitism, a form of nestling down in another soul" (*CW* 3)
and Dionysus' declaration to Ariadne that he is her "labyrinth" (See
also Nietzsche's *DD*, "Klage der Ariadne").

18 The return of Dionysus also recalls for the reader Nietzsche's effort
to overcome the unchallenged valuation of truth as good. One of
the ways he seeks to do this is by *producing the need* for Dionysus
once more, a new taste to combat the cult of suffering and pity, by
overcoming Platonism and restringing the bow, as he suggests in
the preface to *BGE*.

19 See also section 292 in which the philosopher is described as "fatal
human being" [ein verhängnissvoller Mensch]. This might also
be investigated in light of atavism as discussed above and in
Chapter 10.

20 See also Gary Shapiro on masks in *Nietzschean Narratives*
(Bloomington, IN: Indiana University Press, 1989).

CHAPTER 12: "FROM HIGH MOUNTAINS":
NIETZSCHE'S AFTERSONG

1 Our treatment of the poem that ends *BGE* has benefited from
conversations with Rainer Hanshe.

2 See also *GS* 84 for some valuable insights by Nietzsche into the
origin of poetry.

3 Von Stein was Nietzsche's junior by 13 years, a member of Wagner's
inner circle, an associate of Paul Rée and Lou Salomé, and something of a precocious talent in philosophy. He died at the age of 30

from a heart attack and his early death greatly shocked Nietzsche. For some details on his life and work see Young, *Nietzsche: A Philosophical Biography* (Cambridge: Cambridge University Press, 2010), pp. 392–4.

4 According to Burnham this is because the actual name is inconsequential and what matters is the "function," which here is to help open up a new chapter in the history of noble human beings, *Reading Nietzsche: An Analysis of "Beyond Good and Evil"* (Stocksfield: Acumen Press, 2007), p. 232.

5 Nietzsche has already worked this motif in *Z*. For insight see Loeb, *The Death of Nietzsche's Zarathustra* (Cambridge: Cambridge University Press, 2010), pp. 103–5. In addition, Loeb points out that Nietzsche associates the great noon with the moment when all gods are dead, when the shadows of God no longer darken the human mind, and when the sun of human knowledge is at its peak (p. 230).

6 Burnham, *Reading Nietzsche*, p. 233. Burnham considers seven reasons why Nietzsche might have wished to imitate in his poem the moment of Christ's crucifixion.

7 Lampert, *Nietzsche's Task: An Interpretation of "Beyond Good and Evil"* (New Haven, CT: Yale University Press, 2001), p. 299.

8 Lampert suggests that the poem recapitulates in shorter compass the main event of part IV of *Z*, namely, conquering the disappointment of the realization that the friends initially attracted to his teaching are not the ones required by his task, and this overcoming then gives way to his hope in new friends (2001, p. 298). He also sees a parallel between the ending of the poem in *BGE* and the ending of *Z* in part III under the original plan: both end by transforming a cataclysmic image taken from the Bible. *Z* III culminates with "The Seven Seals," an apocalyptic image taken from the book of Revelation (p. 299).

9 Burnham, *Reading Nietzsche*, p. 230.

10 "Zarathustra" symbolizes the self-overcoming of morality—the metaphysics of morality that divides the world into positive (good) and negative (evil)—and the victor of God and the will nothingness; see also *TI*, "How the 'Real World' Finally Became a Fable": "(Noon; moment of the shortest shadow; end of the longest error; pinnacle of humanity; INCIPIT ZARATHUSTRA)."

11 Burnham, *Reading Nietzsche*, p. 230.

12 Ibid.

INDEX

transcendental unity of
apperception *see also*
Kant 86, 87
translation 13, 211, 237n13
truth *see also will to truth* 8–10,
12–14, 16, 19, 22, 27, 29–32,
37, 39, 41, 44–5, 49, 52,
54–6, 60, 66, 73, 74, 83, 92,
98, 113, 121, 140–1, 144,
153, 154, 155, 159, 164–5,
167–9, 189, 193, 206–7, 209,
211, 212, 217, 219, 235n23,
235n25, 244n10, 254n18
types 20, 21, 24, 25, 26, 64, 75,
95–6, 112, 142, 143, 150–1,
172–3, 178, 179, 189, 201,
231n16, 241n3, 249n2,
250n8
tyranny 114–15, 128, 182, 184,
186, 193, 194

understanding 6, 46, 53, 55, 58,
68, 74, 103, 112, 124, 126,
203, 248n17
Utilitarianism 161

values 2, 9, 14, 17–20, 29–32,
35, 44–6, 49, 51, 54, 61–2,
64, 66–8, 80–4, 90–2, 102,
113, 119–20, 123–5, 129,
141, 144–6, 152, 170–3,
184, 186, 188–9, 191–2,
197–9, 202, 203, 207, 218,
253n13
revaluation of 9, 58, 80–4, 90,
122, 126–7, 189, 229n2,
252n21
Vattimo, Gianni 145, 245n25
Vedanta philosophy 87
Veil of Maya 154, 177
virtue 14, 19, 21, 22, 24, 27, 55,
61, 71, 83, 101, 123, 124,

138, 142–3, 145, 148–9,
154–5, 157–8, 159–61,
166–7, 172, 187, 196, 213,
218, 242n20, 247n12,
254n14
Voltaire 53, 73

Wagner, Richard 2, 4, 15, 24,
25, 63, 82, 105–9, 135,
174–5, 179–80, 182–3,
187, 189–90, 218, 239n13,
239n14, 240n19, 249n2,
250n6, 251n18, 253n9,
255n3
war 6, 18, 139, 142, 144, 145–7,
165, 179, 190, 244n14,
246n31, 246n32
Wesendonck, Mathilde 239n13
White, Alan 248n16
Whitlock, Greg 230n10, 231n17,
250n8, 250n9
will 3, 9, 11, 12, 14, 18, 19, 20,
23, 31, 32–7, 39, 42–3, 45–7,
49–51, 57, 59, 63, 69, 72,
74–5, 82–3, 86, 93, 96, 105,
119, 120, 127–8, 133, 138–9,
142, 147, 148, 160, 162–3,
165, 172, 176–7, 187, 194–5,
217, 230n14
will to knowledge 54–5, 122, 163,
177, 182, 217, 248n17
will to power (concept) 3, 9–12,
34–6, 42, 43, 47, 48–50, 53,
62, 69, 73–5, 80, 84–6, 104,
111, 116, 125, 141–2, 155,
158–9, 162, 164, 182, 193,
199, 217, 224, 248n16
will to truth *see also truth* 29, 31,
45, 52, 54, 60, 141, 167
Williams, Bernard 234n18
Wissenschaft see also science
and *gay science* 5, 77, 131